D0760931

ROBERTO BOLAÑO'S FICTION

Columbia University Press
Publishers Since 1893
New York   Chichester, West Sussex
cup.columbia.edu

Copyright © 2014 Columbia University Press

Library of Congress Cataloging-in-Publication Data
Andrews, Chris, 1962-
Roberto Bolaño's fiction : an expanding universe / Chris Andrews.
      pages cm
   Includes bibliographical references and index.
   ISBN 978-0-231-16806-9 (cloth : alk. paper) — ISBN 978-0-231-53753-7
(electronic)
   1. Bolaño, Roberto, 1953-2003—Fictional works. I. Title.
   PQ8098.12.O38Z55   2014
   863'.64—dc23

                                                        2013039656

Columbia University Press books are printed on permanent and durable
acid-free paper.

This book is printed on paper with recycled content.
Printed in the United States of America
c 10 9 8 7 6 5 4 3 2 1

Cover design: Frances Baca
Cover image: © Anna Oswaldo Cruz 1998

CHRIS ANDREWS

ROBERTO BOLAÑO'S FICTION

An Expanding Universe

Columbia University Press / New York

CONTENTS

CONTENTS

ACKNOWLEDGMENTS

I AM VERY grateful to the Australian Research Council for the Discovery Project Grant that supported the writing of this book. I would also like to thank Philip Leventhal of Columbia University Press for his early interest in the project and his guidance, Leslie Kriesel for her perspicacious editing, Victoria Baker for the thought she put into the index, Luciana Scocco for her resourceful research assistance, and Masako Ogawa for finding and translating commentary on Bolaño's fiction in Japanese.

Many friends and colleagues have helped me in various ways, with their questions, comments, conversation, invitations, hospitality, and encouragement. In particular I would like to thank Esther Allen, Dina Al-Kassim, Robert Amutio, Karim Benmiloud, Hugo Bowne-Anderson, Susan Bernofsky, Sara Castro-Klaren, Jing Luciana Chen, Wilfrido Corral, John Culbert, Ignacio Echevarría, William Egginton, Barbara Epler, Ignacio de Ferrari, Ivor Indyk, Gail Jones, Ignacio López Vicuña, Celina Manzoni, Bruno Montané, Christian Moire, Fernando Moreno, Alfonso Montelongo, Carmen Pérez de Vega, Carmelo Pinto, Sarah Pollack, Cristina Rocha, Rodrigo Rojas, José Ramón Ruisánchez, Samuel Rutter, Natalie Saint-Martin, Manuel Vicuña, Natasha Wimmer, Oswaldo Zavala, Danielle Zaslavsky, and the two anonymous reviewers for Columbia University Press. My deepest debt of gratitude is to Michelle de Kretser, who suggested that

I write this book in the first place, and whose eye for hitches at all levels has improved it greatly. The remaining mistakes are down to me.

Material from a number of articles has been reworked for inclusion here, and I am grateful to the editors and presses for permitting separate publication:

"Algo va a pasar: Los cuentos de Roberto Bolaño." In *Roberto Bolaño: Una literatura infinita*, ed. Fernando Moreno, 33–40. Centre de recherches Latino-américaines/Archivos, Université de Poitiers—CNRS: Poitiers, 2005.

"Varieties of Evil." *Meanjin* 66, no. 3 (2007): 200–206.

"La experiencia episódica y la narrativa de Roberto Bolaño." In *Bolaño salvaje*, ed. Gustavo Faverón and Edmundo Paz Soldán, 53–71. Barcelona: Candaya, 2008.

"Bolaño y la incertidumbre." In *Fuera de quicio: Bolaño en el tiempo de sus espectros*, ed. Raúl Rodríguez Freire, 249–254. Santiago: Ripio, 2012.

INTRODUCTION

T HIS IS A book of literary criticism. Although I have had the lucky privilege of being one of Roberto Bolaño's translators, translation will not be my main concern in the following pages. And although Bolaño responded to my queries in the last year and a half of his life, I have no biographical revelations to offer. These opening disclaimers made, I would like to comment briefly on the ways the critical approach adopted here is related—indirectly—to the work of translation and to the life of the author studied.

A translator is, by necessity, a slow reader and a rereader, which is not to say a model reader in all respects, for there are features of a literary work that a translator may not be in the best position to see, simply because he or she is so close to the text and proceeding so slowly through it, except in the final revising. This closeness and slowness can, however, confer a special perspective, because they counteract the reader's natural tendency to hierarchize the contents of a text, privileging plot over subplot, or protagonists over minor characters, or action over atmosphere. Translators, I have noticed, are sometimes haunted by quiet places in a narrative that may seem unremarkable both to general readers, absorbed in the story, and to academic critics, who understandably focus on the aspects of a text that are relevant to their guiding hypotheses. Because translators are obliged to distribute their attention evenly, they spend considerable amounts of time on passages that other readers may hurry through, and in those stretches of textual "noise" they may begin to discern or construe messages. The hypotheses that guided this study were no doubt shaped to some degree by a desire to formulate and organize the messages emitted, as it seemed to me, by inconspicuous recesses of Bolaño's work in which I had lingered as a translator. But my discussion is not limited to the books that I translated; it ranges over the interconnected series of narratives that begins with *Nazi Literature in the Americas* (originally published in 1996) and ends with the stories that appeared posthumously in *The Secret of Evil*. These narratives can be regarded as forming a single, openly structured edifice whose two sustaining pillars are *The Savage Detectives* and *2666,* and for which *Woes of the True Policeman* served as a preparatory model.

My second opening disclaimer was that I had no biographical revelations to offer. I would, however, like to echo the testimonies of others who came into contact with Roberto Bolaño in the final years of his life.[1] He responded to my queries with a degree of openness and generosity that was remarkable in a man with so many claims on his time and (as he knew, though not precisely) so little time left. I will be arguing in chapter 7 that generosity and openness are strongly valued in Bolaño's fiction, which is also informed by an antihierarchical worldview apparent not only in the behavior of the characters but also in the narrative techniques employed. I believe that these conclusions could have been soundly reached on the basis of the published fiction alone, but I suspect that I came to them more quickly because of the impression left by my correspondence with the writer, as well as by Bolaño's interviews, usefully collected by Andrés Braithwaite in *Bolaño por sí mismo* and by Sybil Pérez in *The Last Interview and Other Conversations*. Bolaño's work insistently invites us to construct a figure of the author, which we should distinguish conceptually from the writer Roberto Bolaño, as I shall argue in chapter 2; but in Bolaño's case author and writer have much in common, and to be curious about the relations between them is not necessarily to be under a naïve illusion.

Rather than reconstructing the life from which Bolaño's works emerged or scrutinizing what happened, linguistically, when they crossed from

Spanish into English, I will be concentrating here on the published fiction itself and asking how it was (and is) composed, how it manages narrative tension, how Bolaño's characters experience their selves in time, how they damage and protect one another, and what ethical and political values are implied by their interactions.

Those are the book's central questions, and the answers to them occupy chapters 2 to 7. In the first chapter, however, I will be asking a different sort of question: Why has Bolaño's fiction been well received in the English-speaking world? Because this is a question about reception on a large scale, about what happened to the works, culturally, when they came into English, and not about their internal workings or immediate effects, chapter 1 stands at a certain remove from those that follow. I will come to the fiction via the publishing phenomenon. Many readers of this book will have done likewise. For some the phenomenon will seem a self-evident necessity. Others will have wondered, "Why Bolaño?" I hope to give both groups of readers pause and food for thought by arguing that while a series of reasons for Bolaño's success in translation can be proposed, the phenomenon was (and is) contingent in important ways. Bolaño knew that this is always the case, and he made the contingency of reception a recurrent theme in his fiction, as I will show in the last section of chapter 1, where the work of textual analysis really begins.

That work continues to the end of the book, but with a gradual shift of emphasis that it may be useful to signal here. Very broadly speaking, the shift is from form to content to value, and it is accompanied by a change in the conceptual background of my analysis from narratology to philosophy. This movement does not take the discussion out of the ambit of literary criticism, for, as I said, textual analysis continues to the end, and the later chapters, which are more focused on content and implicit values, nevertheless keep literary mediation in view and make a point of differentiating fiction from philosophical reflection, investigative journalism, and political activism. In addition, form, content, and value are related in ways that link the earlier chapters to the later ones: Bolaño's decentralization of narrative tension (chapter 3), for example, is consistent with his anarchism (chapter 7), and his compositional process of overinterpretation (chapter 2) builds on the attentive openness that his fiction defends (chapter 7). Bolaño's work is not neatly designed; it sprawls, but it has a deep and intricate coherence, which will be reflected by the internal references in this book.

Chapters 2 and 3 address formal and technical questions, from the point of view of the writer and of the individual reader respectively. Bolaño could not have become a publishing phenomenon had he not first been a creative phenomenon. Chapter 2 begins by asking how he could have produced so much genuinely inventive fiction in such a short period. The avowedly partial answer is that he made use of four processes, all of which can be applied over and over: expansion, circulating characters, metarepresentation, and overinterpretation. These terms will be explained in the four sections of chapter 2, but the meaning of each can be roughly indicated here in a sentence. Bolaño expanded or "exploded" his own published texts, blowing them up by adding new characters and episodes as well as circumstantial details. He also allowed characters to circulate or migrate from text to text, sometimes altering their names and properties. Within his novels and stories, he included representations of imagined texts and artworks, that is, metarepresentations. Finally, some of his characters and narrators are over-interpreters: they seize on details, invest them with significance, and invent stories to connect and explain them. These four processes do not operate as constraints; in fact, Bolaño uses some of them to relax the realist conventions requiring consistency in characterization and psychological plausibility in behavior, and this gives his "fiction-making system" (as Nora Catelli has called it) an unusual degree of free play.

The joint operation of Bolaño's compositional processes has resulted in a highly complex body of work. Chapter 2 maps that complexity, incompletely of course, by tracing links between the various novels and stories. I hope that this will enable readers to envisage more fully the web of connections by virtue of which all the later fiction (from *Nazi Literature in the Americas* on) hangs together as a whole. This can and should, I think, be a vertiginous experience, especially since Bolaño trains his readers in suspicion, so that the more assiduous among them are likely to end up discerning dubiously warranted connections. Having perhaps provoked a certain dizziness, it is my further hope that chapter 2 will subsequently serve as a memory aid, helping readers to orient themselves in the labyrinth of Bolaño's work, the structure of which has, fortunately, been further complicated by the posthumous publication of *Woes of the True Policeman*.

In chapter 3 the perspective shifts: I move from exploring how Bolaño composed his work to examining how that work affects the individual reader, and specifically how it generates and manages narrative tension. Bolaño is not to be counted among the novelists who regard "mere storytelling" as atavistic. Indeed, his capacity to maintain narrative tension while eluding predictability and eschewing familiar plot shapes prompts the reflection: what could be "mere" about storytelling in itself, as opposed to a particular set of narrative clichés? It is true that Bolaño's fiction sometimes produces generic suspense, which depends on the reader's familiarity with the conventions of a genre, such as the horror movie. More often, however, suspense arises from uncertainty about the kind of story that is being told. Bolaño's narratives often seem to conceal what Ricardo Piglia calls a "secret story," but they rarely expose it unequivocally at the end, as the classic short story does.[2] In the long novels, the production of narrative tension is decentralized, depending more on glimpses into the lives of marginal characters than on the answer to an overarching question. The characters are not all given equal time and space, but many of those who appear in passing are granted a dignity equal to that of the protagonists, who are not always clearly distinguishable as such.

Many of Bolaño's stories take the form of a quest or an investigation, and this might seem to contradict what I said in the previous paragraph about eschewing familiar plot shapes. But the quests and investigations are not well formed by conventional standards. Bolaño's searchers and detectives typically fail: disappearance is the norm and findings are fluky. His fiction is poor in revelations: the information gaps that it opens as it proceeds are very often left open. By contrast, it is rich in surprises; uncomfortable with generic rules and with its own emergent regularities, it remains unsettled and unsettling. The late stories of *The Insufferable Gaucho*, in particular, drift in a way that suggests a utopia of unending narration. A Bolaño story will often break off abruptly, but this frequently occurs at the beginning of a new phase in the protagonist's life. What Ignacio Echevarría has aptly called

Bolaño's "poetics of inconclusiveness" (SE viii) is a poetics of continuity as well as of fragmentation.

Having devoted two chapters to formal and technical aspects of Bolaño's fiction, I turn, in chapter 4, to a question that arises at the intersection of narrative form and characterization: How do Bolaño's characters experience their selves in time? Typically, the more sympathetic characters are little inclined to fashion selves through storytelling or to live their lives in a narrative mode. They tend to be aimless, like the drifting heroine of "Anne Moore's Life" or Auxilio Lacouture in *Amulet*. There are three reasons for this. One is psychological: in Bolaño's fiction, as for the philosopher Galen Strawson, the Episodic life, lived with no sense that one's present self was there in the further past or will be there in the further future, is not intrinsically inferior to the Diachronic life, in which the self is felt to have long-term continuity. There is also a historical reason: many of the stories that Bolaño tells are of Latin American lives uprooted and disoriented by political turmoil. And, finally, he has a marked aesthetic preference for discontinuous, inconclusive, drifting narrative forms.

Not all of Bolaño's characters are aimless and Episodic. The priest, poet, and critic Sebastián Urrutia Lacroix in *By Night in Chile* is strongly Diachronic, and he embarks on his career with a definite plan, but as he tells the story of his life, his sense of self disintegrates. His case illustrates three dangers that have been emphasized by critics of the narrative identity theories developed by Paul Ricoeur and Alasdair MacIntyre, among others: an unrealistic ideal of control, self-deception, and moral tunnel vision, or what Cora Diamond calls "missing the adventure."[3] Overall, Bolaño's fiction suggests that not everyone wishes or should wish to possess a self unified in the way that Nietzsche recommends, that is, by setting before oneself "an exalted and noble 'to this end.'"[4]

Although the experience of reading Bolaño can be invigorating and amusing, his fictional universe is indisputably harsh and dark. The possibility of violence is never remote; life and well-being are frequently threatened by harms that it is not hyperbolic to call evil. Chapters 5 and 6 focus on these aspects of Bolaño's fiction. Chapter 5 compares his handling of potential and actual violent conflict with the duels in the work of his key precursor, Jorge Luis Borges. On a first impression, Bolaño would seem to have inherited Borges's nostalgia for the warrior ethic and the honor code. Yet if we compare the confrontations in Bolaño's work with Borges's best-known fighting stories (from *Fictions* and *The Aleph*), systematic differences emerge. In Bolaño, physical violence is not inevitable; it functions as a test of courage but is not, as in the work of Borges, epiphanic, revealing a destiny and an identity. The confrontations narrated by Bolaño are generally intermediate rather than culminating moments in a life story, and they are interpersonal rather than personal affairs: characters generally accept the risk of violence in order to prevent harm to others rather than to defend their own honor. These contrasts with Borges are, however, somewhat misleading, because they do not take into account later stories in which the Argentine author abandons the notion of the epiphanic duel. It turns out that where physical conflict is concerned, Bolaño more closely resembles the later Borges.

Fights in Bolaño's work test courage, but courage is not simply a matter of decisive action. As Walter Benjamin affirms in his commentary on Hölderlin's "The Poet's Courage" and "Timidity," it also involves, essentially, a kind of passivity. We see this in Bolaño's work when characters face down violence, withstanding the fear of harm and humiliation, and when they endure long-term hardships. His ideal of heroism combines a readiness to sacrifice oneself with what he calls a "slow-motion luxury" (B 122): a capacity to take one's time, to dilate and distort it, whether in an actual emergency, in the face of imminent danger, or when holding on with no end in sight.

Conflict is endemic in Bolaño's fiction and has to be faced because certain characters are driven by the will not just to dominate but also to destroy the lives of others. Bolaño narrates many occurrences that conform to Claudia Card's secular definition of evils as "reasonably foreseeable intolerable harms produced by inexcusable wrongs."[5] These come about through the actions of four kinds of characters, which I will study in chapter 6: the accomplice, the dictator, the sociopath, and the administrator. The dictator Pinochet (*By Night in Chile*) and the sociopath Wieder (*Distant Star*) are portrayed from a distance, through the eyes of others, in satirical and fantastic modes respectively. The administrator Sammer (*2666*) and the accomplice Urrutia Lacroix (*By Night in Chile*) speak for themselves, drawing the reader into their mental worlds but signally failing to justify what they have done. Bolaño's work presents an anatomy of evil, distinguishing its varieties and showing how they can interact "symbiotically" to produce atrocities. Yet this naturalistic anatomizing does not get to the bottom of the phenomenon. *Distant Star* leaves open the possibility that the evil embodied by Carlos Wieder may be not only sociopathic but also diabolical in the archaic sense of the word. Similarly, in *2666*, the "secret of the world," which is somehow hidden in the crimes of Santa Teresa, according to Klaus Haas (2666 348), has a supernatural resonance that is subtly sustained by the inclusion of uncanny details. The short story "The Secret of Evil" breaks off before delivering what its title promises: the key to the darkest, innermost space of Bolaño's fictional universe. For reasons that relate both to practicalities in his represented worlds and to narrative technique, there is a secret of evil in his writing that must remain a secret.

Bolaño's fiction may seem anomic, ethically flat or blank, partly because it is pervaded by violence and partly because it represents prostitution, pornography, and drug use in a matter-of-fact way. In chapter 7 I will attempt to counter that impression by clarifying the values implicit in the novels and stories. I will argue that, like the French philosopher Ruwen Ogien, Bolaño is an ethical minimalist, an enemy of paternalism, and that his fiction disavows the idea of duties to the self. But that is not to say that nothing matters in his work. His characters live in ethically and politically oriented worlds. A small number of them are genuinely villainous or heroic, but most are far from either extreme. The complexity of the major characters is gradually revealed by the various situations in which they find themselves. In a sense, however, what really matters in Bolaño's fiction is relatively simple: we are clearly invited to admire or reprove a small number of personal qualities. The cardinal virtues are courage and generosity. Are these enough to provide direction and meaning? Jean Franco thinks not and says that "Bolaño often sounds like a romantic anarchist."[6] I will argue that those terms are descriptively accurate but need not be understood as pejorative. Bolaño is an anarchist in the way that he privileges voluntary associations and spontaneous forms of solidarity over institutions, and in the deeply antihierarchical set of his thought, which underlies his decentralization of interest and narrative tension, most obviously in part II of *The Savage Detectives* and "The Part About the Crimes" in *2666*. His anarchism shows its critical edge in fierce stigmatization of a salient vice: servile attraction to the famous and the powerful.

Bolaño's romanticism is apparent in his privileging of poetry, understood broadly, not as a kind of text or specialized activity, but as an adventurous (which is not to say spectacular) way of living. In his fiction, poetry comes to stand synecdochically for youthful or neotenic openness, which is not a function of biological youth and can be clearly demonstrated only by characters who are at least relatively old. This openness, in Bolaño's work, is partly a matter of action and persistence but also, crucially, a matter of attention and becoming. He once joked in an interview that immaturity is an arduous achievement. This was something more than a joke. In the case of Benno von Archimboldi, Bolaño's paradigmatic great writer, becoming immature means placing trust in the risky game of imaginative composition, with no certitude that the investment will turn out to be justifiable. Archimboldi's achieved immaturity is not, however, equivalent to an impermeable self-absorption. When his sister tells him about her son's imprisonment in Mexico, he sets off to "take care of it all" (2666 891). This is one of the moments at which Bolaño marks a limit to the value of art. In his fiction it matters greatly that art should not be subservient to the policies of any institution, but art cannot be the only thing that matters, and it can certainly matter too much (as it does to the radical aesthete and accomplice in torture María Canales in *By Night in Chile*).

This book begins and ends by reflecting on the uncertainties that attend the reception and the effects of literary works. Bolaño's fiction takes lucid account of those uncertainties, and that is not the least of its claims on the interest of present and future readers. A book of criticism too, even as it "travels side by side with the Work" (SD 456), goes uncertainly into the world. I hope that this one will be clear enough either to persuade its readers or to allow them to see precisely where their disagreements lie. And I hope that after focusing attention steadily on the details of Bolaño's fiction it will provide some interesting outward routes via the works cited, not all of which are by authors who are currently conspicuous in literary studies.

ABBREVIATIONS

ENGLISH EDITIONS OF THE WORKS OF ROBERTO BOLAÑO

2666	*2666*
A	*Amulet*
BNC	*By Night in Chile*
BP	*Between Parentheses*
DS	*Distant Star*
IG	*The Insufferable Gaucho*
LEE	*Last Evenings on Earth*
LI	*The Last Interview and Other Conversations*
NLA	*Nazi Literature in the Americas*
R	*The Return*
SD	*The Savage Detectives*
SE	*The Secret of Evil*
SR	*The Skating Rink*
UU	*The Unknown University*
WTP	*Woes of the True Policeman*

SPANISH EDITIONS OF THE WORKS OF ROBERTO BOLAÑO

2666s	*2666*
B	*Bolaño por sí mismo*
LDS	*Los detectives salvajes*
ED	*Estrella distante*
LNA	*La literatura nazi en América*
PA	*Putas asesinas*

See Bibliography for bibliographical details.

NOTE ON TRANSLATIONS

HAVE QUOTED from published translations where possible. Where I have quoted from a source for which I have not been able to find a published translation, the translation is my own, unless otherwise indicated. When citing passages from the work of Bolaño, I have occasionally modified my own published translations. There was no need to tamper with those of Natasha Wimmer and Laura Healy.

ROBERTO BOLAÑO'S FICTION

1

THE ANOMALOUS CASE
OF ROBERTO BOLAÑO

ANOMALY

HE RECEPTION OF Roberto Bolaño's work in English began in an unremarkable way. When Christopher Maclehose, publisher at the Harvill Press in England, bought UK rights for *Nocturno de Chile* (*By Night in Chile*) in 2001, Bolaño was already a well-established author in the Spanish-speaking world. In 1998 his first long novel, *Los detectives salvajes* (*The Savage Detectives*), had won the Premio Herralde de Novela and the Premio Rómulo Gallegos. The second of these prizes, in particular, is a mark of consecration in the Hispanic literary field, and it had been won, before Bolaño, by Mario Vargas Llosa, Gabriel García Márquez, Carlos Fuentes, and Javier Marías. By the end of 2001, *La literatura nazi en América* (*Nazi Literature in the Americas*) and *Estrella distante* (*Distant Star*) had appeared in German and Italian, and the French translator Robert Amutio, who had been trying to interest a publisher in Bolaño's work since 1996, had finally succeeded: Christian Bourgois had bought the rights to the two books already out in Italy and Germany.[1]

By Night in Chile (2003) was positively reviewed and sold modestly (775 copies in the first 12 months). *Distant Star* (2004) was also well received by critics, but sold more slowly still. So far, this story conforms to a familiar pattern: an author recognized as important in his or her source culture is translated into English and published by a small press after having been translated into several other languages. Often the story stops here. Since substantial sales are not accompanying critical success, the publisher understandably decides to cut her losses and take risks on more promising new names as yet untainted by failure in the marketplace.

This, however, is not what happened in the case of Bolaño. The Harvill Press bought UK rights for a third book, a selection of stories from *Llamadas telefónicas* and *Putas asesinas*, for which Bolaño chose the title *Last Evenings on Earth* shortly before his death in July 2003. Across the Atlantic, Barbara Epler at New Directions, who had acquired and published the translations of *By Night in Chile* and *Distant Star* with a prompt enthusiasm, negotiated with Harvill-Secker (the Harvill Press having been taken over by Random House and merged with the Secker and Warburg list in 2005) to bring out the book of stories in the United States before it appeared in the UK. It was published in May 2006. By this stage a certain excitement had begun to develop around Bolaño's work in North America. Susan Sontag had provided an endorsement for *By Night in Chile*. Francine Prose read the story "Gómez Palacio" in *The New Yorker* and discovered in it, as she wrote in the *The New York Times*, "something extraordinarily beautiful and (at least to me) entirely new."[2] Bolaño's reception was already beginning to break with the sadly familiar pattern.

The publication of *The Savage Detectives* by Farrar, Straus and Giroux in 2007 was a breakthrough. The novel was reviewed widely and at length, with almost unanimous enthusiasm. In its first year, *The Savage Detectives* sold 22,000 copies in hardcover, a remarkable success for a translated book.[3] But the climactic moment in Bolaño's posthumous North American campaign was undoubtedly the publication of *2666* in November 2008, which, to reclaim a term overused by marketing departments, truly was an event. When proof copies of the book began to circulate, Leon Neyfakh claimed in *The New York Observer* that carrying one was like "driving an open-top Porsche."[4] The reviews were even more numerous, and, overall, even more positive. Within days of publication, Farrar, Straus rushed out a second printing, bringing the total to more than 75,000 copies.[5]

In 2007, Ilan Stavans wrote: "Not since Gabriel García Márquez, whose masterpiece, *One Hundred Years of Solitude*, turns 40 this year, has a Latin

American redrawn the map of world literature so emphatically as Roberto Bolaño does with *The Savage Detectives*."[6] Looking back in 2009, Jean Franco used the same yardstick: "Not since the publication in English of *One Hundred Years of Solitude* has there been such a rapturous critical reception of a Latin American author in Britain and the USA."[7] Indeed, it is extremely rare for literary works translated into English from any language to achieve such a degree of serious critical attention and commercial success without the backing of the Nobel Prize committee. Franco is right, however, to stress the *critical* reception, because Bolaño is not the biggest selling novelist in translation of the last ten years. Setting aside crime fiction (and the Stieg Larsson phenomenon in particular), Bolaño is no match for Carlos Ruiz Zafón when it comes to shifting stock.[8] Critics and writers are not, however, claiming in significant numbers that Ruiz Zafón has opened up new possibilities for fiction writing.

Why has the case of Bolaño proved to be exceptional? What caused and is causing the Bolaño anomaly? At least seven explanations can be proposed, which I will characterize very baldly as follows, before considering each in turn:

Bolaño is an exceptional writer
Bolaño is an American writer
Bolaño is a translatable writer
Bolaño has given rise to a myth
Bolaño supplies a lack in North American fiction
Men like Bolaño's books
Bolaño has been misread.

SINGULARITY

Bolaño is an exceptional writer: I begin with this explanation because I take it to be, quite clearly, the most powerful of the seven. The claim has been made repeatedly in reviews, but I would like to frame it here in somewhat more theoretical terms, and to foreshadow the ways it will be developed in later chapters of this book.

Bolaño has created what the sociologist Pierre Bourdieu would call a new position in the literary field. Bourdieu argues that artistic and intellectual fields contain a large but finite number of positions, defined by oppositions that "go without saying." Every now and then, however, those oppositions are upset by a "heretic" who rejects both terms of what is taken to be an inescapable either/or alternative. In *The Rules of Art*, Bourdieu provides an abstract formula for the "double rupture" that the heretic feels impelled to effect: "I detest X (a writer, a manner, movement, theory, etc. . . .) but I also detest just as much the opposite of X."[9] And in *Pascalian Meditations* he proposes a general model for what he calls "symbolic revolutions." Discussing the "impossible position" in which Baudelaire placed himself, he writes:

> This position, generating an extraordinary *tension* and *violence*, was produced, one could even say invented, by Baudelaire himself, by setting himself in opposition to positions which were opposed to each other and by trying to bring together properties and projects that were profoundly opposed and socially incompatible, *without conciliatory concessions*.[10]

At the vanguard of the art-for-art's-sake movement, Baudelaire broke simultaneously with bourgeois didacticism and with socially committed realism, combining the formal rigor of the Parnassian school with content that was felt by the judicial authorities to be morally lax in the extreme.[11]

Bourdieu's notion of "symbolic revolution" can help us to come to grips with what is exceptional about Bolaño's writing. As a poet, like his alter ego Arturo Belano in *The Savage Detectives*, he broke with the two dominant and opposed schools of poetry in the Mexico of his youth: socially committed peasant poetry (*la poesía campesina*) and the international aestheticism of Octavio Paz and his followers. Like Belano and his gang of "visceral realists," the poet Bolaño put himself in an impossible, or as Juan Garcia Madero says, "unsustainable" position, "between a rock and a hard place" (SD 19). The *infrarealista* movement led by Bolaño and Mario Santiago in the mid-1970s had no established place in the literary field, like the visceral realist movement as described in *The Savage Detectives*:

the visceral realists weren't part of any camp, not the neo-PRI-ists or the champions of otherness, the neo-Stalinists or the aesthetes, those who drew a government salary or those who lived off the university, the sellers or the buyers, those who clung to tradition or those who masked their ignorance with arrogance, the whites or the blacks, the Latin American-ists or the cosmopolites. (SD 320)

The only solution was to change the structure of the field by inventing a new position within it—"We were all in complete agreement that Mexican poetry must be transformed" (SD 19)—a venture in which both the *infra-realistas* and the visceral realists seem to have failed, although in the posthu-mously published "Death of Ulises" we learn that Ulises Lima (a character based on Mario Santiago) has a hard core of followers who regard him as "Mexico's greatest poet" (SE 134).

As a novelist, Bolaño was generally hostile to the prominent writers of the so-called Boom generation. In his correspondence with Horacio Castellanos Moya, he referred to the "fusty private club full of cobwebs, presided over by Vargas Llosa, García Marquez, Fuentes and other ptero-dactyls."[12] And in 2001, he said in an interview: "Even if I was starving to death, I wouldn't accept any charity from the Boom" (B 99). This is, in part, the expression of a visceral antipathy toward particular writers of his father's generation and the social postures that they had adopted, but for Bolaño the Boom had also created a serious aesthetic problem: its surviv-ing writers and especially their epigones had led Latin American fiction into a dead end.

As readers we have reached a point at which there is, apparently, no way out. As writers we have literally come to a precipice. There's no crossing place in sight, but we have to get across; that's our job, to find some way to get across. Obviously, at this point, the tradition of the fathers (and some of the grandfathers) is no use; on the contrary, it becomes a burden. If we don't want to plummet over the precipice, we have to invent, we have to be daring, not that daring is any guarantee. (B 99)

The implication here is that what some scholars have dubbed the "post-Boom," with its return to reader-friendly storytelling, as represented by the fiction of Antonio Skármeta and Isabel Allende, fails to get across the precipice because it abdicates literature's duty to keep making the structure new: "Structure is never a superfluous resource. If the story you're telling is inane or dead or ultrafamiliar, the right structure can save it (although, it has to be admitted, not for long), but put a really good story in a structure that has passed its use-by date, so to speak, and not even God will be able to save it" (B 98).[13]

Toward the end of his life, Bolaño became increasingly fractious and truculent in his public remarks about other writers, as in "The Myths of Cthulhu" (IG 147–164). Ignacio Echevarría attributes this development to the influence of Nicanor Parra (BP 4), but it may also have been a reaction to the broad positive consensus developing around Bolaño's work in the last five years of his life.[14] His literary habits had been formed by the practice of dissent, and symbolic conflict was his element. In an interview for the Chilean television program *Off the Record* in 1998, he predicted that the imminent publication of *The Savage Detectives* would dispel the misunderstanding or hypocrisy on which the critical consensus had been based and force readers to choose their camps, for or against: "Up until now the critics in Spain have treated me very, very well, and one of the driving forces behind the writing of *The Savage Detectives* was a desire to shatter that unanimity. . . . I'm sure I'm going to make a horde of enemies in Spain; well, you always have a horde of enemies, but they keep quiet. Now there's no way they can keep quiet."[15] As a prediction, this fell wide of the mark, but it is symptomatic of the sense in which Bolaño was working against his own success in the final years of his life. Another such indication is the choice he made in 2002 to publish the jagged and disorienting *Antwerp*, a manuscript dating back to 1979, rather than the much more straightforward *The Third Reich*, written in 1989 and published posthumously in 2010. Of *Antwerp* he said in his last interview that it was the only novel of which he was not ashamed, perhaps because it remained unintelligible (LI 117).[16]

Was this nostalgia for what Alberto Medina has termed "the ethical voluptuousness of the marginal" (553), by which I take him to mean the pleasant sense that one has remained pure and uncorrupted by honors and commercial success?[17] I think it would be wrong to draw such a conclusion, for two reasons. First, Bolaño was closely acquainted with the practical discomfort of a marginality unsupported by cultural institutions. And second, in his work, marginality is no guarantee of aesthetic achievement or ethical integrity, as I will argue below. Bolaño was nostalgic not for marginality as such, which may be solitary and tranquil, but for the stimulation of collective embattlement and rupture.

His "Infrarealist manifesto," written in 1976, was entitled "Leave It All, Again."[18] This is a voluntary echo of André Breton's "Leave everything":

> Leave everything.
> Leave Dada.
> Leave your wife, leave your mistress.
> Leave your hopes and fears.
> Drop your kids in the middle of nowhere.
> Leave the substance for the shadow.
> Leave behind, if need be, your comfortable life and promising future.
> Take to the highways.[19]

Breton, in turn, was knowingly echoing the Gospels: "If any man come to me, and hate not his father, and mother, and children, and brethren, and sisters, yea, and his own life also, he cannot be my disciple" (Luke 14:26, see also Matthew 10:37). Like Jesus of Nazareth, Breton needed to break social and familial bonds in order to assure the solidarity of his disciples. Similarly, as both Francisco Segovia and Ignacio Echevarría have remarked, Bolaño was inclined to echo the Christic ultimatum: "He that is not with me is against me" (Matthew 12:30).[20] While his late polemical texts are not direct bids for loyalty, they do separate wheat from chaff, or sheep from goats, in a way that recalls the team-building rhetoric of the historical avant-gardes. From "Leave It All, Again" (1976) to the "The Myths of Cthulhu" (2003), Bolaño retained and nurtured a habit of conflict and confrontation.[21]

The invention of a new position in the literary field is not, however, simply a matter of ruptures or rejections. It also requires, as Bourdieu argued, the combining of properties and projects that are generally held to be incompatible. Bolaño effected at least three such distinctive combinations, bringing together poetic figuration and narrative tension, elegiac themes and energizing effect, literariness and distance from literature.

The expression "poetic prose" is often used to mean slow, meditative, richly textured prose, but there is not much of that to be found in Bolaño's work. His training as a postsurrealist poet is apparent in a different way: passages of plain, quickly paced narration are interrupted by bursts of imagery or by lists. Metaphors and similes, on one hand, and enumeration or lists, on the other, are poetic in a basic, formal sense: they project "the principle of equivalence from the axis of selection into the axis of combination," thus fulfilling Roman Jakobson's poetic function.[22] Bolaño's metaphors and similes often clearly exceed an illustrative role. As in much modern poetry, the vehicles strike out on their own, while the tenors momentarily take a back seat. This is what happens when Sebastián Urrutia Lacroix, in *By Night in Chile*, compares the half-closed eyes of his mentor Farewell to "empty bear traps ruined by time and rain and freezing cold" (BNC 100), or when, at the beginning of *Amulet*, Auxilio Lacouture says: "Let me stretch time out like a plastic surgeon stretching the skin of a patient under anesthesia" (A 2).

Unlike Jorge Luis Borges, the Latin American writer whom he most admired, Bolaño rarely indulges in the kind of enumeration that Leo Spitzer dubbed chaotic and traced back to Whitman, whose heterogeneous lists suggest a random sampling from the inexhaustible inventory of everything there is.[23] Bolaño's lists are generally of a different and older type: the epic catalogue, which takes a limited set and attempts to exhaust its elements (heroes of the Trojan War in Book II of the *Iliad*, ships of the Trojans' Etruscan allies in Book X of the *Aeneid*, winds in Book X of Milton's *Paradise Lost*, whales in Chapter XXXII of *Moby-Dick*). The possible meanings of Wieder's name in *Distant Star* (DS 40–42), Juan García Madero's catechism of poetic terminology in *The Savage Detectives* (SD 527–531), Elvira Campos's list of phobias in *2666* (381–383), and the discontinuous catalogue of victims in "The Part About the Crimes" all belong to this exhaustive, epic type.

The poetic function comes to the fore at certain moments in most literary prose, but rarely does it obtrude as indiscreetly and independently as in Bolaño's metaphorical volleys and prodigal lists. Nevertheless the reader is drawn on by a desire to know what is going to happen, because even when the prose has digressed orthogonally, as it were, to explore a paradigm, a narrative question invariably hangs over it. As I will argue in chapter 3, Bolaño's novels and stories expertly manage narrative tension, and suspense in particular, although they rarely dissipate it in anything approaching a dénouement, governed as they are by what Ignacio Echevarría has called a "poetics of inconclusiveness" (SE viii).

In coupling elegy and energy, Bolaño effected a second distinctive combination. Much of what he wrote was an elegy for the generation of Latin Americans who came to maturity, often abruptly, in the 1970s, the decade of the coups in Chile (1973), Uruguay (1973), and Argentina (1976). In the speech that he gave on accepting the Rómulo Gallegos Prize, he said:

> to a great extent everything that I've written is a love letter or a farewell letter to my own generation, those of us who were born in the 1950s and who at a certain moment chose military service, though in this case it would be more accurate to say militancy, and we gave the little we had— the great deal that we had, which was our youth—to a cause that we thought was the most generous cause in the world and in a certain way it was, but in reality it wasn't. (BP 35)

The stories Bolaño tells are mainly stories of failure. As he said in an interview, "From a literary point of view, the loser always yields far more than a winner" (B 117). And yet many readers have vouched for the energizing effect of his fiction. Jonathan Beckman, for example, has written: "Readers may leave *2666* bemused . . . but the experience will nonetheless have been moving and invigorating."[24] Horacio Castellanos Moya has described how "the force and the magnetism" of Bolaño's prose in *The Savage Detectives* kept "taking him by the throat" and plunging him back into the novel's world, even though he was reading it in "the worst possible conditions," after exhausting days spent coordinating news coverage of the Mexican elections in 2000.[25] There are, I think, two reasons for this apparently paradoxical effect. First, the failures of Bolaño's characters are almost always contingent rather than chosen or willed, however unconsciously. His characters are rarely motivated by a taste for failure or "wrecked by success," as Freud put it, that is, precipitated into neurosis by the fulfillment of a long-cherished wish.[26] Failure is simply something that happens to them, an accident produced by an external cause, as death is, according to Spinoza.[27] In this sense, it would be more accurate to speak of defeat, as Ignacio Echevarría has pointed out.[28] Nor is failure or defeat necessarily a cause for lamentation. Looking back over his avant-garde youth and the grand plans for Stridentopolis that he hatched along with his friends, Amadeo Salvatierra in *The Savage Detectives* says, "I saw our struggles and dreams all tangled up in the same failure, and that failure was called joy" (SD 336). The struggles and dreams may have come to nothing in the end, but while the stridentists pursued them, their power to act was augmented; even as they were failing, they were affected by a joyous passion.[29]

The second reason for the invigorating effect of Bolaño's stories of failure concerns their forms and rhythms. His prose has a contagious, joyful energy, even when treating desolate themes. This energy springs in part from a literally expansive quality: it moves forward by expanding and opening up what has already been written, from the scale of the sentence up to that of the book, as I will explain in chapter 2. In this sense, Bolaño is an anti-Beckett: the failures of his characters are not mirrored by shrinking forms and deliberate lexical asceticism but belied by verbal proliferation.

I come now to the third distinctive combination of qualities mentioned above, the combination of literariness and distance from literature. In an interview Bolaño said that in Barcelona he had learned to live outside literature, by which I think he meant that he had learned to live with people for whom Literature with a capital L was not important.[30] This openness is something that Simone Darrieux likes about Arturo Belano in *The Savage Detectives*: "he always seemed to be thinking in terms of literature, but he wasn't a fanatic, he didn't look down on you if you'd never in your life read Jacques Rigaut, he even liked Agatha Christie too" (SD 207). In the first part of *2666*, the critics Pelletier and Espinoza discover, as they come to the end of their studious youths, that much as they love the work of Archimboldi, it cannot fill their lives. What matters to them most is what is happening in the group they form with their colleagues Norton and Morini (2666 29). Their voyage to Mexico in search of the great and enigmatic Archimboldi takes them away from literature and toward a world where fiction is a luxury and journalism a dangerous vocation. Inverting Bolaño's trajectory, the European critics (Espinoza in particular) learn, in Mexico, to live outside literature. But their learning is told, of course, in a literary work. This is literature questioning itself from within: not relinquishing its hard-won autonomy, but rejecting certain extravagant claims made on its behalf by radical aesthetes.

Bolaño is both an intensely literary author and one for whom the importance of literature is relative. His books are full of writers and his appetite for reading was immense, but he did not use literature as a sanctuary or a sacrificial altar. Nor did he idolize action. He would not have agreed that "the world was made in order to result in a beautiful book," as Jules Huret reports Mallarmé saying, nor that "true life is elsewhere," to commandeer a phrase from Rimbaud's *A Season in Hell*.[31] For Bolaño, literature was part of life, quite as real as the rest, and vitally important, but a part. He might have subscribed to the opinion of his compatriot Alejandro Zambra, who reflects at the end of *Formas de volver a casa* (*Ways of Going Home*) that the "strange trade" of writing is "necessary and insufficient."[32] Bolaño's books keep sending us to the paper or electronic archives (to find out, for example, whether this or that proper name refers to a real person) but they also, crucially, keep sending us back to what is happening among us here and now.

An anonymous essay in *N + 1* makes this point in a lively and somewhat hyperbolic way:

> In Bolaño, literature is a helpless, undignified, and not especially pleasant compulsion, like smoking. At one point you started and now you can't stop; it's become a habit and an identity. Nothing is so consistent across Bolaño's work as the suspicion that literature is chiefly bullshit, rationalizing the misery, delusions, and/or narcissism of various careerists, flakes, and losers. Yet Bolaño somehow also treats literature as his and his characters' sole excuse for existing. This basic Bolaño aporia—literature is all that matters, literature doesn't matter at all—can be a glib paradox for others. He seems to have meant it sincerely, even desperately, something one would feel without knowing the first thing about his life.[33]

This is hyperbolic because, as we have just seen in the case of Pelletier and Espinoza, literature is not all that matters in Bolaño's work; nor is it devoid of value. It is not practiced *exclusively* by careerists, flakes, and losers; and besides, many of the flakes and losers are, in their various ways, admirable and endearing characters. Rather than an aporia or insurmountable contradiction, we are faced with an unusual combination of belief and critical distance. Writers need to believe in literature in order to keep going, and this need becomes more urgent as the public turns gradually from writing to audiovisual media. But they do not have to subscribe to all the articles of a common creed. In chapter 7 I will argue that a minimalist ethics is implicit in Bolaño's fiction. His belief in literature is similarly minimalist. Just as his fiction implicitly but firmly upholds a small number of ethical principles, his approach to writing is grounded in a small number of strong commitments: to a pantheon of favorite authors and a band of friends, to the purity and promise of young writers, and to a certain idea of poetry.[34]

Beyond his core loyalties, Bolaño had little time for literary life in general. A savage critic of careerists, he was quick to spot the resentments and vanities that flourish in a social world structured by dramatic differences in reputation. Of Alejandro Jodorowsky, he wrote: "I remember him saying that Nicanor [Parra], on his way somewhere, had stayed at his house. In this statement I glimpsed a childlike pride which since then I have noticed again and again in the majority of writers" (LEE 213). Bolaño's critical distance with regard to literary life was in part the product of an atypical trajectory, marked by emigration and a long period of social marginality. Succeeding late, in the last five years of his life, he maintained the dispositions of an outsider.[35]

SYMPTOM

In the previous section, I sketched an explanation for Bolaño's North American reception in terms of his singularity as a writer. I would like now to return to the list proposed at the beginning of this chapter and gloss each of the remaining explanations, all of which take his success to be symptomatic of a situation. My glosses will be brief, for three reasons. First, this is primarily a book of literary criticism, not a study of reception.[36] Second, without conducting serious empirical research, it is very difficult to assess the relative powers of these symptomatic explanations. And third, as I will argue below, even the most meticulous empirical research could not provide a complete explanation for a cultural phenomenon of this kind, in which contingencies and uncertainty play a significant part.

BOLAÑO IS AN AMERICAN WRITER

The enthusiastic reception of Bolaño's fiction in North America might be related to the fact that he is a transnational writer who set his fiction in Chile and Mexico, where he grew up, but also in other American countries, which he constructed elaborately in imagination and fantasy. *Nazi Literature in the Americas*, a biographical survey of imaginary writers who flirted with or espoused far-right ideologies, is a pan-American book. The largest contingent of fictional authors is from Argentina (nine), followed by the United States (seven). A number of important characters in Bolaño's other books are North Americans: the African American journalist Oscar Fate, who is the focal character in the "Part About Fate" in *2666*, Barbara Patterson in *The Savage Detectives*, and Anne Moore in "Anne Moore's Life," Bolaño's longest short story, which might be more aptly described as an accelerated novel.

The heartland of Bolaño's fictional world is the state of Sonora in northwest Mexico, and in particular that state's northeast corner, where the imaginary city of Santa Teresa is located. The paths of his characters converge on this region. The four fugitives in *The Savage Detectives* (Belano, Lima, Madero, Lupe) end up there, running away from Lupe's pimp and searching for the vanished poet Cesárea Tinajero. Of the band of four European critics in *2666*, three also go to Sonora, trying to track down the reclusive German writer Benno von Archimboldi. Imprisoned in Santa Teresa on suspicion of crimes that closely resemble the real murders of young women in Ciudad Juárez, Archimboldi's nephew, Klaus Haas, says to the journalist Fate, "No one pays attention to these killings, but the secret of the world is hidden in them" (2666 348); and Bolaño, in his notes for the book, mentions a "hidden center" buried beneath the book's "physical center" (896). These centers are located in an infamously troubled border zone, and the breakdown of law and order there is a problem that urgently concerns the United States, whose consumers sustain the drug industry and the *maquiladoras*. So it is not surprising that *2666* has commanded the attention of North American readers; it speaks to them of a social catastrophe in which they are implicated, however indirectly.

In that sense it is an uncomfortable book, but there is a different sense in which Bolaño's work may seem to sit comfortably with North American preconceptions. The Argentine critic Josefina Ludmer, formerly a professor at Yale, has said of her students there: "To put it simplistically, what interests them is Latin American barbarity: the dictatorships, magical realism. . . . In other words, what they don't have. That's what they're interested in importing and reading; why would they want to read more of the same?"[37] Ludmer formulates a general tendency, observable in international publishing choices as well as student preferences. To be interesting, the foreign must be exotic, which often means in practice that the subtly different is displaced by what differs obtrusively. Bolaño is an exceptional writer, but his success in the United States does not represent an exception to this tendency, because barbarity is not scarce in his work, and that has given it "hooks," as people say in the publishing trade.

In a penetrating article on the reception of *The Savage Detectives*, Sarah Pollack writes:

> Unwittingly—or perhaps even with a provocative deliberation—*The Savage Detectives* plays into a series of opposing characteristics that the United States has historically employed in its self-definition vis-à-vis its neighbors to the south: hardworking vs. lazy; mature vs. adolescent; responsible vs. reckless; upstanding vs. delinquent. In a nutshell, Sarmiento's dichotomy, as old as Latin America itself: civilized vs. savage. Regarded from this standpoint, *The Savage Detectives* is a very comfortable choice for the United States to represent Latin America and Latin American literature, offering both the pleasure of the savage and the superiority of the civilized.[38]

Pollack's article is a study of reception, "a reading of a reading," but the reading that she criticizes has not been imposed arbitrarily; to some disputable degree, *The Savage Detectives* "plays into" it, from the title on. It would, however, be rash to assume that the novel, or Bolaño's work in general, superimposes the north/south and civilization/barbarity distinctions in a simple way or reproduces stereotypes automatically.

The passage cited above from Pollack's article follows a quotation from *The Savage Detectives* in which the North American character Barbara Patterson is complaining about her feckless Mexican boyfriend, Rafael Barrios, who has come back with her to Los Angeles, where he does nothing but take showers "and watch TV until dawn or go out for beers or play soccer with the fucking Chicanos in the neighborhood" (SD 324). The boyfriend is certainly a layabout, but if this trait is typical, it is typical of the young men in the visceral realist group, not of the women or of the other Mexicans in the novel. Those young men are disinclined to "make something" of their lives, and although Barbara Patterson finds that disinclination exasperating in Rafael's case (SD 301–303), it is one aspect of a stance that the novel as a whole celebrates and memorializes, as I will argue in chapter 7. While playing into the reading that Pollack criticizes, *The Savage Detectives* also plays it false, notably by valuing resistance to social aging, a resistance associated not with Latin America but with poetry.

It might be claimed that *2666* reinforces the stereotypical civilization/barbarity distinction in a darker way by describing in detail the bodies of 109 women killed in Santa Teresa, south of the border. Three connected points can be made in reply. First, the number of women's bodies found in "The Part About the Crimes" exactly matches the number found in and around Ciudad Juárez in the corresponding period (see appendix). Bolaño has not exaggerated the magnitude of the atrocity. Second, the impunity of the criminals in *2666* may reflect a stereotypical lawlessness, but here reality and stereotype coincide. This is what the detective Miguel Loya is telling the congresswoman Azucena Esquivel Plata when he says that "in Mexico a person can be more or less dead":

No, I said, almost hissing, no one can be more or less dead, in Mexico or anywhere else in the world. Stop talking like a tour guide. Either my friend is alive, which means I want you to find her, or my friend is dead, which means I want the people who killed her. Loya smiled. What are you laughing at? I asked him. The tour guide part was funny, he said. I'm sick of Mexicans who talk and act as if this is all *Pedro Páramo*, I said. Maybe it is, said Loya. (2666 624)

Loya does not mean that it can be impossible to distinguish a living person from an apparition, as it is for Juan Preciado in the first part of Juan Rulfo's novel *Pedro Páramo*, but that Preciado's predicament has a real analogue: when a person has fallen foul of organized crime and disappeared (especially when the criminal organization has infiltrated government agencies), it is sometimes impossible to find out what has happened. It is precisely this coincidence of reality and stereotype that the congresswoman finds intolerable.

The third point is that the crimes in Santa Teresa reveal a human potential that is universal, if more contained in most other places. Barbarity is amply manifest in the historical horrors of "The Part About Archimboldi," set in Germany and Eastern Europe before, during, and after the Second World War. More surprisingly, it also inhabits the distinguished university professors Pelletier and Espinoza, citizens of the European Union in the 1990s. When a taxi driver insults their friend and lover Liz Norton, they beat him until he is "bleeding from every orifice in the head, except the eyes" (74).

To sum up this first symptomatic explanation: Bolaño is an American writer who is recognizably Latin for readers from the north, but the reading that makes his work "a comfortable choice" is reductive.

BOLAÑO IS A TRANSLATABLE WRITER

Another factor contributing to Bolaño's reception in North America may be that his prose is relatively amenable to translation. By this I do not mean that he writes in a bland, neutral, "international" style, devoid of local particularities; on the contrary, Bolaño makes extensive use of regional varieties of Spanish in first-person narration. This characteristic is bound to be lost to a large extent in translation, even when the target language also has a broad range of regional varieties, as English does, since using, for instance,

Australian idioms in translating distinctively Chilean speech would in all likelihood be confusing even for an Australian reader. What I mean by "relatively amenable to translation" is that a relatively high proportion of the linguistic features on which Bolaño's style depends are transferable from Spanish to English without major loss. A short list of those features would include the headlong sentence, which persists in accumulating clauses by coordination; the "swirling" word repetition described by the Colombian poet Dario Jaramillo as an irritating tic;[39] the bursts of bold postsurrealist imagery mentioned above, often introduced by "as if"; and the strategic deployment of the narrator's uncertainty and/or memory lapses as rapid transitions. Naturally there are shifts and losses, but Bolaño's style, which as the translator Natasha Wimmer has said, has an "underlying plainness,"[40] is more robust and better withstands translation than a style in which wordplay or subtle sound patterning, or both, are central, like that of the great Cuban writer José Lezama Lima, who remains little known in the English-speaking world, in spite of Gregory Rabassa's resourceful version of *Paradiso*.

For some writers and critics, a style that depends on larger-scale, relatively translatable features is necessarily coarse and inferior. The Colombian novelist Fernando Vallejo, for example, has said, in a typically provocative sally, that Bolaño's use of language is on a level with "Me Tarzan, you Cheetah."[41] But to make such a judgment is to subscribe to the limited "acoustico-decorative" conception of style criticized by Borges in "The Superstitious Ethics of the Reader." According to that conception, Bolaño would not be a stylist at all, but he would be in fine company, with Montaigne, Cervantes, and Dostoyevsky. As Borges argues, against Flaubert, the stylistically perfect page, in which nothing can be changed without occasioning an important loss of quality, is the most vulnerable to misprints, mistranslations, and misreadings, while the truly immortal page can withstand such accidents without losing its "soul."[42] This argument, a version of which was canvassed by Flaubert himself in a letter to Louise Colet,[43] is reprised and radicalized by Bolaño in an article entitled "Translation Is an Anvil":

> How to recognize a work of art? How to separate it, even if just for a moment, from its critical apparatus, its exegetes, its tireless plagiarizers,

its belittlers, its final lonely fate? Easy. Let it be translated. Let its translator be far from brilliant. Rip pages from it at random. Leave it lying in an attic. If after all of this a kid comes along and reads it, and after reading it makes it his own, and is faithful to it (or unfaithful, whichever) and reinterprets it and accompanies it on its voyage to the edge, and both are enriched and the kid adds an ounce of value to its original value, then we have something before us, a machine or a book, capable of speaking to all human beings: not a plowed field but a mountain, not the image of a dark forest but the dark forest, not a flock of birds but the Nightingale. (BP 241)

There has not yet been time for all the phases of this rigorous testing, and Wimmer clearly fails to satisfy the condition of being "far from brilliant," but it is not too soon to say that Bolaño's work is living up to the ideal of robustness and fecundity defended in this passage, because it has already been taken up and used by writers, not all of them "kids," who have read it in English, but also in many other languages.[44]

If we are convinced by Borges's arguments in "The Superstitious Ethics of the Reader," we can either concede that style is only one of the factors that contribute to literary value or expand the notion to take in a larger range of linguistic features, from the level of the sentence up to the syntactic and semantic organization of whole works. Indeed, we could go further still, with the Argentine writer César Aira, and think of style as a continuum that stretches all the way from word choices to life choices. In "Absolute Particularities," an essay on style thus broadly conceived, Aira argues that although writing is an organization of lived experience, some parts of life are already organized like written texts, for example a trip with its departure, return, and intervening episodes.[45] The prodigy, says Aira, can make literature from any kind of experience; it need not present itself in intelligible chunks; it can be chaotic, boring, or dismal. He cites Kafka the office worker, Borges the bookworm, Proust in his cork-lined refuge, and Joyce: "exiled, alcoholic, myopic, unhappily married, making a supreme work of art from the degree zero of experience: an ordinary day in the life of an ordinary man in a modern city" (12). At the other end of the spectrum is the writer who no longer needs to write because his or her experience has assumed a satisfyingly literary shape.

The example that Aira gives is Rimbaud. "Each writer," according to Aira, "works out his own combination, his niche at an intermediate point, and this working out constitutes his personal myth. The particular figure that each writer cuts is the formula that he has invented to organize the complex of perceptions and feelings, and, through that organization, to turn it into experience from which to write" (12). In Aira's essay, "personal myth," "formula," and "style" are synonyms for a principle that organizes the whole constituted by a life and a life's work. And this all-inclusive, existential notion of style leads us to a third symptomatic explanation for Bolaño's success in North America, which is that a myth has intensified and sustained public interest in his work.

BOLAÑO HAS GIVEN RISE TO A MYTH

Bolaño's life did and does provide stuff for myth-making: his wandering youth; his years of poverty; his imprisonment in Chile after the coup in 1973; his reputation as an *enfant terrible* on the Mexican poetic scene in the mid 1970s; his sudden rise to fame when he won the Rómulo Gallegos prize in 1998 for *The Savage Detectives*; the prodigious productivity of his later years; the meganovel he was known to be writing when he died at the age of fifty, from liver failure, while waiting for a transplant.

The facts have sometimes been embellished, as Bolaño himself remarked in an interview: "I was held for eight days. . . . When I was first published in Germany they said it was a month; the first book didn't sell too well, so they put it up to three months on the second book; and on the third book it was four . . . the way things are going, I'll have been in prison all along" (B 38). In 2008, the literary agent Andrew Wylie, who represents the Bolaño estate, wrote to *The New York Times* in response to what he and the author's widow saw as a similar case of embellishment or fabrication in a review of *2666* by Jonathan Lethem:

Roberto Bolaño's widow, Carolina López, and I would like to clarify that Roberto never suffered any form of addiction to drugs, including heroin. This longstanding misunderstanding seems to have been conjured from the coincidence of Roberto's illness and the subject matter of his story "The Beach" [*sic*]. Though written in the first person, that story is truly a work of fiction.[46]

"Beach" begins like this: "I gave up heroin and went home and began the methadone treatment administered at the outpatient clinic" (BP 260). The text was first published in August 2000 in the Madrid newspaper *El Mundo*, in a series with the general title "Story: The Worst Summer of My Life," then collected in the posthumous volumes *Between Parentheses* and *The Secret of Evil*. In *Between Parentheses*, the piece appears in a section entitled "Scenes," in which the other texts (newspaper columns and a speech) are all nonfictional. The book's editor, Ignacio Echevarría, writes in his introduction that "Beach" could figure "in any of Bolaño's story collections" (BP 7), but some of the texts in those collections, as Echevarría points out elsewhere (SE ix), are autobiographical: their first-person narrator strongly resembles the real Roberto Bolaño as well as the characters referred to in the third person as B and Arturo Belano. "I," B, and Belano overlap. Consequently, it is not at all surprising that "Beach" has been read autobiographically. Such readings may have resulted from a mistaken inference, but they were not the deceptive product of a conjuring act.

It is, however, symptomatic that Bolaño's supposed heroin addiction has been routinely mentioned in English-language reviews. It is a detail that enriches the myth. A number of critics have taken issue with the mythologizing of Bolaño, notably Scott Esposito, Sarah Pollack, Horacio Castellanos Moya, Christopher Domínguez Michael, and Juan Antonio Masoliver Ródenas.[47] Fundamentally, these critics have three objections: that the mythologizing falsifies, that it confirms stereotypes, and that it distracts from the work. The first two objections are related. The myth that has circulated in reviewing, blogging, and conversations has, to some degree, distorted Bolaño's life by assimilating him to familiar figures of the artist: the *poète maudit*, the Beat. Hopefully, one day, a well-researched biography will serve as a corrective, conveying a complexity that journalistic portraits cannot capture for simple reasons of space.

The third objection—that mythologizing distracts from the work—is more problematic. Certainly, biographical curiosity can erode the autonomy of imaginative literature by implying that the fiction is only interesting if it can be attached to an interesting real-life story. But should we attempt to keep work and life rigorously apart? Authorities as different as Marcel Proust, C. S. Lewis, and Roland Barthes have argued that we should. Proust was scandalized by the blindness of Sainte-Beuve, who could not see beyond Baudelaire's unimpressive showing in the salons, taking him to be a very minor talent, an eccentric, and calling *Les fleurs du mal*, "This little lodge, which the poet has built himself on the tip of the Kamtschatka of literature, I call it 'the Baudelaire Folly.'"[48] For Proust, the real author is a "creative self," quite unrelated to the "social self" who fascinates the biographical critic. Lewis, for his part, was irritated by what he called the Personal Heresy, a modern and at bottom atheistic error, based on "the proposition that all poetry is *about* the poet's state of mind."[49] For Lewis, the real author is the nation or the race, a somewhat disturbing position, as E. M. W. Tillyard politely suggests in his reply, pointing out that Lewis's sentiments fall in with a "strong modern tendency, *whose limits are not easily drawn*, to belittle the individual in comparison with the race."[50] The emphasis is mine: the two men were debating in the mid-1930s, and Tillyard seems to have been more alive than his interlocutor to the sinister potential of the strong modern tendency in question. At the end of the 1960s, Barthes wanted to free the reader from the author's tyranny and usher in the modern "scriptor," who is born at the same time as the text and is the instrument of a purely verbal and intransitive process of writing.[51] For Barthes, as for Mallarmé, the real author is language itself (143).

These arguments for replacing the author with a creative self, a nation, a race, or a language, persuasive as they may be, are fundamentally normative arguments with other critics about how criticism should be written and about how literature should be taught, rather than descriptive accounts of what happens at an earlier stage, when we read. And unless we have been very purely schooled, we tend, as we read a literary text, to construct an author (conceptually distinct from the empirical writer) who is the agent of the action that is the text. As Alexander Nehamas puts it in his article "Writer, Text, Work, Author": "We become interested in whoever it is who can be said to have produced that text and to be manifested in its characteristics."[52] Not the historical individual who sat down and wrote it (the writer), but the kind of person we imagine him or her to have been as we read (the author).

Nehamas's conceptual distinction has clarified the question of the author's death invaluably, but it does not negate the existence of connections between a given writer and the authors that we, as readers, variously construct by interpreting his or her work. Writer and author are related in many ways, as are Proust's social and creative selves, although the relations are often far more complex, indirect, and twisted than Sainte-Beuve could imagine. To be drawn on from book to book by interest in an author is not necessarily to be the victim of a myth or a marketing strategy. Barthes himself confessed, in *The Pleasure of the Text*, that he was motivated by a desire for the author "in the text," that is, the author in the sense defined by Nehamas.[53] And to be curious about the relations between an author and a writer is to discover both how the work is a subset of the actions that compose a life and just how distinct that subset can be. A style, in Aira's extended sense of the word, is always complex and difficult to grasp as a whole, but that does not invalidate the notion. When Rubén Medina informs us that Bolaño was rarely present among the *infrarealistas* who disturbed poetry readings with their heckling, but that he always took care to find out what had happened and recorded the events meticulously in his notebooks, we learn something worth knowing about his existential style, something that examination of the works alone would not reveal.[54]

BOLAÑO SUPPLIES A LACK IN NORTH AMERICAN FICTION

I have just suggested that the North American myth of Bolaño has assimilated him to a familiar figure of the writer. But a fourth symptomatic explanation of his success might contradict that claim: Bolaño has succeeded not because he resembles writers already popular in North America but because he supplies a lack in North American fiction. Such an explanation might draw on the "polysystems theory" of the Israeli translation scholar Itamar Even-Zohar, who conceptualizes national literary fields as nests of systems in which translated literature can be peripheral, as it usually is in English, or central, as Hebrew translations of Russian texts were in Israel between the world wars:

> The dynamics of the polysystem create turning points, that is to say, histori-
> cal moments where established models are no longer tenable for a younger
> generation. At such moments, even in central literatures, translated litera-
> ture may assume a central position. This is all the more true when at a
> turning point no item in the indigenous stock is taken to be acceptable, as
> a result of which a literary "vacuum" appears.[55]

Perhaps the indigenous stock of the United States is so abundantly supplied with highly professional fiction that Bolaño's defiantly messy and inconclusive books have served, for some younger writers, not so much as models to imitate but as examples of sheer boldness, encouraging them to take new risks of their own. That would be one way to understand Nicole Krauss's statement, quoted on the jacket of *Nazi Literature in the Americas*: "When I read Bolaño, I think: Everything is possible again." In a review of *2666*, Jonathan Lethem remarked: "Bolaño seems to make sport of violating nearly all of the foremost writing-school rules, against dream sequences, against mirrors as symbols, against barely disguised nods to his acquaintances, and so on."[56] Beyond the community of writers, readers too may have begun to weary of fiction that buys the rules and aims for high grades; they too may have been stimulated and relieved by Bolaño's unprofessional conduct in this regard. As Barbara Epler has written: "We are tired of dull fiction and sick of trick ponies. One reason why he has loomed so large in the USA is his absolute polarity from every aspect of the boring creative writing world."[57]

MEN LIKE BOLAÑO'S BOOKS

A fifth symptomatic explanation for Bolaño's fortunes in North America might take its cues from feminist criticism. It would be absurd to suggest that *only* men like Bolaño's books—the first two collections of essays on his work were edited by women (Celina Manzoni and Patricia Espinosa), his first publisher in the United States was a woman (Barbara Epler), and he has had influential female readers, including Susan Sontag and Patti Smith—but it is also obvious that he is a writer who appeals to men.[58] Why is this a possible explanation for his success? In a study conducted in 2005, Lisa Jardine and Annie Watkins interviewed 100 academics, critics, and writers about their reading habits and concluded that "Men who read fiction tend to read fiction by men, while women read fiction by both women and men. Consequently, fiction by women remains 'special interest,' while fiction by men still sets the standard for quality, narrative and style."[59] More empirical research is needed in this area, but if Jardine and Watkins' conclusions are sound, literary fiction by men simply has a larger potential audience.

Bolaño's success has been critical as well as commercial, and in this respect as well, gender may not have been indifferent. Fiction by men still seems to have a better chance of being taken seriously and qualified as "great."[60] Some of Bolaño's books may have symbolic advantages that flow not directly from a man's name on the cover but from forms and themes that men tend, statistically, to favor. A "great" book is often a big book: one whose text is long, whose story is extensive in space and time, and that can give an impression of exhaustiveness.[61] *2666* satisfies these conditions. Reviewing the novel in *The Australian*, Don Anderson wrote, "Bolaño suggests several of his great contemporaries or antecedents: Thomas Pynchon, Robert Musil, James Joyce, William Gaddis, William Vollman, Don DeLillo, say, over-reachers all, Men of the Big Book, because only a big book can—presumptuous, Promethean thought—encompass the universe."[62] Other reviewers have added other men to Anderson's list: Murakami Haruki (*The Wind-Up Bird Chronicle*) and David Foster Wallace (*Infinite Jest*). In discussions of maximalist versus minimalist postmodern fiction, the maximalist standard-bearers are nearly all men, while the minimalists are a more or less evenly mixed group.[63]

Logically enough, "greatness" correlates with size, but it also seems, still, to correlate with epic themes, in the Homeric sense: war and adventurous voyaging, both of which figure strongly in Bolaño's novels. (*2666* and *The Third Reich*, in particular, draw on his extensive and detailed knowledge of military history and war games.)[64] I am not suggesting that these themes were chosen in a bid for glory, or questioning the principle of neutrality defended by Henry James in "The Art of Fiction"—"we must grant the art-ist his idea, his subject, his donnée: our criticism is applied only to what he makes of it"[65]—I am noting that Bolaño's themes, especially in the two long novels, tally with an ancient and gendered conception of what makes for great literature. What Virginia Woolf referred to, in 1918, as "the very dif-ficult question of the difference between the man's and the woman's view of what constitutes the importance of any subject" is still a difficult question.[66]

BOLAÑO HAS BEEN MISREAD

Having briefly reviewed six symptomatic explanations for the enthusiastic reception of Bolaño's fiction in North America, all of which, I think, have some validity, I move now to an explanation that is, in my view, invalid, although it is seductive from the point of view of the source culture: "Bolaño has been misread."

Pierre Bourdieu uses the term *allodoxia* for the phenomenon of false rec-ognition, which he likens to mistakenly identifying a friend or acquaintance in the street.[67] In the domain of culture, Bourdieu says, allodoxia is an effect of middlebrow goodwill:

> This pure but empty goodwill which, for lack of the guidelines needed to apply it, does not know which way to turn, exposes the petit bourgeois to cultural allodoxia, that is, all the mistaken identifications and false recog-nitions which betray the gap between acknowledgement and knowledge. Allodoxia, the heterodoxy experienced as if it were orthodoxy that is engen-dered by this undifferentiated reverence, in which avidity combines with anxiety, leads the petit bourgeois to take light opera for "serious music," popularization for science, an imitation for the genuine article, and to find in this at once worried and over-assured false recognition the source of a satisfaction which still owes something to the sense of distinction.[68]

It might be suggested that this is what has happened in Bolaño's case: the North American public was waiting for the next big thing from the south, and fixed on a writer with a suitable profile but without the genuine aesthetic merits of the more deserving X (insert here the name of a novelist highly reputed in Latin America, but little known beyond academic circles in the north). Alberto Manguel sees the reception of Bolaño in English as an instance of such a mistake:

> No doubt Bolaño was a skillful writer and wrote at least a couple of books that are well worth reading. *Distant Star* and *By Night in Chile* are two excellent, forceful novels; the rest are light playful experiments, not very successful, with little intelligence and less ambition. . . . It is not an author's fault if certain impressionable critics (as well as his agent, and his publishers . . .) have decided, without irony, that he must also take on the role of a Latin American messiah in the world of letters.[69]

Leaving aside the very surprising dismissal of *The Savage Detectives* and *2666* as a "light playful experiments" without ambition, the review places English-speaking readers, including the cultural elite, in the position of Bourdieu's anxious and gullible petit bourgeois. The implication is that even elites are prone to allodoxia when choosing among foreign cultural products. In other words, foreigners get it wrong, as Philip Larkin said in his *Paris Review* interview: "Foreigners' ideas of good English poems are dreadfully crude: Byron and Poe and so on. The Russians liking Burns."[70] Since Byron, Poe, and Burns are not renowned for the subtlety of their sound patterning, Larkin may be subscribing here to the limiting "acoustico-decorative" notion of style criticized by Borges in "The Superstitious Ethics of the Reader." He is certainly assuming that any value that Byron, Poe, and Burns might have acquired in another cultural context must be spurious. César Aira takes this curmudgeonly line of argument and twists it radically in an essay entitled "The Incomprehensible":

> Within a historical community, a book is necessarily "over-understood" [*sobreentendido*]. . . . We understand too well and the book teeters dangerously on the brink of the obvious. We have the misfortune of sharing the conditions in which it was produced. . . . But with the books we love, distances begin to open up straight away. . . . Inevitably, time begins to

pass, and that temporal distance will always continue to grow. Also, books move in space, they leave the neighborhood, the city, the society that produced them, and end up in other languages, other worlds, in an endless voyage towards the incomprehensible. The ship that transports them is misunderstanding. For an Argentine, the idea that a Cuban could understand Borges or Arlt is as ridiculous as it must be for a Cuban to hear an Argentine claiming to understand Lezama Lima. When books are stripped of over-understanding, all we can do is love them. The phrase, "to love for the wrong reasons" is what logicians call a nonsensical proposition; anyone who has loved knows that.[71]

For Aira, as for Larkin, foreigners get it wrong, but we are all foreigners in relation to the works of the past written in our mother tongue, and those of the present as well if they are written in dialects other than our own. The fall from "over-understanding" into misunderstanding is both inevitable and fortunate. The destiny of misunderstanding is to "engender further misunderstandings, to multiply them and make them more effective, to turn them into truths to be used for living and creating" (23).

Bolaño has surely been misunderstood in Aira's sense of the word. How could it have been otherwise? But that does not mean that he has usurped a recognition rightly due to another. Indeed, his work's capacity to generate effective and productive misreadings (as well as reductive ones) may be a sign of its vigor.

UNCERTAINTY

In the preceding sections I have considered seven possible explanations for Bolaño's positive reception in the United States. The first (that he is an exceptional writer) seems to me the strongest, and the last (that he has been misread) invalid. All the others have, I think, some degree of explanatory power, but even taken together, I am not convinced that they fully explain what has happened.

It is tempting for both fans and detractors to regard Bolaño's success as predictable. For fans it may seem a necessary consequence of the work's inherent quality: the books are so good that they had to succeed. For detractors, success is an effect of hype, and some may see it as proof that Bolaño never was a truly literary author, since the truly literary authors are, by definition, those who do not succeed in the marketplace. Dissenting from both of these views, I would argue that the exceptional qualities of the books did not guarantee their success, and that the market might not have been so friendly to them, in spite of the hype.

There are three reasons why I believe this is so. First, good books well translated into English have a way of sinking. Why, for example, are the extraordinary later novels of Manuel Puig, translated by Suzanne Jill Levine, so inconspicuous? Second, people well placed to predict the fortunes of *2666* in English, like the book's publisher, Lorin Stein, and its translator, Natasha Wimmer, have said that they were apprehensive about its reception, because it is an extremely somber work and has little of the comic relief and idiomatic variety that made *The Savage Detectives* so engaging.[72] Critic and Bolaño-watcher Scott Esposito voiced similar doubts in his blog as he read a proof copy.[73] And yet those doubts were not confirmed.

My third and most important reason for questioning the necessity of Bolaño's success is that research by sociologists and economists has shown that uncertainty is built into cultural markets. A recent book by the French sociologist Pierre-Michel Menger argues that uncertainty is a constitutive principle of creative activity from the composition of the work to its distribution and evaluation. Among a host of sources, he cites an "Experimental Study of Inequality and Unpredictability in an Artificial Cultural Market" conducted by Matthew J. Salganik, Peter Sheridan Dodds, and Duncan J. Watts. These researchers created an artificial music market in which successive groups of consumers chose songs with and without information on what others had chosen. The songs were then ranked according to strictly individual choices and according to socially influenced choices. Sagalnik, Dodds, and Watts observed that the "best" songs as determined by the first ranking never did very badly in the second, and the "worst" songs never did extremely well, but almost any other result was possible.

The more information participants have regarding the decisions of others, the greater agreement they will seem to display regarding their musical preferences; thus the characteristics of success will seem predictable in retrospect. On the other hand, looking across different realizations of the same process, we see that as social influence increases . . . , which particular products turn out to be regarded as good or bad becomes increasingly unpredictable. . . . We conjecture, therefore, that experts fail to predict success not because they are incompetent judges or misinformed about the preferences of others, but because when individual decisions are subject to social influence, markets do not simply aggregate pre-existing individual preferences. In such a world, there are inherent limits on the predictability of outcomes, irrespective of how much skill or information one has.[74]

If Sagalnik, Dodds, and Watts are right, and if Menger's more general conclusions are sound, symptomatic explanations of the kind proposed above cannot be complete, even when taken together. And to complete them it would not be enough to consider the singularity of Bolaño's work. One would also have to reconstruct the singular event history of its reception in English, taking into account contingencies such as the fact that Susan Sontag read *By Night in Chile* shortly before she died and recommended it enthusiastically. She lent her name to be conjured with, but she might have chosen to read something else. Then it happened that Deborah Treisman at *The New Yorker* chose to publish the story "Gómez Palacio" in 2005. A different fiction editor might have turned the story down, as *The Paris Review* had done. Then there is the contingent fact that *2666* came out less than two years after *The Savage Detectives*, and throughout that time the blogosphere was abuzz with eager chat about the huge posthumous novel on the way. As the publication date approached, a countdown effect intensified the excitement, which might have lapsed somewhat had the lag between the publications of the two translations been longer. Or not: the excitement might have continued to build.

Menger's "uncertainty principle" is not breaking news; he has generalized and theorized what people working in the arts have long known intuitively.

The economist Richard Caves calls the uncertainty of demand for cultural products the "nobody knows" property, in honor of the screenwriter William Goldman's much quoted remark on the motion picture industry: "Nobody knows anything."[75] Many cultural mediators (publishers, film producers, gallery owners, and so on) will admit that uncertainty makes their work exciting. But the uncertainty principle is not always easy to accept for artists and audiences. As Menger notes, it is often ignored by supposing either that the value of an artwork is simply revealed by its reception or that the work's value is a pure social and marketing construction.[76] The first supposition tempts successful writers and their admirers, who sometimes argue that x thousand readers can't be wrong (but wrong about *what*, exactly?). The second supposition tempts unsuccessful writers and their admirers, who sometimes argue that "They (i.e., the marketing departments) can sell anything" (although counterexamples are not hard to find).

The uncertainty principle can be hard to accept because it is cruel. Not only does it follow from the principle that success is unfairly distributed overall; it also follows that the distribution of success is not even systematically unfair, so individual failure cannot be regarded as a guarantee of merit. If we recognize the validity of the uncertainty principle we will also have to relinquish the consoling "scheme of compensatory justice" according to which, as Menger writes, "the quickest successes are the most ephemeral, and inversely, consecration will be all the more durable and widespread if it has been slow to come" (10). The reverse of the principle's cruelty is a curious sort of kindness (or is it a further cruel twist?): since "nobody knows," since differences of quality or talent are incompletely observable, large numbers of candidates can go on hoping to succeed in the creative professions in spite of the Pareto Principle, which applies to the arts as well as to many economic systems: 20 percent of the participating individuals concentrate 80 percent of the gains (7).

As it happens, the uncertainty principle is illustrated in the fiction of Roberto Bolaño, who wrote obsessively about writers and their fortunes. In Bolaño's fictional universe, the talent of a writer and the quality of his or her work can be uncertain, even for the writer's inner circle, while reputations are both unreliable and unstable over time.

Two stories from *Last Evenings on Earth*, "Henri Simon Leprince" and "Dentist," dramatize uncertainty about literary talent. Having written a long poem on the "mystery and martyrdom of minor poets" in a fit of inspiration, Henri Simon Leprince realizes that he does not himself belong to that category (LEE 23). He burns the poem. So is he more or less than a minor talent? The story does not give us grounds to decide. "There is something elusive, something indefinable about him that people find repellent" (22). But that something may be simply the smell of failure: "Perhaps they sense that Leprince is tainted by the years he has spent in the underworld of sad magazines and the gutter press, from which no man escapes, except the exceedingly strong, brilliant, and bestial" (22). Leprince finally accepts "his lot as a bad writer" (25), but the lot in his case may be social rather than ontological.

"Dentist," which I shall discuss in more detail in chapter 3, begins like this: "He wasn't Rimbaud, he was just an Indian boy" (LEE 188). By the end of the story, however, the reliability of that assertion is in doubt. The narrator's dentist friend has presented the boy, José Ramírez, as a literary prodigy, but the narrator is skeptical, thinking that his friend's judgment has been muddled by love. Finally the narrator reads some of Ramírez's work: "The story was four pages long; maybe that's why I chose it, because it was short, but when I got to the end, I felt as if I had read a novel. . . . Earlier, I had been almost falling asleep myself, but now I felt wide awake and absolutely sober" (207). Clearly there is something very special about this text. "The mystery of art and its secret nature," which the narrator subsequently understands in a dream "for barely a second" (209), remains a mystery, and so does its connection with the work of the young Ramírez. Is he Rimbaud reincarnate or a deluded kid from Irapuato? Like "Henri Simon Leprince," this story leaves the crucial question hanging.

In Bolaño's work reputations are unreliable guides to talent. There are good writers who are justly celebrated, like Benno von Archimboldi in *2666*, and good writers who are neglected, like "Sensini" in the story of the same name (LEE 1–18). There are bad writers who triumph, like the careerists Marco Antonio Palacios and Hernando García León at the Madrid Book Fair in *The Savage Detectives* (SD 462–466), and there are many, many bad writers who remain entirely obscure, like the flakes and losers who largely populate *Nazi Literature in the Americas*.

Not only do reputations fail to inform us reliably about talent; they are also fundamentally unstable. That is the lesson of Auxilio Lacouture's crazy prophecies near the end of *Amulet*:

> For Marcel Proust, a desperate and prolonged period of oblivion shall begin in the year 2033. Ezra Pound shall disappear from certain libraries in the year 2089. Vachel Lindsay shall appeal to the masses in the year 2101. . . . All statues tumble eventually, by divine intervention or the power of dynamite, like the statue of Heine. So let us not place too much trust in statues. (A 159–161)

Bolaño is not setting up Lacouture as an arbiter of compensatory justice, but giving us an imaginative illustration of a position that he attributed to the critic Iñaki Echavarne in *The Savage Detectives*: "And one day the Work dies, as all things must die and come to an end" (SD 456). Or as he crisply put it in an interview: "there is no immortality" (B 96).

Bolaño once said, "Success is no virtue, it's just an accident" (B 47). This is a typically provocative oversimplification, but it points toward an important truth. Both in his fiction and in conversation, he saw, more clearly than those who would claim that his success in North America was predictable, how literary writing is, as Menger writes, "modeled by uncertainty," from the conception of the work to its long-term reception.[77] Although it can be difficult to accept the uncertainty principle for the psychological reasons outlined above, doing so should leave us a little freer and more independent in our judgments, less inclined to revise them upward, as the fortunate publisher of the long-seller sometimes does, or downward, as believers in the intrinsic virtue of the marginal sometimes do when the object of their early enthusiasm loses its social distinctiveness.

2

BOLAÑO'S FICTION-MAKING SYSTEM

THE BULK OF Bolaño's massive oeuvre in prose was written in the last ten years of his life. Javier Cercas has remarked: "it is nothing short of astonishing that he wrote what he wrote between 1996, the year of *Distant Star*, and 2003, the year of his death."[1] The astonishing thing is not the sheer volume of his production, which is matched by many authors of commercial fiction, but the combination of high productivity and genuine inventiveness. Commenting on this aspect of the Bolaño anomaly, Nora Catelli has written:

> The work of Roberto Bolaño gives a clear and almost unquestionable impression of ease. While so many of his colleagues struggle to put together a barely convincing storyline, trying to convince us (and themselves) that the result reveals ontological reticence rather than weak plotting, Bolaño seems to have no difficulty finding and developing plots. And the way in which he does this is so fluid that it might be mistaken for natural. Yet there is nothing nineteenth-century about it: his skill is not naïve, and his use of narrative resources is not complacent. Indeed it could be said that Bolaño has constructed a fiction-making system that is as simple as it is rigorous.[2]

What is this system? How does it work? Is it really simple and rigorous?

Bolaño's fiction invites us to read genetically, that is, looking for traces of method in the finished work. This chapter examines four processes discerned by genetic reading: expansion, circulating characters, metarepresentation, and overinterpretation. The first two facilitate composition in an obvious way because they are modes of recycling. The second two, as we shall see, also contribute to the proliferation of Bolaño's fiction by providing a means of linking heterogeneous stories and kinds of discourse, and by enlarging the range of thoughts and actions that are psychologically plausible for a given character, thus allowing the writer greater freedom in developing the plot. None of the processes examined in this chapter is radically new, but Bolaño employs each distinctively, and their joint operation accounts in part, and of course *only* in part, for his extraordinary productivity.

EXPANSION

Perhaps the most striking of the four is expansion. Bolaño revisited previously published texts and expanded them from within, scaling up the rhetorical figure of tmesis, which cuts a word and inserts another (often an expletive) into the cut, as in "neverthebloodyless." This can be observed most clearly in *Distant Star* (*Estrella distante*, 1996), which expands "Carlos Ramírez Hoffman," the final chapter of *Nazi Literature in the Americas* (*La literatura nazi en América*, 1995), and in *Amulet* (*Amuleto*, 1999), which expands chapter 4 in part II of *The Savage Detectives* (*Los detectives salvajes*, 1998).

In the prologue to *Distant Star*, the author explains that he blew up the final chapter of *Nazi Literature in the Americas* at the prompting of "a fellow Chilean, Arturo B," who "would have preferred a longer story that, rather than mirroring or exploding others, was, in itself, a mirror and an explosion" (DS 1). The explosion that occurs in *Distant Star* does not totally destroy the earlier text but breaks it into fragments, which are conserved and exploited in the new, ampler structure. This too is signaled in the prologue: "My role was limited to preparing refreshments, consulting a few books, and discussing the reuse of numerous paragraphs with

Arturo and the increasingly animated ghost of Pierre Menard" (DS 1). Pierre Menard, eponymous hero of a famous story by Jorge Luis Borges, is invoked here as the patron saint of rewriting. Just as Menard's fragments of the *Quijote* are verbally identical to the original, many paragraphs and passages of *Distant Star* are reproduced from "Carlos Ramírez Hoffman" without changes, except for the names of the characters.[3]

In order to observe and describe the effects of this expansion I will compare the two texts, beginning on a small scale with a single episode common to both. First, however, I need to clarify the meanings of some technical terms that will be used in the analysis. Broadly speaking, two kinds of new element can be introduced into an existing narrative while respecting its overall shape: descriptive details and subsidiary actions, or, to use Barthes's terminology in "Introduction to the Structural Analysis of Narrative," indices and catalyzers.[4] Indices, for Barthes, are elements referring to more or less diffuse concepts that are nevertheless important to the meaning of the story: they inform us about a character's personality or identity; they suggest an atmosphere or situate the action in a social space. Catalyzers are functions or actions that do not have significant consequences for the way things turn out, as opposed to the cardinal functions or nuclei, but serve to connect those key moments, which constitute the story's armature.

Bolaño expands by adding both indices and catalyzers, as we can see if we compare the two versions of the episode in which Stevens/Ruiz-Tagle visits the Venegas/Garmendia twins at their country home (NLA 180–181; DS 19–23). The scene contains four nuclei: 1) Stevens/Ruiz-Tagle arrives at the house in Nacimiento; 2) he is invited to stay the night; 3) he murders the girls' aunt; and 4) he and his men murder the girls. Even in the short version, however, these nuclei are connected by catalyzers: the girls read out poems after dinner, Stevens hears a car approaching as he goes to the aunt's room, and so on. In rewriting this episode for *Distant Star*, Bolaño added further catalyzers. In "Carlos Ramírez Hoffman," "someone knocks at the door, and it is Emilio Stevens. The Venegas girls are pleased to see him" (NLA 181). In *Distant Star* a gap is opened up between Ruiz-Tagle's knocking and the appearance of the twins: "Someone knocks at the front door. Knocks and knocks and finally the maid opens the door and there is

Ruiz-Tagle. He says he has come to see the twins. The maid doesn't let him in and says she will go and call the girls. Ruiz-Tagle waits patiently, seated in a cane armchair on the broad porch" (DS 19). Indices are also multiplied: for example, the broad porch and cane chair in the passage just quoted and the paintings by the twins' dead parents, which, along with plates from the area around Nacimiento, line the corridors of the house (DS 22). None of these descriptive details is present in "Carlos Ramírez Hoffman."

As Barthes observes, the categories of index and catalyzer are not mutually exclusive, and it turns out that many of the expansions in this scene are what we might call indicial catalyzers, that is, actions that serve to link nuclei but also to tell us something about the nature of the actor (96–97). With the benefit of hindsight, Ruiz-Tagle's persistence in knocking at the door and patience in waiting can be seen as indices of a disquieting imperturbability. Similarly, his firm refusal to read his own poems has a sinister resonance, especially for rereaders, who know that his new work involves performing and documenting atrocities: "He says he has nearly finished something new, but until it is finished and corrected, he would prefer not to talk about it" (DS 20).

It would seem, then, that the expansion *completes*, adding atmospheric detail and actions that illustrate character, making it possible to imagine the scene more vividly and understand it more deeply. A detailed comparison of the reused content shows that in the expanded version hypotheses become statements, the possible becomes probable, and hesitations are resolved:

after dinner they *probably* read out poems (NLA 181)	After dinner they stay up late talking, and the twins read some poems (DS 20)
not Stevens, he ... smiles in a mysterious, knowing way, or *perhaps* he doesn't even smile, just flatly says no (NLA 181).	He smiles, shrugs, says, No, sorry, no, no, no (DS 20)
perhaps he has slept with María Venegas, *perhaps* not (NLA 181)	He has *probably* slept with Veronica Garmendia (DS 21)
and then he cuts the aunt's throat, *no*, he stabs her in the heart, it's cleaner, quicker (NLA 181)	Straight away, with a single stroke of the knife, he cuts her throat (DS 22)

Unequivocal statements in the first version are also reinforced:

they bombard him with questions, invite him to dinner (NLA 181)	Ruiz-Tagle is invited to dinner, *of course*, and in his honor they prepare a feast (DS 19)
then [they] say he's welcome to stay the night (NLA 181)	*Naturally*, they invite him to sleep the night (DS 20)
not Stevens, he doesn't want to read anything (NLA 181)	He, *of course*, doesn't read anything (DS 20)

So the second version would seem to be not only more complete but also more definite.

On the evidence gathered so far from the two versions of this episode, we might be tempted to regard "Carlos Ramírez Hoffman" as a preparatory sketch, tentative and gappy. Yet there is a sense in which it is more self-sufficient than *Distant Star*, because it is strongly centered on the protagonist, while the novel is insistently digressive and compromises the unity of the story that it expands. Chapters 4 and 5 of *Distant Star*, for example, are devoted to the poets Juan Stein and Diego Soto: friends, rivals, and doubles of each other. Moreover, within these digressive chapters, Bolaño digresses to double the doubles, telling the stories of Juan Stein's namesake in Puerto Montt (DS 61–64) and Lorenzo, also known as Petra, the armless gay artist (DS 72–76): "in a way, Petra is to Soto what Juan Stein's double is to the Juan Stein we knew" (DS 72). The expansion completes the earlier version, but also exceeds its frame by introducing new episodes and characters. Rather than simply rounding out the story, it produces disunity. It exploits and explodes.

This excessive aspect of the process is apparent in the episode of Stevens/Ruiz-Tagle's visit to the twins' country house. The longest segment of new material concerns the after-dinner reading and discussion of poetry:

And Ruiz-Tagle politely obliging, talking about signifier and signified, about Joyce Mansour, Sylvia Plath and Alejandra Pizarnik (although the twins say, No, no, we don't like Pizarnik, by which they really mean that they don't *write* like Pizarnik), and the aunt nodding attentively as Ruiz-Tagle goes on to mention Violeta and Nicanor Parra (I met Violeta, in her tent, I did, says poor Ema Oyarzún), and then Enrique Lihn and "civil poetry," and here if the twins were more attentive they would see an ironic glint in his eye (civil poetry, I'll give you civil poetry), and finally, in full flight now, he starts talking about Jorge Cáceres, the Chilean surrealist who died in 1949 at the age of twenty-six. (DS 20)

The multiplication of brackets is symptomatic: the parenthetic asides seem to be waiting for elaboration. Why do the twins disavow an affinity with Pizarnik? How did Ema Oyarzún come to meet Violeta Parra in her tent? What is the nature of the relation between Lihn's "civil poetry" and that of Ruiz-Tagle/Wieder? From each of these narrative stubs, a digression could depart.

We saw that where content is reused in this episode, doubts are resolved, but the new content introduces new doubts and alternatives, as in the following examples:

a car appears on the dirt road, but the twins don't hear, because they're playing the piano or busy in the orchard or stacking firewood at the back of the house with their aunt and the maid. (DS 19)

And then the twins get up, or perhaps it's only Veronica who goes to look in her father's sizeable library. (DS 21)

From time to time the Garmendia sisters, or maybe just Angelica, used to talk about republishing the complete works of Cáceres. (DS 21)

So in the end it is far from clear that the expanded version is more complete or definite, since the expansion opens new alternatives and leaves unexploited narrative stubs. It could be expanded again, and it was.

In "Carlos Ramírez Hoffman," the Chilean detective Romero, who is trying to locate Ramírez Hoffman, asks the narrator to watch four pornographic films. It turns out that most of the crew who made the films, five actors and a cameraman, have been murdered, and Romero believes that Ramírez Hoffman, working as a second cameraman under the name R. P. English, was the killer (NLA 200). In *Distant Star*, Romero visits an actress named Joanna Silvestri in the hope of confirming this hypothesis. She remembers English but is unable to identify him as the man who appears in an old photograph of Wieder, the renamed Ramírez Hoffman (DS 125–128). In "Joanna Silvestri," from the collection *Llamadas telefónicas* (*Phone Calls*), published in 1997, the year after *Distant Star*, the actress recalls working in Los Angeles and visiting an old friend, the legendary porn star Jack Holmes, who was dying of AIDS. The story is an interior monologue that records Joanna's thoughts during the visit of the Chilean detective, who is mentioned, although not named, at the beginning and the end (R 81, 96–97).

"Joanna Silvestri" is an expansion of an expansion, and had Bolaño lived longer, he may well have used the process yet again, expanding a section of this story, which, like the new content in *Distant Star*, contains intriguing stubs. For example, when Joanna goes to Los Angeles, she finds that the prevailing mood in the pornography industry has improved and attributes this to the death of Adolfo Pantoliano, "who was a thug and a crook of the worst kind" (R 84). Holmes says to Joanna: "But you know old Adolfo got killed?" (R 89). She knows, but even a keen reader of Bolaño may be excused for having forgotten that the poet John Lee Brook of the Aryan Brotherhood, whose life and works are recounted in *Nazi Literature in the Americas*, confessed, when on trial for another murder, to killing Pantoliano and the actors Suzy Webster and Dan Carmine (NLA 152). Was Brook the real killer? And if so, what was his motive? The story of Adolfo Pantoliano's life and death remains to be developed.

Considered in the abstract, Bolaño's process of expansion would seem to comport a grave risk, that of slowing the pace of the narrative to the point of tedium. Guillermo Martínez has highlighted this danger in a typology of recent Argentine fiction. The novels of the "fundamentalists of language," he says, "are easily recognizable by their Saer-like slowness: the characters take no less than thirty pages to open a freezer, turn off a tap or go down to look in the letterbox."[5] But Bolaño is not a fundamentalist of language. In practice, his expansions obviate the risk of tedium in two ways. First, they slow the pace of the narrative strategically, when the reader is already anxious or curious about the outcome of an event sequence, and this, as skilled storytellers have always known, is a way of increasing narrative tension. For example, in the scene of Stevens/Ruiz-Tagle's visit to the twins' country house, the expansion delays the violent outcome while foreshadowing it with touches of dramatic irony: "in their innocence they think they understand, but they don't understand at all . . . and here if the twins were more attentive they would see an ironic glint in his eye" (DS 20).

The second way Bolaño's expansions avert dullness is by introducing new characters and stories. When they do this, the pace of the discourse relative to the story may actually quicken. A new character appears when Ruiz-Tagle visits the twins in *Distant Star*: the maid, Amalia Maluenda, the only member of the household to survive. Her escape serves to qualify Wieder's almost supernatural self-possession: "Wieder has already left the aunt's room and is going into the maid's. But the bed is empty. For a moment Wieder doesn't know what to do; he is seized by a desire to kick the bed, smash up the rickety old chest of drawers in which Amalia Maluenda's clothes are piled" (DS 22). She also reappears to testify at Wieder's trial in absentia and to situate his crimes in a historical context:

> In her memory, the night of the crime was one episode in a long history of killing and injustice. Her account of the events was swept up in a cyclical, epic poem, which, as her dumbfounded listeners came to realize, was partly her story, the story of the Chilean citizen Amalia Maluenda, who used to work for the Garmendias, and partly the story of the Chilean nation. A story of terror. . . . Remembering the black night of the crime, she said she had heard the music of the Spanish. When asked to clarify what she meant by "the music of the Spanish," she replied: "Rage, sir, sheer, futile rage." (DS 111)

Wieder, as I will argue in chapter 6, is a sociopath, an exceptional case, but his crimes are part of a pattern of violence. The story of Amalia Maluenda is a minor digression, but it also serves to sketch a historical and political hinterland that is absent from "Carlos Ramírez Hoffman." Bolaño's explosive expansions lengthen the stories retold but also, by opening them out, broaden their significance.

CIRCULATING CHARACTERS

We have already seen that Bolaño's characters circulate from text to text. This process has a long history, at which it will be useful to glance in order to grasp its peculiarities in Bolaño's work. Daniel Aranda has shown that although Balzac was not the first novelist to reuse characters of his own invention, he did set his stamp on the technique decisively by combining strongly particularized realist characterization (as in Rétif de la Bretonne) with congruent reappearances in a temporally and spatially unified world encompassing the individual novels (as in Fenimore Cooper).[6] When Aranda writes of a "chronology that organizes the inter-novelistic existences of his creatures," he is referring to Balzac's intentions as declared in the 1842 preface to *The Human Comedy* rather than the detail of the execution, since, as Fernand Lotte has pointed out, the series contains many chronological inconsistencies, as well as surprising changes in psychology, behavior, physiognomy, and other traits.[7] In *The Prisoner*, Proust's narrator implies that such inconsistencies are a small price to pay for a coherence that may be imperfect but has grown out of the fictional material, rather than being imposed on it by a pre-established plan:

> This unity was an afterthought, but not artificial. Otherwise it would have crumbled into dust, like so many systematic constructions by mediocre writers who, by lavish use of titles and subtitles, try to make it look as if they have followed a single transcendent design. Not artificial, perhaps all the more real for being an afterthought, born in a moment of enthusiasm when it is discovered between parts which only need to come together, a unity which was unaware of itself, and which therefore is vital and not born of logic, which has not ruled out variety or put a damper on execution.[8]

Proust is pleading his own cause here as well as defending Balzac, for although *In Search of Lost Time* has, as he wrote in a letter to Benjamin Crémieux, a "rigorous composition," its coherence, like that of *The Human Comedy*, was emergent, and indeed still emerging when he died.[9]

In 1998, Bolaño said in an interview: "in a very humble way, I think of all my prose works and even a part of my poetry as a whole. Not just in stylistic terms, but in terms of plot as well: there is a continual dialogue among the characters and they keep appearing and disappearing" (B 112). This might suggest that his prose works all belong to a single temporally and spatially unified world, as the novels of Balzac's *Human Comedy* do, at least according to the 1842 preface. But Bolaño's wording should give us pause. When he says that there is a continual dialogue among the characters, he is speaking metaphorically and thinking of how his characters relate to one another from text to text. The relations are not necessarily identities; they may be resemblances or analogies.

When characters reappear in Balzac and Proust, they are often initially unrecognizable, but the identity that connects their various appearances is generally established in the end. In Bolaño's work, as we shall see, identity sometimes remains undecidable, and this quandary affects major as well as minor characters. The reappearances sometimes leave unsolved what analytical philosophers call the "reidentification problem": how can we tell whether "a particular encountered on one occasion or described in respect of one occasion is *the same individual* as a particular encountered on another occasion or described in respect of another occasion"?[10] It is not simply that Bolaño, like Balzac and Proust, did not have time to iron out inconsistencies (all three writers died prematurely, at fifty), or that he was, as Fernand Lotte says of Balzac, insufficiently systematic in his planning.[11] Inconsistency is a part of his work's design. By allowing characters to return *differently*, Bolaño was able to build on written and published texts without being strictly constrained by them.

The adverb "strictly" is crucial. Had the earlier texts not exercised any constraint at all, Bolaño's prose works would not have formed a whole at the level of plot. Here it is illuminating to compare his fiction with that of a contemporary whom he admired: César Aira (BP 146–147). Aira's characters undergo radical changes in the course of a single book. In *Las noches de Flores* (*The Nights of Flores*), an elderly couple, Aldo and Rosita, have taken up pizza delivery to supplement their income after the financial crisis of 2001 in Argentina. They come across "a strange being, half-bat, half-parrot," whose name is Nardo Sollozo.[12] Toward the end of the novel we learn that this being is in fact a dwarf in disguise, wearing a Batman costume, working as a police informant. The charming retirees, meanwhile, turn out to be the novel's real monsters. Aldo is a criminal, nicknamed Cloroformo because he used chloroform to kidnap minors and sell them into sexual slavery. Rosita is not a woman but one of Cloroformo's partners in crime, known to the authorities as Resplandor (Shining, as in the title of Stephen King's novel). We are faced here with not a revelation but a metamorphosis that affects the characters' names and properties and is born of the unconstrained improvisation that Aira has explained in interviews. By multiplying radical shifts of this kind, he cultivates disunity at the level of plot.

Bolaño's books, by contrast, are strongly interconnected by diegetic continuities, although he gave a somewhat misleading impression when he said that he thought of *all* of his prose works as constituting a whole. Like Balzac, he did not have a totalizing conception of his fiction at the outset. His "moment of enthusiasm" (to use Proust's phrase) seems to have occurred in 1995, when he had the idea of rewriting the final chapter of *Nazi Literature in the Americas*.[13] No characters from his previous novels (*Antwerp, Monsieur Pain, The Skating Rink, The Third Reich*) reappear in other books. But *Nazi Literature in the Americas* functioned like an incubator. As well as providing the scenario for *Distant Star*, it produced Daniela de Montecristo (NLA 85–86), who speaks in "Daniela" (SE 117–119); the Romanian general Eugen Entrescu, whose genital endowment and crucifixion, exposed and narrated in *2666* (679–693, 745–747), are briefly noted in *Nazi Literature*'s "Epilogue for Monsters" (NLA 209); and the pornographer Adolfo Pantoliano (NLA 152, 212), whose death is regretted by no one in "Joanna Silvestri" (R 84).[14]

The "moment of enthusiasm" in which Bolaño grasped the potential unity of his fiction (which may not have been a singular moment: I am borrowing Proust's expression simply to indicate a shift in practice) coincides with his adoption of two processes discussed in this chapter: expansion and circulating characters. I have already suggested that his use of the second is distinctively complex, and now it is time to tease out that complexity. Broadly speaking, there are three ways characters circulate in Bolaño's fiction: return, renaming, and transfiguration. Sometimes characters simply return, with the same name and the same properties, or new properties that are compatible with those manifested in an earlier appearance. Such is the case of the Chilean detective Abel Romero, who appears first in *Nazi Literature in the Americas*, then reappears in *Distant Star* and *The Savage Detectives*. Sometimes characters are renamed: they come back with a new name but with unchanged or compatible properties, like Carlos Wieder in *Distant Star*, who corresponds to Carlos Ramírez Hoffman in *Nazi Literature in the Americas*. And sometimes characters are transfigured: their properties change to the point of incompatibility while the name remains the same or is recognizably similar. This is what happens with Lalo Cura in "Prefiguration of Lalo Cura" (R 99–116) and *2666*, and with J. M. G. Arcimboldi and Benno von Archimboldi in *The Savage Detectives* and *2666*.

Renaming and transfiguration raise obvious questions. Why change names if the character is recognizably the same? And why reuse a name for a character who cannot be the same individual? These questions are idle if understood psychologically, as bearing on the causes of Bolaño's decisions, but worth asking if recast in terms of the effects produced by his fiction-making system. One effect of renaming is to enrich the significance of the character's set of names. Carlos Wieder is a case in point. His surname means "again" in German, as Bibiano O'Ryan points out at the beginning of a philological fantasia (DS 40–42). This signals his status as a repetition or revenant, but also alludes to his role in the "second coming" of the Second World War, as the narrator's fellow prisoner Norberto sees it, with a crazy lucidity (DS 27). And the name may also be read as an ironic interlingual pun on *vida*—"life" in Spanish—since Wieder not only exalts death in his aerial poems but also kills repeatedly.

The change of name from Ramírez Hoffman to Wieder is consistent with the character's practice of pseudonymity in both *Nazi Literature in the Americas* and *Distant Star*, and with his fundamental elusiveness ("in fact he had *always* been an absent figure" [DS 104]). As well as using a false name before the military coup, Ramírez Hoffman/Wieder seems to have used a string of pseudonyms in his later literary and cinematographic career: Octavio Pacheco (a compound of the names of the Mexican writers Octavio Paz and José Emilio Pacheco), Masanobu, Juan Sauer, Jules Defoe, and R. P. English. No firm evidence, however, links these names to Ramírez Hoffman/Wieder, so we cannot be sure exactly what to include in the set of the aviator-poet's works and deeds. And nothing guarantees that either Ramírez Hoffman or Wieder is a true, legally valid name after all. His renaming adds a new and richly significant element to a conjectural set of names, which may be incomplete and may include names that refer to other individuals.

Other cases of renaming in *Distant Star* emphasize the story's inscription in a national context. Whereas Ramírez Hoffman goes by the name of Emilio Stevens before the coup, Wieder uses the alias Alberto Ruiz-Tagle. Ruiz-Tagle is a dynastic name in Chile: Eduardo Frei Ruiz-Tagle was president from 1994 to 2000; the writer Carlos Ruiz-Tagle Gandarillas was coauthor of the humorous best-seller *Revolution in Chile* (1962), originally published under the pseudonym Sillie Utternut; and the engineer Eugenio Ruiz-Tagle Orrego was one of the victims of the infamous "Caravan of Death," an airborne death squad that executed and "disappeared" at least seventy-five prisoners in October 1973.[15] This explains Bibiano O'Ryan's remark: "What a nerve . . . stealing a good name like that" (DS 45). As for O'Ryan's name (changed from Cecilio Macaduck in "Carlos Ramírez Hoffman"), it resonates with that of Chile's founding father, Bernardo O'Higgins (1778–1842).

The correspondences between characters in "Carlos Ramírez Hoffman" and *Distant Star* are clear and unequivocal. The renamed characters in the later novel are more developed, but their new properties and actions are consistent with those of their predecessors. Elsewhere in Bolaño's work, however, a name is shared by characters whose properties are not fully compatible, in which case the relation between them is one of transfiguration rather than renaming. Lalo Cura in "Prefiguration of Lalo Cura," for example, does not have the same background and life story as Lalo Cura in *2666*. In "Prefiguration of Lalo Cura," he is the son of a renegade priest (known as "el cura") and Connie Sánchez, who acts in the surreal pornographic films of Helmut Bittrich, and he grows up in Medellín, Colombia (R 99–100). In *2666*, he is the son of a woman named María Expósito who lives outside Villaviciosa, a fictional town in the Mexican state of Sonora, and his father is either one of a pair of students from Mexico City with whom María slept in 1976 (2666 558). These students are not named, but anyone who has read *The Savage Detectives* will guess that they are Ulises Lima and Arturo Belano.[16] The two Lalo Curas grow up in different countries and different social worlds. Some of their properties are clearly incompatible. Why then have they been given the same name? The principal effect of this choice is to underline certain characteristics that they *do* share: they belong to the same generation of Latin Americans; both have grown up without a father; and both are well acquainted with violence. Each in his way is the product of a society going mad and devouring its children: the madness suggested by the punning name (Lalo Cura/*la locura* = madness) is surely collective and contagious.[17]

When Bolaño renames a character who is recognizably the same, he enriches and compounds the significance of the character's names. When he reuses a name for a character who is discernibly different, he further exploits the single name's connotative potential. In both cases we are faced with multiple versions of a character, inconsistent in at least one respect. Bolaño did not complacently publish his drafts or publicly document his creative process, but neither did he remove all traces of his work's genesis. His characters are not strictly constrained by their first versions: they evolve; their names and properties are allowed to change in response to new fictional environments. He systematically relaxes the requirement of consistency that Balzac attempted to meet in *The Human Comedy*. This gives his fiction-making system a degree of free play unavailable to writers in a more strictly realist tradition. It also creates intriguing puzzles for the reader.

Sometimes the reappearances of Bolaño's characters seem calculated to unsettle the distinction between the same and the other. Just as his detectives face problems of identification—Romero suspects but is not able to confirm that the cameraman R. P. English was in fact Carlos Wieder (DS 125–128); Juan García Madero is not sure that the Cesárea Tinaja described in a 1928 newspaper article is the Cesárea Tinajero for whom he and his friends are searching (SD 541)—so Bolaño's readers may find themselves wondering whether characters appearing in different parts of his work are in fact one and the same. In *The Savage Detectives*, it seems quite likely that Jacobo Urenda's French wife, Simone, who asks her husband to describe Arturo Belano and says that she understands his desire to get himself killed in Africa (SD 499), is the Simone Darrieux who initiated Belano into the world of sadomasochism in Mexico (SD 207–208). Looking beyond the novel, it is also tempting to identify the unnamed "Andalucian girl" in María Teresa Solsona Ribot's monologue (SD 490–492) with Clara in "Clara" (R 69–80). But when I wonder whether the unnamed Chilean sock sales-man in "Crimes" (SF 77–84) is Carlos Wieder, whom some claim to have seen selling socks and ties in Valparaíso (DS 97), I may have crossed over into paranoid reading. In *The Savage Detectives* Belano tells Guillem Piña that "there were similarities between his last book and his new book that fell into the realm of games that were impossible to decipher" (SD 446). The remark applies just as aptly to the books of Roberto Bolaño.

The problems of identification that I have been examining are raised in a systematic and strategic way by the characters who resemble Bolaño himself, as we can see in the stories. Many are told in the first person by an "I" whose properties are consistent both from story to story and with the widely accessible biographical information about the writer Roberto Bolaño ("Sensini," "Mauricio 'The Eye' Silva," "Gómez Palacio," "Dentist," "Dance Card," "Cell Mates," "Clara," "Meeting with Enrique Lihn," "Jim," "Colonia Lindavista," "The Room Next Door," and "I Can't Read"). Seven stories feature Arturo Belano, either as a first-person narrator involved in the action ("Enrique Martín," "The Grub"), or as a main character in third-person narration ("Detectives," "Photos," "The Old Man of the Mountain," "Death of Ulises," and "The Days of Chaos"). Belano, of course, as his name suggests, has much in common with Bolaño; he is a fictional alter ego. But there are clear departures from autobiography in "Photos" (set in Liberia in 1996), "Death of Ulises" (set in Mexico around the year 2000), and "The Days of Chaos" (set in 2005 and presumably in Spain), since Bolaño was not present in those places at those times.

In addition to the autobiographical stories and the stories about Belano, there are five third-person stories about a character called B ("A Literary Adventure," "Phone Calls," "Last Evenings on Earth," "Days of 1978," and "Vagabond in France and Belgium"). How B differs from Bolaño and from Belano is not at all clear. As well as alluding to Kafka's K, B could be an abbreviation of either surname, and the character named B serves as a transition between the autobiographical "I" and the fictional alter ego. The use of the initial flags the possibility of fabulation, informing the reader that she is entering the fatally ill-defined territory of autofiction.

METAREPRESENTATION

The two processes that I have discussed so far—expansion and circulating characters—contribute to the productivity of Bolaño's fiction-making system in an obvious way because they involve the reuse of elements from earlier texts, both published and unpublished. They allow Bolaño's work to feed on itself.[18] The process that I will examine in this section, by contrast, facilitates the inclusion of new elements derived from the work of imaginary others. *Nazi Literature in the Americas*, *Distant Star*, and *Woes of the True Policeman* contain numerous descriptions of poems, stories, novels, essays, artworks, and war games created by fictional characters. These descriptions are instances of *metarepresentation*: the representation of a text or artwork within another text. I will be using this rather cumbersome term, rather than "embedding" or "nesting," in order to maintain a useful distinction made by Paisley Livingston. According to Livingston, nesting takes place when artistic structures are "presented or made observable" in the nesting work rather than "merely described or evoked."[19] Mere descriptions and evocations fall into the broader category of metarepresentation. "What nesting makes possible," Livingston writes, "is a direct gauging or appreciation of an artistic structure on display" (238). The distinction is hard to draw with absolute clarity because a description of a work will often contain direct quotations from it, which present it or make it observable to some degree.

Nonetheless, in Bolaño's fiction, descriptions far outweigh quotations. He rarely gives us full-blown works-within-works.

In an analysis of Borges's "pseudosummaries," or simulated summaries of imaginary texts, Gérard Genette proposes a distinction that coincides with the one drawn by Livingston between nesting proper and other kinds of metarepresentation. As Genette points out, the pseudosummary is not an apocryphal text "since the supposed text has not actually been *produced* but only *described*, with no attempt at stylistic imitation."[20] A double distance opens up between the actual writer (Borges) and the text described: it is supposedly the work of another, and it is accessible only through the filter of a summary. Borges's pseudosummaries are typically thought experiments that allow him to explore an idea and its corollaries while dispensing with the accumulation of circumstantial details, a task for which he expresses his distaste in the introduction to *The Garden of Forking Paths*: "It is a laborious madness and an impoverishing one, the madness of composing vast books— setting out in five hundred pages an idea that can be perfectly related orally in five minutes. The better way to go about it is to pretend that those books already exist, and offer a summary, a commentary on them."[21] Borges's conversation, as recorded by Bioy Casares in his posthumous *Borges*, swarms with such ideas, only some of which were elaborated in stories. His descriptions of imaginary works are exercises in potential literature, and like the cofounder of the Oulipo, François Le Lionnais, he was often content simply to proffer an abstract scheme or a tantalizing sketch, such as his account of Herbert Quain's *April March*, a "regressive, ramifying fiction" (108–109), or of Ts'ui Pen's *The Garden of Forking Paths*, which ramifies forward as well (126–127).

Bolaño is deeply indebted to Borges in his use of metarepresentation. He too favors the pseudosummary rather than nesting in the strict sense, but he uses it to quite different ends. His descriptions of imaginary works often have a broadly realist function; they enrich characterization "by showing what sort of thing the portrayed artist or writer makes."[22] While Borges is less interested in Herbert Quain or Ts'ui Pen than in their works, Bolaño, in *Nazi Literature in the Americas*, often presents works as actions that manifest a particular character, sometimes in a quite straightforward way. For example, in the summary of *The Fighting Years of an American Falangist in Europe*, we learn that Jesús Fernández Gómez "marvels at his own youth: he writes of his body, his sexual potency, the length of his member, how well he holds his liquor . . . and his ability to go for days without sleep" (NLA 38–39). Sometimes, however, the manifestation of character is more complex. Even when an author is presented as ridiculous or despicable, his or her work may be formally interesting. Carlos Ramírez Hoffman and Willy Schürholz, for example, explore new media for poetry: the sky and the surface of the earth (NLA 188–189, 96).[23] Ernesto Pérez Masón writes a novel whose fundamental theme remains ambiguous throughout: "*The Enterprise of the Masons* . . . in which it is never entirely clear whether Pérez Masón is talking about the business acumen of his ancestors or the members of a Masonic lodge who met at the end of the nineteenth century . . . to plan the Cuban Revolution and the worldwide revolution to follow" (NLA 56). Harry Sibelius's *The True Son of Job* employs a strategy akin to the Oulipo's chimera: the structure of Arnold Toynbee's *Hitler's Europe* is populated with stories and characters from other works (NLA 122–123).[24] The point that Bolaño is making is that even if there is a statistical correlation between avant-garde aesthetic practice and progressive politics (which explains why Schürholz is initially supported by poets opposed to the military regime in Chile [NLA 94]), the two are not causally related. Artistic experimenters, like Schürholz and Ramírez Hoffman, may be advocates or agents of conservative revolutions.

So far, I have been stressing the broadly realist function of Bolaño's metarepresentations in *Nazi Literature in the Americas*: the imaginary works may be absurd, but they serve to characterize their authors and sometimes, as we have just seen, to illustrate the complex relations between aesthetic and political positions. To read the metarepresentations only in this way would be, however, to miss something important. They also have a ludic function: Bolaño takes advantage of the double distance opened up by the pseudosummaries to indulge his tastes for citation, enumeration, and the conjuring up of literary oddities.

The account of Edelmira Thompson de Mendiluce's *Poe's Room* contains a long and slightly modified extract from Poe's essay "The Philosophy of

Furniture" (NLA 9–11), originally quoted in Julio Cortázar's translation (LNA 16–18), which runs through items present in an ideal room. This extract contributes only in a marginal way to the characterization of Edelmira Thompson and owes its place in the chapter primarily to Bolaño's love of lists. Similarly, the descriptions of Luiz Fontaine da Souza's successive refutations of *Being and Nothingness* serve as pretexts for stringing together Sartre's section headings and thereby accumulating items of philosophical jargon (NLA 51–52). While the pseudosummaries in the stories of Borges describe works that he seems to have seen no point in fully realizing, Bolaño sometimes summarizes works whose realization seems intrinsically unlikely. It is one thing to offer two readings of the title *The Enterprise of the Masons*, and another to construct a novel that maintains the ambiguity throughout. Similarly, the global ambiguities that characterize Irma Carrasco's *Vulture Hill* (plea for a return to nineteenth-century values or prefiguration of the apocalypse?), Segundo José Heredia's *Saturnalia* (real or dreamed atrocities?), and Argentino Schiaffino's *The Great Buenos Aires Restaurant Novel* (stag night, wake, gastronomical gathering, or trap set for a traitor?) would require a Jamesian subtlety of execution that seems to exceed the capacities of the imaginary authors concerned (NLA 81, 114, 168).[25] In these ludic pseudosummaries, which evoke improbable fictional objects, constraints on plausibility are relaxed and speculative imagination is given free rein. By attributing the works to unstable eccentrics and describing them from a distance, in impressionistic summaries, Bolaño grants himself a facilitating license.

Metarepresentation is more frequent and extensive in *Nazi Literature in the Americas* and *Distant Star* than in the books that followed. It is curiously rare in *The Savage Detectives*, given that the novel is centered on a group of poets. The only visceral realist poem presented in the novel is Cesárea Tinajero's "Sión," which is wordless apart from its title (SD 353). As Mark Ford has written: "We get not one single example of the work of Belano or Lima . . . or Juan García Madero."[26] Perhaps it is not surprising that their poems are not quoted, or, as Livingston would say, nested, given the book's discursive modes: the longest part (II) is made up of spoken monologues, while García Madero's diary (parts I and III) is not so much a poet's notebook as a record of day-to-day life. Nevertheless, it *is* surprising that visceral realist poems are so rarely described or discussed. When Ulises Lima reads a poem at Julio César Álamo's workshop, at the beginning of the novel, Juan García Madero says that it is the best poem he has ever heard but does not explain why (6). Belano and Lima tell the Argentine poet Fabio Ernesto Logiacomo that they write "poem-novels," but all we find out about these hybrids is that they are "very long" and influenced by "some French poets" (136–137). The most explicit description of what the visceral realists produce is given by Norman Bolzman, remembering a poem that Ulises Lima read aloud in Tel Aviv, which was "essentially a collection of fragments about a Mediterranean city, Tel Aviv, I guess, and a bum or a mendicant poet" (265). It is not, as Alan Pauls claims, that "there is no work," but the work is largely occulted.[27]

There are three converging reasons for this, which relate to the nature of the visceral realist project, to Bolaño's technique of structuring his narratives around gaps, and to a difficulty intrinsic to nesting and metarepresentation. The visceral realists are portrayed as persisting in the sweeping avant-garde project of "transforming life" (as Rimbaud wrote) rather than simply adding titles to library catalogues.[28] They hope to do away with the distinction that, for Yeats, imposed a grievous choice: "The intellect of man is forced to choose / Perfection of the life, or of the work."[29] And for them, poetry is not just a way of combining words but a way of organizing or disorganizing both life and work. Opening up the notion of poetry like this necessarily reduces the weight given to texts. Nevertheless, like the Mexican stridentists or the French surrealists, they do reserve a central place for poetry in the restricted, technical sense of the word, and it remains puzzling that their own poems are so little described, if not quoted, in *The Savage Detectives*. This, however, is not the only baffling gap in the book. We never hear Belano or Lima's account of events; we do not know to whom the monologues in part II are addressed, with one exception;[30] and, perhaps most tantalizingly, Juan García Madero says nothing about Cesárea Tinajero's notebooks, except that he has read them (SD 575). The novel is structured around these gaps, which encourage the reader to engage in meaning projection, as Wolfgang Iser might have said, but also delimit a potential space for the writer's later invention.[31]

As well as being part of a pattern of deliberate gaps, the occultation of the visceral realists' poetry responds to a difficulty that is intrinsic to nesting and metarepresentation. As Paisley Livingston writes:

> It is easy enough for an author to describe a character as a genius who has written a brilliant poem, painted a masterpiece or composed great music, whereas ostension of this figure's brilliantly original artistic structures is another matter, as the attempt to concoct a structure in which genial artistic and aesthetic features can be observed sometimes backfires. Although proper uptake of the context constructed by the matrix work is crucial to our comprehension of any nested structures it may contain, the observability of that structure may in turn establish a significant constraint on what is genuinely fictional (in the sense of "appropriately imaginable" with regard to the work). Conceptual possibility is trumped by salience.[32]

Even if Ulises Lima and Cesárea Tinajero are meant to be appreciated as artists of life, whether or not they are also interesting and original writers is not a matter of indifference in the fictional world of *The Savage Detectives*. If García Madero had quoted the poem that Lima read out at Álamo's workshop, as he quotes a poem by Efrén Rebolledo elsewhere (SD 11), a reader who failed to share his enthusiasm might regard him as deluded, and this would make a significant difference to the way the novel is read. If it is not "appropriately imaginable" that Lima is a poet of exceptional talent, *The Savage Detectives* must be read either as parody, like most of the "articles" in *Nazi Literature in the Americas*, or as a story of how youthful illusions were lost. The first option is not really sustainable, for although *The Savage Detectives* has parodic enclaves, they function by contrast with a fundamentally serious matrix. Some support for the second option might be found in the monologues of Laura Jáuregi and Daniel Grossman (SD 154, 427), but as I will be arguing in chapter 7, the novel as a whole laments the loss of youthful energy and openness rather than welcoming the lucidity that comes from the loss of youthful illusions. It resists Daniel Grossman's conclusion: "Youth is a scam" (SD 427).

Bolaño's extreme parsimony in describing the poems of Lima and the notebooks of Cesárea Tinajero protects the credibility of these characters as writers. He made a similar strategic decision in *2666*, where there is very little metarepresentation of Benno von Archimboldi's novels. It is instructive to compare the relatively long pseudosummaries of seven novels by J. M. G. Arcimboldi in *Woes of the True Policeman* (141–159) with the succinct descriptions, in one or two sentences, scattered through *2666*.[33] J. M. G. Arcimboldi is a semicomic character, playfully handled, so Bolaño can afford to present his books as improbable curiosities.[34] But for the figure of Benno von Archimboldi to be convincing, the reader must be able to imagine that his novels are brilliantly original, and that is facilitated principally by showing how they have magnetized the lives of the critics Pelletier, Norton, Espinoza, and Morini.

Given Bolaño's employment of the expansive process, one might have expected him to use pseudosummaries to sketch out parts of future stories or novels. In fact he does this rarely and only in a marginal way. Two of the pseudosummaries in "Carlos Ramírez Hoffman" are expanded in *Distant Star*—Octavio Pacheco's one-act play and *Interview with Juan Sauer* (NLA 194–195; DS 94–95, 97)—but most of the descriptions of imaginary works in the later text are entirely new. On the evidence of the material published so far, Bolaño never made a whole new text by expanding a pseudosummary, although in *Distant Star* he does briefly describe a work that resembles his own *previous* book, *Nazi Literature in the Americas*: "*The Warlocks Return* is a highly readable study of fascist literary movements in South America from 1972 to 1989" (DS 108). As a rule, in Bolaño's fiction, metarepresentations serve to expand but are not themselves expanded.

Nevertheless, there are complex relations of narrative level among Bolaño's books as well as within them. The fictional character Arturo Belano, one of the heroes of *The Savage Detectives,* may also be the principal author of *Distant Star*'s new parts, that is, of most of the text. (I say that he *may* be, because the coauthor's surname is not given in full: he is referred to, in the prologue, as "a fellow Chilean, Arturo B" [DS 1]). And according to Bolaño's notes for *2666*, Belano is the narrator of that novel (*2666* 898). So both *Distant Star* and *2666* could be seen as metarepresentational with respect to the discontinuous narrative of Belano's life composed by *The Savage Detectives*, *Amulet*, and the seven short stories in which Belano features ("Enrique Martín," "The Grub," "Detectives," "Photos," "The Old Man of the Mountain," "Death of Ulises," and "The Days of Chaos"). Might we then say that *Distant Star* and *2666* are nested? Not without stretching the concept, for in neither case is there something that can be convincingly identified as a matrix work: the prologue to *Distant Star* is no more than a prologue, after all, and the note that indicates the meta-representational status of *2666* has been extracted from an as-yet unpublished paratext. *Distant Star* and *2666* seem to be subordinate to the story of Belano, but do not sit inside any of the texts in which that story is told.

This situation raises questions about how the pieces fit together. If Belano is the narrator of *2666*, how did he come to invent or discover that novel's plethoric materials? We know very little, in fact, about the life and literary career of Arturo Belano after his experiences in Liberia in 1996 (SD 496–518; R 181–190). All we have to go on are "Death of Ulises" (SE 127–134), set around the year 2000, when Belano is forty-six and has become a well-known writer (132), and "The Days of Chaos" (SE 143–144), whose action takes place in 2005. Like the gaps within *The Savage Detectives*, the gaps between texts, in which Belano, for instance, presumably returns from Liberia to Spain and writes the novels that bring him a measure of fame, have a double function: they intrigue the reader, but also mark out a space that the writer may partly fill with future inventions ("partly" because, as we saw in the first section of this chapter, Bolaño's expansions open new gaps even as they fill old ones). This is one way his fiction-making system sustains the continuity of its operation.

OVERINTERPRETATION

The three processes that I have discussed so far—expansion, circulating characters, and metarepresentation—are conducted by an agent external to the fiction: the writer. The process of overinterpretation is ultimately a writerly process too, but is often delegated to characters. This means that it functions at two levels. At the diegetic level, it affects the ways the over-interpreting characters think and act. At the discursive level, it allows the writer to manipulate those characters more freely because their behavior is no longer bound by what would be expected of normal, balanced people. The delusional or fantasist thought of the overinterpreting characters also permits the writer to introduce elaborate subsidiary narratives that manipulate real or realistic givens without regard for verifiability or plausibility.

The term "overinterpretation" will be used nonpejoratively here to refer to the way certain characters and narrators seize on minimal details, invest them with weighty significance, and invent stories to connect and explain them. I call this *over*interpretation because it ignores the criteria of economy and coherence that, according to Umberto Eco, guide standard forensic and scientific inquiries. These criteria bring the process of interpretation to a close when a putative clue has received a relatively simple explanation that fits with the rest of the evidence.[35] Bolaño's overinterpreters make something out of nothing, or join too many dots, to borrow a metaphor from Richard Rorty.[36] Some are paranoid and suffer from delusions, but others manifest a benign, creative form of apophenia, which the psychologist Klaus Conrad defined in 1958 as "unmotivated seeing of connections [accompanied by] a specific feeling of abnormal meaningfulness."[37]

As I noted in the previous section, the fictional character Arturo Belano strongly resembles the real writer Roberto Bolaño—up to a point. In *The Savage Detectives* that point can be located in chapter 22 of part II, which recounts how Belano challenged the critic Iñaki Echavarne to a duel. This chapter, as Ignacio Echevarría has commented, strains plausibility.[38] I would add that it marks the stage at which the lives of Belano and Bolaño clearly diverge. After the duel, Belano renounces literature and goes to Africa, where he works as a war correspondent in Angola, Rwanda, and Liberia. If, in Mexico, Arturo Belano played the "André Breton of the third world," as Luscious Skin says (SD 152, see also 89), in Africa he takes up the role of Arthur Rimbaud and provisionally disappears.

Why does Belano challenge Echavarne to a duel? How has his honor been affronted? He is convinced that Echavarne, whom he is yet to meet, is about to write a devastating review of his new book, but the reasons for this conviction are, as Guillem Piña tries to point out, extremely specious:

> And how do you know that he's going to review your new book when it isn't even in the bookstores yet? Because the other day, he said, while I was at the publishing house, he called the head of publicity and asked for my latest novel. So? I said. So I was sitting there, across from the head of publicity, and she said Hello, Iñaki, what a coincidence, Arturo Belano is right here across from me, and that bastard Echavarne didn't say anything. What was he supposed to say? Hello, at least, said Arturo. And since he didn't say anything, you've decided that he's going to tear you apart? (SD 447)

At the end of his monologue, Piña says that when he found out that Belano had bought an air ticket to Dar es Salaam, he realized that his friend had gone "completely insane" (449). Rather than a revelation, this is a suspicion confirmed. Piña has agreed to be Belano's second in the duel, knowing that he is being drawn into a kind of madness: "The proposition seemed crazy and unwarranted. You don't challenge a man for something he hasn't done yet, I thought" (448). Belano's madness has a clinical label: paranoia.

Both Arturo Belano in this episode and B in "A Literary Adventure" (LEE 42–53) exhibit paranoid behavior and suffer from persecutory delusions. While Belano has very flimsy grounds for anticipating a hostile review, B suspects that A's positive reviews of his books are preliminary steps in a long-term plan to destroy his literary reputation: "He's praising my book to the skies, thinks B, so he can let it drop back to earth later on" (43). Belano challenges Echavarne to a duel; B is determined to meet A face to face and have it out. And just as Echavarne thinks at first that the challenge must be a joke, so it seems unlikely that from A's point of view there is any score to settle. When the hostess at a party says to B, "There's a friend waiting for you down there," gesturing toward an arbor in the garden, B jumps to two highly dubious conclusions: "It must be A, he thinks, from which he immediately deduces: he must be armed" (48). But when the two writers finally meet, A, who has invited B to dinner, shows no sign of hostility (53).

Although B seems to be deluded about A's motivation and actions, the delusion serves as an instrument of discovery, focusing B's attention on objects that would probably escape scrutiny in the daily life of more balanced individuals. His powers of observation are keen, like those of Daniel Paul Schreber, whose case of paranoia was studied by Freud.[39] Here, for example, he considers the message on A's answering machine:

> By the time he has listened to this invitation several times, without leaving a message, B has formed some hypotheses about A and his partner and the mysterious entity they constitute. First, the woman's voice. She is young, much younger than A and B, energetic by the sound of it, determined to carve out her place in A's life and make sure that place is respected. Poor fool, thinks B. Then A's voice. Supremely serene, the voice of Cato. This guy is a year younger than me, thinks B, but he sounds fifteen or twenty years older. Finally, the message: Why the joyful tone? Why do they suppose that if it's important the caller is going to stop trying and be content to leave his or her number? Why do they take turns, as if they were reading out a play? To make it clear that two people live there? Or to show the world what a wonderful couple they make? All these questions remain unanswered, of course. (LEE 49–50)

Hypotheses proliferate to account for details that seem relevant only within B's paranoid frame of mind. But this is not to say that a more reasonable character would notice the same details and deem them irrelevant. B's noticing, as well as his hypothesizing, seems to be intensified by his paranoid suspicions, giving his imagination more material to work with. And that material does not always reinforce the delusional structure directly; sometimes it enriches an imagined scene, as when A's partner answers the phone and goes away to fetch him: "B can hear voices; she must have left the receiver on a table or a chair or hanging from the wall in the kitchen. . . . Suddenly there is silence on the line, as if the woman had sealed B's ears with wax" (51). Sounds are converted into images and an imagined tactile sensation. By means of this hyperacute perception and speculative interpreting, which fills a pause with signs, B imagines his way into A's apartment and private life. Considering the story as a whole, his paranoid reading of the reviews, which leads to his persistent telephone calls, precipitates an invitation to dinner. B's overinterpretation drives the story forward and produces the "adventure" to which its title alludes. For the writer Bolaño, B's persecutory delusion makes it plausible that he should persecute the apparently well-meaning A, just as Belano's delusion in *The Savage Detectives* attenuates but does not entirely cancel out the implausibility of his duel with Echavarne.

When Belano flies off to Africa after the duel, he acquires an emblematic dimension: he becomes the Poet Who Disappeared. It is significant that this is where the purely fictional part of Belano's life story begins. In Bolaño's work it is often through overinterpretive scrutiny of the factual that fiction achieves full autonomy and characters come to stand for something beyond their particularities. This can be clearly observed in three stories that describe (or include descriptions of) photographs of French writers: "Last Evenings on Earth," "Photos," and "Labyrinth." By contrast with the examples of the process that I have examined so far, the overinterpretation that occurs in these stories is not markedly paranoid and delusional. It manifests a form of apophenia that is benign and can even (as in "Photos") prove to be salutary.

In "Last Evenings on Earth" the character B, on holiday with his father in Acapulco, pores over an anthology of French surrealist poetry translated by Aldo Pellegrini. He is particularly fascinated by the figure of Gui Rosey: "In the afternoon, on the beach, while his father is stretched out asleep in a deck chair, B rereads Gui Rosey's poems and the brief story of his life or his death" (LEE 136). There follows a detailed narrative account of how Rosey disappeared in a port city in southern France during the Second World War (136–137). B's thoughts return insistently to Rosey throughout "Last Evenings on Earth," not because of his poems (B finds the work of Desnos and Éluard far more interesting [138]), but because Rosey emblematizes the fate of the minor poet—disappearance—which he feels he will share, as we see at the end of the story: "B thinks of Gui Rosey, who disappeared from the face of the earth without a trace, quiet as a lamb, while the Nazi hymns rose into a blood-red sky, and he sees himself as Gui Rosey, a Gui Rosey buried in some vacant lot in Acapulco, vanished for ever" (LEE 157).

For Bolaño, this fate has a paradoxical grandeur. Speaking of Rosey in an interview with Philippe Lançon, he said: "I find his end more moving than that of Walter Benjamin, because he isn't saved by his work. The cemetery of minor poets is tragic and wretched. Mainly because the minor poet knows that he's minor. If you're Rimbaud and you know it, what does it matter? But if you're Gui Rosey and you know it, that's something!"[40] Disappearing absolutely requires greater courage, Bolaño seems to be saying here. The real *poètes maudits* are not the ones in Verlaine's book—Tristan Corbière, Arthur Rimbaud, Stéphane Mallarmé, Marceline Desbordes-Valmore, Villiers de L'Isle-Adam, and Pauvre Lelian himself (the name is an anagram of Paul Verlaine)—whose works are widely available today, but those who are bound for real oblivion unless, like Henri Lefebvre in Bolaño's story "Vagabond in France and Belgium" (LEE 173–174), they happen to be mentioned by a writer of renown.

"Last Evenings on Earth" suggests that B has read the story of Gui Rosey's life in the anthology that he has brought to Acapulco. But Pellegrini's biographical note is succinct: "Born in Paris on the 27th of August 1896. Participated in the activities of the Surrealists from 1932. Last seen in Marseilles in 1941, among the Surrealist refugees hoping to leave France. There has been no news of him since."[41] All the details of Rosey's disappearance have been invented by B:

> At the *pension* where he is staying, no one knows what has happened; his suitcases and books are there, undisturbed, so he clearly hasn't tried to leave without paying (as guests at certain *pensions* on the Côte d'Azur are prone to do). His friends try to find him. They visit all the hospitals and police stations in the area. No one can tell them anything. One morning the visas arrive. Most of them board a ship and set off for the United States. Those who remain, who will never get visas, soon forget about Rosey and his disappearance; people are disappearing all the time, in large numbers, and they have to look out for themselves. (LEE 136–137)

That Bolaño shared B's fascination with Rosey is shown by the poem "The Great Pit" in *The Unknown University* (674–681), in which the minor surrealist's body is swept by a current into the depths of an ocean trench. "Last Evenings on Earth" and "The Great Pit" might seem to be imaginatively filling gaps in the historical record, but as Robert Amutio has pointed out, Aldo Pellegrini, in spite of his encyclopedic devotion to the surrealist cause, was wrong or at least misleading in his note on the life of Rosey, who did not disappear absolutely. He survived the war and returned to writing poetry after a long period of silence.[42]

When informed by Amutio of Pellegrini's mistake, Bolaño, it seems, was not disappointed but interested by the fictional potential of what had really happened: "After the war, he gets married, leads a modest life. He buys a car and drives around France with his wife. Then he gets old and dies. I don't know which of the two destinies is the more terrible."[43] What is striking about this oral sketch is its resemblance to the end of "Henri Simon Leprince," the story of a fictional French poet who joins the Resistance, survives the war, and continues to write in complete obscurity: "For some, his presence, his fragility, his terrifying sovereignty serve as a spur or reminder" (LEE 25). Whether Rosey disappears abruptly or slowly fades away, he stands, like Leprince, for something larger than himself. B's overinterpretation of his photograph and biographical note in "Last Evenings on Earth" allows the writer Bolaño to join two causally unrelated stories via the figure of the Minor Poet.

At the discursive level, photographs of poets function similarly in "Photos," serving the writer's fiction-making system by connecting stories across time and space and activating emblematic figures. The effect that they have on the overinterpreting character, however, is very different. Rather than nourishing melancholy, they revive a faltering desire to live. Arturo Belano, stranded in a Liberian village devastated by civil war, is flicking through an anthology of francophone poetry that includes author photos and biographical notes. At first the story seems to be a haphazard sequence of unrelated descriptions, but soon the still images begin to move and interact. Belano's first interpretation of the photograph and biography of Claude de Burine leads to the hypothesis of her disappearance, based on three "clues." First, she has not published a book since 1969 (R 183), but as the narrator points out on the following page, the anthology that Belano is browsing through was published in 1973, so the lapse of time is hardly a compelling reason to speculate about her disappearance (especially since her previous book was published in 1963). Second, her great theme is love, inexhaustible love: "and when Belano reads that, it all makes sense in his overheated brain: someone who *dit l'amour* could perfectly well disappear at the age of 38" (R 183). The third "clue" follows immediately: "*especially* if that person is the double of Little Orphan Annie" (R 183). As the narrator suggests, only an overheated brain would conclude on the basis of this evidence that Claude de Burine had vanished (she lived, in fact, until 2005, and published many more books of poems).

The melancholic tilt of Belano's overinterpretation is reversed by his encounter with the image and the bibliography of Dominique Tron, whom he sees as a French double of his younger self: "Belano thinks about his own youth, when he used to churn it out like Tron" (R 184). Tron's abundant titles with their infectious energy effect a subtle but decisive shift in Belano's state of mind. He begins to imagine an improbable relationship between the poets whose images he has been animating independently: "he sees Claude de Burine again, the photo-portrait of Claude de Burine, in her lonely poet's tower, watching the adolescent cyclone that is Dominique Tron, who wrote *La souffrance est inutile*, and perhaps he wrote it for her" (R 185). Although there is something in Claude's eyes that speaks of the "arid, sad and terrible end to come" (R 185), she seems, as she runs toward the arms of Dominique Tron, to have received the message that suffering is futile, as indeed does Belano himself. The romance that he has contrived anticipates his fantasy of an erotic encounter with the supremely desirable Nadia Tuéni: "immaculate, perfectly serene, like the accidental muse of certain poets, or their provisional muse, the one who says, Don't worry, or who says, Worry, but not too much, the one who doesn't speak in dry and definite tones but whispers, whose parting gift is a kind look" (R 188). Nadia Tuéni provisionally figures the muse in whom the poet Bolaño believed, not in a literal, fundamentalist way but without any kind of ironic reserve, to judge from his poem "Muse," prominently placed at the end of *The Unknown University* (804–811).

Belano knows from the biographical note in the anthology that Nadia Tuéni was born in Beirut in 1935, that her father was a Druse and her mother French, that she is married to an orthodox Christian, and that she has written about Lebanon's various ethnic and religious communities. The note describes her as a "poet of tides, hurricanes and shipwrecks" (R 187 188). As a war correspondent, Belano presumably also knows about the civil war in Lebanon, which lasted from 1975 to 1990 ("Photos" is set in 1996, shortly before the end of the first Liberian civil war). In his earlier state of mind, he would have quickly combined these items of information to construct a story about her death or disappearance. But a reorientation has taken place. Looking at the photo of Denise Jallais and remembering Nadia Tuéni, he thinks, "I hope they're alive" (R 189).

Nadia Tuéni died of cancer in 1983, but in "Photos," leading a cohort of forgotten and celebrated poets, she gives Belano the strength to get up and walk. In the earlier part of his African voyage, he had been intent on getting himself killed. Now, clinging to the anthology as to a plank or a buoy, he sets off to resume his life:

> and then Belano shuts the book and stands up, still holding it, grateful, and begins to walk westward, toward the coast, with the book of Francophone poets under his arm, grateful, and his thought speeds ahead of his steps through the jungles and deserts of Liberia, as it did when he was an adolescent in Mexico, and soon his steps lead him away from the village. (R 190)

For the character Belano, overinterpretation has been salutary. It may even have saved him. What it has done for the writer in this case is to allow a tangle of entirely speculative stories to sprout from the protagonist's minimal action, which comes down to this: he sits and leafs through an anthology of poems, then stands up and carries it away.

The mechanisms that we have seen at work in "Last Evenings on Earth" and "Photos" are laid bare in "Labyrinth," a posthumous and apparently unfinished story in which the animating overinterpretation is undertaken not by a character but by the narrator, who is scrutinizing a photograph of the Tel Quel group taken in Paris in "1977 or thereabouts" (SE 48). The narrator begins by describing the physical appearance and clothing of each person in turn, relying exclusively on the photograph and its caption, as if deprived of access to reference books and the Internet, like B on the beach in Acapulco or Belano in the ruined Liberian village. When describing the group's best-known members—Philippe Sollers, Julia Kristeva, and Pierre Guyotat—he is able to replace the initials in the caption with a first name. In the other cases, he guesses or makes an arbitrary choice: "Next to Guyotat is C. Devade. Caroline? Carole? Carla? Colette? Claudine? We'll never know. Let's say, for convenience's sake, that she's called Carla Devade" (50). The reason "we" will never know is not that the name is irrecoverable (the woman in question is the painter Catherine Devade), but that her real name is immaterial to the narrator. Here, as often in Bolaño's work, fabulation is not deferred until the known facts have been gathered; it is not restricted to a gap in the records, but begins as soon as the real has furnished sufficient material to prime the fiction-making system.

Having described each person, the narrator proceeds to imagine the "complex and subtle web of relations among these men and women" (52). This is done by manipulating the characters almost as if they were figurines: "Let's imagine J.-J. Goux, for example, who is looking out at us through his thick submarine spectacles. His space in the photo is momentarily vacant and we see him walking along Rue de l'École de Médecine" (52). Goux goes to a café and waits for a lover who fails to appear. "Let's suppose," the narrator says, "that the person who didn't come was Jacques Henric" (53). The others are likewise combined to form couples, on the basis of the narrator's prior knowledge (Sollers and Kristeva), or a common surname in the caption (C. and M. Devade), or because, like Goux and Henric, they happen to be seated next to each other in the photograph (Pierre Guyotat and Marie-Thérèse Réveillé).

All the members of the group come to life, and we see them reading, eating, wandering around Paris, and making love. But the heart of the story concerns a character who does not appear in the image at all. The narrator notices that the gazes of Marie-Thérèse Réveillé and Carla Devade, who are not looking at the camera, seem to be converging:

Marie-Thérèse Réveillé and Carla Devade look off to the left, at an object beyond Henric's muscular shoulders. There is recognition or acceptance in Carla's gaze: that much is clear from her half-smile and gentle eyes. Marie-Thérèse, however, has a penetrating gaze: her lips are slightly open,

FIGURE 2.1 The Tel Quel group at the Fête de l'humanité, 1970. From left to right: Jacques Henric, Jean-Joseph Goux, Philippe Sollers, Julia Kristeva, Marie-Thérèse Réveillé, Pierre Guyotat, Catherine Devade, Marc Devade.

Courtesy Jacques Henric

as if she were having difficulty breathing, and her eyes are trying to fix on (trying, unsuccessfully, to *nail*) the object of her attention, which is presumably moving. Both women are looking in the same direction, but it's clear that they have quite different emotional reactions to whatever it is they are seeing. Carla's gentleness may be conditioned by ignorance. Marie-Thérèse's insecurity, her defensive yet inquisitorial glare, may result from the sudden stripping away of various layers of experience. (SE 55)

There is a difference between the expressions of the two women in the photograph (see figure 2.1), but what each expresses is interpreted here with a boldness that the pseudo-objective wording ("that much is clear . . . presumably") only serves to underline.

A little later, the object of the women's attention is speculatively identified: "Here we can reasonably conclude that, while Guyotat is looking at a stranger, Marie-Thérèse and Carla are looking at a man they know, although, as is usually (or, in fact, inevitably) the case, their perceptions of him are entirely different" (57). The effect of the analytical style is again ironic, making it clearer that the conclusion has been reached by imaginative rather than deductive means. From this point on, suppositions follow one another in a cascade, leading to the construction of a new character beyond the frame: a young, ambitious, embittered writer from Central America, who has visited the Tel Quel office to pay his respects and been treated with restrained condescension by Sollers and company. The visitor comes from a part of the periphery that has no cachet for these central intellectuals, and he resents their indifference, his nullity in their eyes. But that resentment, the narrator tells us, is, in a sense, superficial. As the writer leaves the office, he bumps into Marie-Thérèse Réveillé on the stairs. They look at each other, and what she sees "beneath the expedient mask of bitterness, is a well of unbearable horror and fear" (60). That is why, when she notices him in the café where the photo is being taken, there is apprehension in her gaze.

Whether the Central American attempts to renew his contact with the group is something "we will never know," for the story comes to a halt after briefly describing figures in the background of the group portrait, including a young boy who recalls the presumed victim of abuse in Julio Cortázar's "Blow-Up" ("Las babas del diablo"). In Cortázar's story as in Bolaño's, a photograph taken in Paris is described in detail, comes to life, and gradually yields its secrets. "Blow-Up" stands behind "Labyrinth" as the boy in the photograph of the Tel Quel group stands behind the intellectuals. Perhaps because it is an unfinished draft, "Labyrinth" shows with a special clarity how the process of overinterpretation works. The narrator fixes on details of the photograph, charges them with significance, and freely constructs a story to connect and make sense of them. The factual serves merely as a springboard or launch pad. Fiction claims its autonomy early on when the narrator arbitrarily chooses a first name for Carla (in fact Catherine) Devade, then supposes relationships among the members of the group. What Barthes might have called the *punctum* of the photograph, the apparently apprehensive gaze of Marie-Thérèse Réveillé, calls forth an explanation in the form of a character who, like Gui Rosey the Minor Poet, Dominique Tron the Kid, and Nadia Tuéni the Muse, clearly belongs to a type in Bolaño's fictional universe: in this case, the Arriviste, the writer intent on using literature as a social ladder, who is irresistibly attracted to the holders and wielders of symbolic power. The Central American is not merely pathetic. The "well of unbearable horror and fear" within him could overflow in violent acts: "[he] could quite easily become a murderer. Perhaps, back in his country, he will, but not here, where the only blood he could possibly shed is his own. This Pol Pot won't kill anyone in Paris. And actually, back in Tegucigalpa or San Salvador, he'll probably end up teaching in a university" (SE 63). This is one expression of an ethical tenet implicit in Bolaño's fiction, which I will discuss in chapter 7: attraction to institutionally vested power and prestige is not a foible but a vice.

In "Labyrinth," the narrator overinterprets as Belano and B did in "Photos" and "Last Evenings on Earth." All three are savage or wild detectives, by which I mean not that they are uncouth, but that they are prone to apophenia, and that their inferences are not constrained by criteria of economy and coherence.[44] In the absence of such criteria, clues can multiply indefinitely and can be connected to form an indefinite number of significant patterns. Particularly energetic or driven interpreters may reach the extreme exemplified by Graham Greenwood in *Distant Star*, who believes that the way to fight evil is by learning to read "not only words but numbers, colors, signs, arrangements of tiny objects, late-night and early-morning television shows, obscure films" (DS 102).

Toward the end of "Labyrinth," new figures emerge from the background: "And there is yet another person: careful examination reveals something protruding from Guyotat's neck like a cancerous growth, which turns out to be made up of a nose, a withered forehead, the outline of an upper lip, the profile of a man who is looking, with a certain gravity, in the same direction as the smoking man" (SE 64). The common object of their gaze, beyond the right-hand edge of the photo, is not identified, but not because of any limits on the narrator's power to interpret. A photographic image becomes a blur beyond a certain degree of magnification, but an obsessive interpreter can always adduce an additional "clue" and explain it by broadening the frame of the investigation. The process of overinterpretation may come to an end when it exhausts its agent or is stopped from outside, socially, by the application of hermeneutic norms, but it does not exhaust itself. The other processes examined in this chapter are also potentially limitless. Metarepresentations may contain further metarepresentations, as the summary of Ansky's notebook in *2666* contains a summary of Ivanov's novel *Sunset* (2666 718–721), and this kind of insertion can be pursued, at the risk of disorienting the reader. A character may return over and over again, renamed or transfigured, multiplying his or her doubles. Expansions, as we saw, may be expanded in turn, since the new material they contain often includes intriguing gaps and stubs. At the end of this survey of Bolaño's compositional processes, we can see that Nora Catelli's description of his "fiction-making system" as "simple" and "rigorous" needs to be qualified. The processes comprised by the system can be simply described, but because of the ways they interact and operate recursively, their results are highly complex. Each works flexibly, not with a programmed rigor: none could be properly called a constraint in the Oulipian sense of the word. In fact, the processes sometimes give Bolaño's fiction-making system extra degrees of freedom by relaxing (though not flouting) the conventional requirements, respected by most realist fiction, that characterization be basically consistent and action psychologically plausible.

It would, of course, be simplistic to suggest that Bolaño's books were turned out by a system consisting solely of the four processes that I have been describing; and it would be absurd to claim that such a system could automatically produce interesting results. As the very unbalanced Raymond Roussel wisely pointed out in *How I Wrote Certain of My Books*: the value of procedures depends on how they are used.[45] Nevertheless, reading genetically, for traces of compositional method, can take us beyond static patterns and give us some insight into the dynamics of Bolaño's fictional universe, if not into the energy that drove its astonishing expansion.

3

SOMETHING IS GOING TO HAPPEN

Narrative Tension

ANY MODERN NOVELISTS, at one time or another, have felt that storytelling is a tedious obligation, a regrettable concession to popular taste. Writing to Louise Colet in 1852, Flaubert reflected wistfully, "What seems beautiful to me, what I should like to write, is a book about nothing, a book dependent on nothing external, which would be held together by the internal strength of its style."[1] In the first of his Clark lectures, given in 1927, E. M. Forster imagined three voices answering the question, "What does a novel do?" The third voice, his own, says regretfully, "Yes, oh dear yes, the novel tells a story."[2] He adds: "I wish that it was not so, that it could be something different—melody, or perception of the truth, not this low atavistic form" (34). In 1963, Alain Robbe-Grillet combatively declared that plot was an obsolete notion; not only was storytelling no longer necessary, it had become "strictly impossible."[3] Ten years later, in the introduction to *Aren't You Rather Young to Be Writing Your Memoirs?*, B. S. Johnson lamented the prevailing backwardness of fiction writers and readers: "surely it must be a confession of failure on the part of any novelist to rely on that primitive, vulgar and idle curiosity of the reader to know 'what happens next.' . . . Why . . . do so many novelists still write as though the revolution that was *Ulysses* had never happened, still rely on the crutch of storytelling?"[4]

By the early 1990s, when Roberto Bolaño began entering stories and novels in literary competitions in Spain in the hope of winning the cash prizes offered by municipalities around the country (LEE 1–2; MP ix), the idea of escaping from the "atavism" of storytelling, though far from dead, had lost some of its freshness and glamor. Bolaño's particular problem was not how to elude that atavism but how to harness it effectively enough to appeal to judging panels. He had been writing and publishing postsurrealist poetry for twenty years. He had written but not published *Antwerp,* in which the story is pulverized thoroughly enough to satisfy the most radical advocates of the "new novel." The disjunctive was, or seemed to be, his element. As Mark Ford has remarked, "his early work rather rigorously eschewed the art of storytelling, but it turned out to be an aspect of writing that Bolaño was amazingly good at."[5] This is not to say that his stories fall into familiar patterns, or that they follow the quasi-Aristotelian guidelines laid down by manuals like Robert McKee's *Story.*[6] Bolaño's fiction is unruly in its structures, as in its implicit attitudes. And yet it has widely proven its effectiveness in holding the reader's interest, in generating and sustaining narrative tension. How it manages to do this is the subject of the present chapter.

Narrative tension, as Jean-Marie Schaeffer has pointed out, is a relatively neglected object of academic study, for two reasons. First, it is "canonical" or normal, and scholars have tended to focus on deviant or subversive modes of narrative functioning. And second, it is often assumed that narrative tension can be explained straightforwardly. On the contrary, as Schaeffer writes, it raises extremely complex problems concerning not only literary, linguistic, and semiotic analysis but also cognitive psychology and the psychology of the emotions.[7] Recent research addressing these problems has drawn extensively on the work of Meir Sternberg, and particularly his identification of three temporal relations between discourse and story, each of which has a distinct emotional effect:

(1) The discourse progresses chronologically, in the same sequence as the story, creating suspense;

(2) The discourse withholds information about something that has already happened—and draws attention to that omission—creating curiosity;

(3) The discourse withholds information about something that has already happened—without indicating that something has been omitted—thus creating surprise when the information is made available.[8]

Raphaël Baroni has observed that this scheme cannot account for surprises produced not by revealing withheld information but simply by confounding expectations.[9] This is true, but as Emma Kafalenos points out, Sternberg uses "surprise" as a narrowly defined technical term.[10] Having noted this difference in definition, we can characterize Bolaño's handling of narrative tension broadly as follows: he cultivates suspense more than curiosity, and surprises the reader by confounding expectations rather than by revealing withheld information.

GENERIC SUSPENSE: *DISTANT STAR*

When a reader is in suspense, she is wondering what is going to happen in the story, engaging in prospection or forming prognoses in a largely subconscious manner.[11] Typically, as Donald Beecher writes, "literary suspense entails liked characters under duress whose futures are perilous and uncertain—futures about which readers hold strong preferences."[12] As soon as the dissonant music begins in a horror film, subliminal memories of other films in the genre begin to shape our prognoses concerning the imminent threat to the protagonist. Sometimes the suspense in Bolaño's fiction works in a similar way. Here, for example, the narrator of *Distant Star* is remembering a letter in which Bibiano O'Ryan recounts a visit to Alberto Ruiz-Tagle's apartment:

> What did Bibiano say about Ruiz-Tagle's apartment? He talked about how bare it was, mostly; he had the feeling it had been *prepared*. He only went there once on his own. He was passing by and, typically, decided to drop in and invite Ruiz-Tagle to go and see a film. He hardly knew the guy, but that didn't stop him. There was a Bergman film showing, I can't remember which one. Bibiano had already been to the apartment

a couple of times with one or the other of the Garmendia sisters, and on both occasions the visit had been expected, so to speak. Both times, the apartment seemed to have been *prepared*, its contents arranged for the eye of the imminent visitor; it was too empty, and there were spaces from which things had obviously been removed. In the letter explaining all this to me (which was written many years later), Bibiano said he felt like Mia Farrow in *Rosemary's Baby*, when she goes into the neighbor's apartment for the first time with John Cassavetes. What was missing from Ruiz-Tagle's apartment was something unnameable (or something that Bibiano, years later, and knowing the full story, or a good part of it at any rate, considered unnameable, but palpably present), as if the host had amputated parts of the interior. (DS 6–7)

Even at this early stage in the novel, it is clear that Bibiano's host is a disquieting character: we know that Ruiz-Tagle is not his real name, that he lives in an apartment with the curtains permanently drawn, and that a "sinister legend" will grow up around him in later years (DS 6). Writing with the benefit of hindsight (shared by rereaders), Bibiano remembers ominous features, or projects them onto his memories. The narrator doubts Bibiano's account— "I don't know how much to believe and how much to put down to my fellow student's imagination" (DS 6)—but his doubts about what really happened (reiterated in parenthetical asides) do not diminish the suspense. On the contrary, they intensify the reader's anxious anticipation by suggesting that what is about to be revealed must be horrific because it may seem exaggerated.

Bolaño's italicization of "prepared" functions as a generic cue, like a discord in a film score. The preparation seems to consist of removing things, and the sense that things have been removed or hidden motivates the comparison with *Rosemary's Baby*, in which Rosemary Woodhouse (played by Mia Farrow) notices that pictures have been taken down in the apartment of her neighbors, Roman and Minnie Castavet. The mention of Polanski's film is a more obvious generic cue, indicating that the novel is venturing into the terrain of classic horror. What is missing from Ruiz-Tagle's apartment is not something that will be revealed to us later, satisfying our curiosity (as when Rosemary Woodhouse sees the sinister paintings, just before discovering that she has borne the child of Satan), but something never to be named, absent yet paradoxically palpable. Although this thing is unnameable, the choice of the verb "amputate" to evoke the way it has been removed foreshadows the photographs that Wieder will later exhibit in a friend's apartment in Providencia, particularly the image of "a severed finger, thrown onto a floor of porous, grey cement" (DS 89).

The double account of Bibiano's first two visits ("Bibiano had already been to the apartment a couple of times with one or the other of the Garmendia sisters") is doubled by the spontaneous visit that he makes on his own. Strangely, the impression that the apartment has been prepared is "even stronger" on this occasion (DS 7). Ruiz-Tagle has not been expecting Bibiano; he shuts the door and makes him wait outside for a few seconds before letting him in, while engaging perhaps in minimal "preparations." What is missing this time, or hidden, can be named, at least speculatively: Bibiano hears a noise and assumes that there is a woman in the apartment. When Ruiz-Tagle says that he has a date with Veronica Garmendia, Bibiano guesses that she is the source of the noise:

> Otherwise why would Ruiz-Tagle, who was normally so discreet, have mentioned her name? But try as he might, he couldn't imagine our star poet in that situation. Neither Veronica nor Angelica Garmendia would stoop to eavesdropping. So who was it? Bibiano never found out. Right then, probably the only thing he knew was that he wanted to get out of there, away from Ruiz-Tagle, and never return to that naked, bleeding apartment. (DS 8)

Again, what is hidden will not be revealed, but the words "naked" and "bleeding" (like "amputated") have a proleptic function: they anticipate the fate of the Garmendia twins (DS 23), and we may presume that they reflect Bibiano's reimagining of the visit, "years later" when he knew "the full story" (DS 7), rather than his experience at the time.

Bibiano's letter records no objective evidence of violence or cruelty, yet it is particularly effective in creating and maintaining suspense. The effect is obtained partly by the multiplication of uncanny details: the apartment's excessive tidiness, the host's rather too fixed smile, the "peculiar odor" ("as if Ruiz-Tagle had cooked something very pungent the night before, something oily and spicy" [DS 8]), and the noise that could well have come from next door. Even Ruiz-Tagle's declared dislike of Bergman's films can be read as an ominous sign: this is a man who has no time for the emotional complexities of domestic life, as we can infer later from the elemental simplicity of the "poems" that he writes in the sky: "Death is friendship," "Death is Chile," "Death is responsibility," and so on (DS 80–82). But the uncanniness of the details depends in part on the frame established by the reference to *Rosemary's Baby*. Insofar as we know that "this is going to be a horror story," as Auxilio Lacouture says at the beginning of *Amulet* (A 1), the suspense created by the scene is generic.

SECRET STORIES

Elsewhere in Bolaño's work, suspense arises from uncertainty about the kind of story that is being told. A model of the short story developed by Ricardo Piglia and Guillermo Martínez can help to explain the functioning of this second kind of suspense, which I will be calling intergeneric. The basic idea is simple. Piglia puts it like this in his essay "Theses on the Short Story": "A short story [*cuento*] always tells two stories [*historias*]."[13] In the classic short story, according to Piglia, there is a visible story in whose interstices a secret story is encoded. At the end, the secret story comes to the surface, producing an effect of surprise. The two stories are governed by different "systems of causality."[14] The key elements have a dual function, participating in the two systems simultaneously. The modern short story, according to Piglia, "abandons the surprise ending and the closed structure; it works the tension between the two stories without ever resolving it," telling "two stories as if they were one" (64).

Martínez has proposed a "slight variation" on Piglia's theses: instead of two stories, he speaks of two logics: the initial logic, that of common sense, and the logic of fiction, of what is going to happen (since there is a tacit pact between writer and reader, according to which "something is going to happen"). At the beginning the two logics coincide, but in the course of the story they come apart; the logic of fiction begins to displace the logic of common sense and "gradually occupies the scene."[15] If the story has been successfully constructed, the ending, according to Martínez, should be a necessary consequence of this transmutation, rather than coming out of nowhere.

The Piglia-Martínez model can bring an aspect of Bolaño's originality into focus and help to explain how his stories generate narrative tension while remaining puzzling and inconclusive. Like the modern short story writers cited by Piglia (Chekhov, Katherine Mansfield, Sherwood Anderson, Joyce), Bolaño "works the tension between the two stories without ever resolving it," and this working takes a variety of forms, which I will illustrate here by examining "Cell Mates," "Dentist," and "Last Evenings on Earth."

"Cell Mates" presents itself initially as an extract from the fictionalized autobiography of Roberto Bolaño. The "cell mates" of the title are the narrator-protagonist and his lover Sofía. Both happened to be imprisoned in the same month of the same year (November 1973), although in different jails, thousands of kilometers apart (R 57). Sofía says that she is losing her mind: like a number of Bolaño's stories—"Phone Calls," "Enrique Martín," "Prefiguration of Lalo Cura"—"Cell Mates" dramatizes encroaching madness. Her diet consists almost entirely of instant mashed potatoes. At one point she seems to be on the brink of suicide: "I got the feeling Sofía was visiting all her ex-lovers. I got the feeling she was saying goodbye to them one by one, but not in a calm or resigned sort of way" (R 61). The narrator does not inquire into the causes of her depression (melancholy is a brute fact in Bolaño's fictional universe), but at certain moments the reader can glimpse the possibility of a fantastic logic that might explain her behavior.

One day, after the end of their relationship, the narrator visits Sofía's apartment on the top floor of a dilapidated building. He knocks at the door: "I thought there was no one there. Then I thought there was no one *living* there" (63). The use of italics brings out an ambiguity: perhaps the apartment is uninhabited, or perhaps there is someone there who is not living. The dwelling does in fact seem to be haunted: "Just as I was about to go, the door opened. It was Sofía. The apartment was dark and the light on the landing went off automatically after twenty seconds. At first, because of the darkness, I didn't realize she was naked" (63). Sofía doesn't let him in, although she is alone: "My boyfriend will be back soon and he doesn't like it if there's anyone here with me, especially a man" (64). "Sounds like this boyfriend of yours is a vampire," replies the narrator, which is, of course, a joke, and Sofía smiles, but it is also a way of picking up the fantastic thread. Why is Sofía waiting naked in a dark, cold apartment? If the boyfriend is not literally a vampire, it seems that he is at least metaphorically sucking the life from her. "They've done something to you," the narrator says, before he is told to go (64).

He does not see Sofía again for more than a year, but some mornings he wakes up with the feeling that he has spent the night with her, as if she were a succubus. Another of Sofía's ex-lovers, Emilio, sometimes has the same impression. It turns out that Sofía and her new boyfriend have tried to kill Emilio, who, in the midst of the fight, noticed a strange resemblance between his attackers: "they were like twins" (66). Here, with the appearance of the doppelgänger, the fictional logic that has been suggested by a series of allusions to fantastic motifs (haunted house, vampire, succubus) reaches its most explicit, but then immediately begins to recede, because Sofía's double, far from being a terrifying figure, is small and weak. Emilio gives him a beating and walks out.

When, after hearing this story, the narrator visits Sofía, her apartment (which he now enters for the first time) still seems to be haunted, and she still seems to be possessed. He sits down in an armchair, "maybe the one Emilio had sat in on the day of the ambush" (67), and the reader cannot help imagining a repetition of the earlier attack. But when the narrator asks Sofía about her boyfriend, she replies, "He's gone away . . . and he's never coming back" (68). The story's last sentence—"Then we got dressed and went out to eat at a pizzeria" (68)—is perhaps the prefiguration of a cure: they leave the dark and empty apartment, in which there is no food at all, "not even a miserable tin of peas," and go to a place that, if not clean and well-lighted, will at least provide something more nutritious to eat than instant mashed potatoes. Common sense reasserts itself, but without entirely dissolving the fantastic atmosphere, since a number of troubling questions remain unanswered: Who or what was Sofía's boyfriend, "the nameless man," her "twin"? (66). Why did he try to kill Emilio? And why did he go away?

In "Cell Mates," the "secret story," as Piglia would say, sinks away before it has fully emerged. There is a similar but more complex movement in "Dentist," whose "visible story" has three distinct components, each of which is an episode in the life of the eponymous dentist, a friend of the narrator. These components are: the death of an Indian woman who has been treated at the dentist's practice; his encounter with the famous painter Cavernas; and his friendship with a young man named José Ramírez who is, so he claims, a literary prodigy. It is not clear what connects these episodes apart from the fact that they all involve the dentist. A possible solution to this problem can be glimpsed when the narrator meets José Ramírez and begins to wonder about his friend's sexuality:

> Then, as the boy sat down with us and exhibited his wintry smile, it occurred to me that perhaps my friend, a confirmed bachelor who could have chosen to live in Mexico City years ago but had preferred to stay in his hometown, Irapuato, had become, or had always been, a homosexual, and that for some obscure reason this fact, kept secret for years, had emerged in the course of our conversation that night about the Indian woman and her cancerous gum. (LEE 193)

Perhaps the dentist blames himself for the death of the Indian woman because he is displacing guilt about his sexuality (188). Perhaps he tells the story of his humiliation by Cavernas because the painter's words touched a nerve: "he asked if I was an out-and-out faggot or if it was just a phase I was going through" (190). Perhaps he considers Ramírez a genius because he has fallen in love. The dentist guesses what his friend is thinking and denies it: "I'm not . . . I'm not that way . . . you know . . . inclined . . . I'm not . . . you didn't think I was, did you?" (201). But perhaps he insists too much.

There is nothing in "Dentist" to disprove the narrator's hypothesis, but having allowed the logic of repressed sexuality to emerge and offer a neat solution to the problem of how the three components of the story fit together, Bolaño leaves that offer aside and introduces a new fictional logic. When José Ramírez presents the two friends with a pile of his stories, the narrator wants at first to borrow them, hoping to avoid the embarrassing obligation to respond on the spot to bad writing. But the dentist orders him to pick a story at random and read it: "So I did. I lowered my eyes, ashamed, chose a story and began to read. The story was four pages long; maybe that's why I chose it, because it was short, but when I got to the end, I felt as if I had read a novel. . . . Earlier, I had been almost falling asleep myself, but now I felt wide awake and absolutely sober" (207). There must be something authentically prodigious about the writing of Ramírez to have produced these psychological and physical effects on the narrator, who is, to extrapolate from the other stories told in the first person, an exacting judge, and, on this occasion, both skeptical and weary before he begins to read. There is no metarepresentation of the story itself in this episode; only its effects are described (as we saw in chapter 2, this is often the case when the fictive writer has real talent). By this point, however, the dentist has already told the narrator about some of Ramírez's work, notably "a story about a child who had to look after his numerous younger brothers and sisters, that was the gist of it, the first part anyway, because then the plot swung around and smashed itself to pieces" (204). This summary can be read as a *mis-en-abyme*: when the narrator reads Ramírez's stories, the plot of "Dentist" swings around, and although it does not smash itself to pieces, it does fail strikingly to pull itself together and accomplish any kind of resolution.

In an earlier disquisition on the nature of art, the dentist spoke of "the secret story": "the one we'll never know, although we're living it from day to day, thinking we're alive, thinking we've got it all under control and the stuff we overlook doesn't matter. But every damn thing matters! It's just that we don't realize" (192). This passage too can be read reflexively, for the dentist seems to be talking not only about art but also about his own life. The "secret story" of "Dentist" seems at first to be one of repression, the story of a man remaining in the closet, or perhaps timidly coming out, but then the plot swings around and a story that is more secret still emerges in the form of an ineffable illumination: "as we left that godforsaken place I realized there was very little we could say about the events of the previous night. Both of us felt happy, but we knew, without a shadow of doubt, and without having to put it into words, that we would not be able to ascertain or reflect on the nature of what we had experienced" (208).

In the final paragraphs of "Dentist," the three components of the visible story are juxtaposed anew: the dentist looks at the engravings by Cavernas hanging on the wall of his apartment; the narrator dreams of José Ramírez's house and "for barely a second" understands "the mystery of art and its secret nature"; but then the old Indian woman who died of gum cancer comes into his dream and erases that miraculous understanding (208–209). The relations among the components remain enigmatic. In addition, if we turn back to the beginning of the story, the first sentence—"He wasn't Rimbaud, he was just an Indian boy"—may throw some doubt on the intrinsic qualities of the texts that produced the illumination.

In both "Cell Mates" and "Dentist," a fictional logic gradually occupies the scene up to a precise moment in the narrative (the attack on Emilio, the narrator's reading of José Ramírez's stories), but the process is then halted or reversed. In "Cell Mates" the initial, autobiographical logic reasserts itself; in "Dentist" a second fictional logic appears, repeating the split that occurs only once per story according to the model proposed by Guillermo Martínez.

Elsewhere, Bolaño disturbs and undermines common-sense logic without allowing a distinct alternative to emerge. "Last Evenings on Earth," in which B and his father spend a few days in Acapulco on vacation, exemplifies this strategy. The apocalyptic title sets the tone: this will be the chronicle of a disaster foretold. B's father goes swimming in spite of the sea's roughness, against the advice of a fisherman (LEE 147). He disappears; the fisherman and two boys cry out in alarm. Although in the end he returns to shore safely, "from this moment on" B "knows the disaster is approaching" (148). In the first part of the story, the disaster looms in the form of an accident; after the episode of the risky swim, B's father dives from a dinghy to recover his wallet and remains submerged for so long that B begins to worry (149). B plunges into the water and sees his father swimming back up with the wallet in his hand: "They look at each other as they pass, but can't alter their trajectories, or at least not straight away, so B's father keeps ascending silently, while B continues his silent descent" (149). This comic incident retrospectively acquires an emblematic significance when the narrator gives us a clue to the nature of the impending disaster: "a singular disaster whose main effect is to distance B from his father" (150).

Father and son are taking a vacation together, presumably to reinforce the filial bond after B's time in Chile, during which he was nearly killed, "twice, at least" (153). But the trip seems to have precisely the opposite effect: "this is the last time we're traveling together, thinks B" (153). It marks the end of a phase, dividing time into a before and an after, and with the benefit of hindsight, again, we can see this temporal discontinuity figured in the curtain of the roadside café where B and his father eat iguana on the way to Acapulco: "B has the intermittent impression that this curtain separates not only the kitchen from the eating area but also one time from another" (132).

Beyond the story's midpoint, the approaching disaster takes on a different although still vague form. It begins to seem not accidental but planned: "It all begins with the reappearance of the ex-diver" (150). B and his father go with this man to a nightspot and a restaurant before arriving at "the scene of the crime," a bar and brothel in the suburbs (153). There the father wins a substantial amount of money at cards. When he attempts to leave with his winnings, the other players make violent threats. B hears his father "accusing the ex-diver of something" (157). Perhaps the ex-diver has collaborated with the other gamblers to lay a trap for the tourists from Mexico City, knowing that B's father is not short of money, since he chose to watch the diving show from the bar of the hotel overlooking the precipice, which charges an exorbitant admission fee (142). Or perhaps the ex-diver simply loses his nerve when it comes to choosing sides. The reason for the father's reproach is not clarified, and the story ends with the beginning of a fight (like "The South" by Jorge Luis Borges, which Bolaño parodies in a later story, "The Insufferable Gaucho"). The ending is not just inconclusive but paradoxical, because if this fight is the foretold disaster, its result does not seem to be to "distance B from his father" (150), but on the contrary to affirm their bond. B realizes that unlike Gui Rosey, the French surrealist poet about whom he has been reading, "he is not alone" (157).

In "Last Evenings on Earth" the initial logic of common sense is perturbed by B's presentiments, but no coherent fictional logic comes to occupy the scene. What begins as the story of a vacation in Acapulco does not turn out to be, in fact, the story of an accident or a conspiracy or an estrangement, as it seemed it would at various points along the way.

And yet the suspense does not flag, because as soon as one threat recedes, another comes to the fore. In addition, Bolaño multiplies anomalous elements that do not turn out to contribute to any secret story apprehensible in retrospect. For example, one evening, while he is reading by the motel pool, B sees a woman who seems to be ill:

> The woman is wearing a loose, light-colored summer dress, cut low, leaving her shoulders bare. He expects her to start walking again, but she stands still, her hand fixed to the edge of the flowerbed, looking down, so B gets up with the book in his hand and goes over to her. The first thing that surprises him is her face. She must be about sixty years old, B guesses, although from a distance, he wouldn't have said she was more than thirty. She is North American, and when B approaches she looks up and smiles at him. Good night, she says, rather incongruously, in Spanish. Are you all right? asks B. The woman doesn't understand and B has to ask again, in English. I'm just thinking, says the woman, smiling at him fixedly. For a few seconds B considers what she has said to him. Thinking, thinking, thinking. And suddenly it seems to him that this declaration conceals a threat. (139–140)

The function of this passage is not to introduce a character who will be instrumental later on (although she does reappear, talking to B's father [146–147]) but to intensify the atmosphere of unspecified menace, which began to develop with the story of Gui Rosey's disappearance (discussed in the final section of chapter 2). Once that atmosphere has reached a certain intensity, Bolaño has only to let B's gaze linger on details—such as the receptionist's "bright little rabbit teeth" shining in the semidarkness (139)—to make them ominous. This story, like much of Bolaño's fiction (particularly "The Part About Amalfitano" and "The Part About Fate" in *2666*), is suffused with a dreamlike unease that is strongly reminiscent of David Lynch's films, an affinity reinforced, in certain passages, by the way Bolaño's prose follows and frames the movements of the characters with a cinematic precision, as when B watches the North American woman returning to her hotel room: "Then the woman says good night and makes a gradual exit: first she goes up the stairs to reception, where she spends a few moments chatting with someone B can't see, then, in silence, she sets off across the hotel lobby, her slim figure framed by successive windows, until she turns into the corridor that leads to the inside stairs" (141). A reader contaminated by B's somewhat paranoid attention to details might find herself wondering at this point to whom the woman spoke. Was it the rabbit-toothed receptionist who was suspiciously insistent in his recommendation of the San Diego nightclub? According to the traditional pact between the writer and the reader of a short story, something is going to happen, and various things do indeed happen in "Last Evenings on Earth," but the nature of those things is at best dimly foreshadowed by generic conventions.

"Cell Mates," "Dentist," and "Last Evenings on Earth" exemplify three ways of exploring the tension between the visible story and the secret story, to use Piglia's terms, or between the logic of common sense and the logic of fiction, as Martínez would say. The logic of fiction can gradually emerge up to a certain point in the story, then recede again, or it can split, or unsettle the logic of common sense without constituting a coherent secret story. These strategies prolong suspense by planting questions that can resonate indefinitely in the reader's mind: Who or what was Sofía's boyfriend? Why did José Ramírez's stories produce such a powerful effect? Of what did B's father accuse the ex-diver? While *Distant Star* expertly manages generic suspense, identifying itself as a tale of horror and exploiting expectations produced by familiarity with the horror genre, "Cell Mates," "Dentist," and "Last Evenings on Earth" create intergeneric suspense: they keep the reader wondering not only what will happen next, but also what kind of story this will turn out to be, really, in the end.

THE DECENTRALIZATION OF NARRATIVE TENSION: *2666*

So far in this chapter I have been discussing suspense in short stories and scenes from a short novel. As many critics have remarked, Bolaño's long novels are largely composed of linked stories. The linking complicates the production of narrative tension, as I will show in this section, with examples from 2666. Here I will adopt what Noël Carrol, in *The Philosophy of Horror*, calls an "erotetic" or "tacit question model" of narrative, that is, I will formulate the implicit questions raised by the text on a range of scales, from the scale of the novel as a whole down to that of particular episodes.[16] In 2666 tension is heightened by means of fragmentation and alternation, and, as in part II of *The Savage Detectives*, it is decentralized or devolved, depending more on the briefly told stories of marginal characters than on the answer to an overarching question.

Considered as a whole, 2666 is an intellectual quest narrative: like *The Savage Detectives*, it recounts the search for a disappeared writer. At this high level of generality, the quest creates suspense, raising the implicit question: Will the critics find and meet Benno Von Archimboldi? But that question loses much of its urgency early in the first part of the novel, when Pelletier and Espinoza realize that "the search for Archimboldi could never fill their lives" (29). The investigation undertaken by the critics in Sonora, unlike that of Belano and Lima in *The Savage Detectives*, is fruitless, and Pelletier and Espinoza reach the conclusion that although Archimboldi is present in Santa Teresa, they will not find him: "'Archimboldi is here,' said Pelletier, 'and we're here, and this is the closest we'll ever be to him'" (159). It is not until the very end of the novel, when Archimboldi sets off for Mexico to help his nephew Klaus Haas, imprisoned in Santa Teresa (893), that the possibility of an encounter between the critics and the great writer reemerges. What might seem initially to be the mainspring of the novel's suspense hardly operates in its three central parts and in most of the final part.

Nevertheless, a complex embedding of implicit questions ensures that narrative tension is maintained. For example, in "The Part About the Critics," as the quest for Archimboldi loses its urgency, the relationships among the critics intensify, raising the following suspense questions: Which of the male critics will Norton choose? And will the friendship among them survive the erotic complications produced by her hesitation? These are shadowed by the curiosity question: Is Norton simply indecisive or is there a destructive will behind her changes of mind, as her "friend" Alex Pritchard suggests when he says to Pelletier, "Beware of the Medusa" (69)?

At the highest level of generality, then, "The Part About the Critics" is an intellectual quest. At the next level down, it is a story about friendship and love. At a lower level again, it recounts a series of troubling incidents, which can be read as parables about civilization and barbarity. In the anecdote of the little gaucho consumed by murderous rage after losing a horse race against a visiting German (20–23), barbarity is represented by the local boy and civilization by all the other characters, but of those who hear this story in Germany, only Archimboldi can solve the "riddle" of the boy's rage because, in his way, he is barbaric too (his publisher Bubis calls him "a Germanic barbarian" [839]). The artist Edwin Johns brings barbarity into the world of art when he cuts off his painting hand, has it embalmed, and turns it into the centerpiece of a self-portrait (52–53). Even more disturbingly, the critics Pelletier and Espinoza, who have known and assumed "all along" that they are "civilized beings, beings capable of noble sentiments" (41), turn out to be capable of barbaric violence too: they respond to the insult of a Pakistani taxi driver with a brutal physical attack (73–75). The point of this episode, as of Johns's action art and Archimboldi's empathy with the little gaucho, seems to be that the barbaric may be lodged at the apparent heart of civilization, an idea that inevitably recalls thesis VII of Walter Benjamin's "On the Concept of History."[17] Although these incidents do not form a single subplot, they are dramatically arranged as well as thematically linked: first the little gaucho, seething with fury; then the painter's self-mutilation; finally the critics' violent attack on a third party. In this sequence, barbarity is progressively realized in action, and at the same time, it comes closer to home, that is, to the central characters in the narrative.

In *2666*, as well as embedding stories within stories, Bolaño sustains and heightens narrative tension by means of fragmentation and alternation. Near the end of "The Part About the Critics," for example, Espinoza and Pelletier receive almost identical e-mails from Norton explaining the decision that she has finally made (140–141), but what she has decided to do—break off her intimate relationship with them and move in with Morini—is withheld for fifteen pages, in which sections of the long e-mail, relating, among other things, the death of Edwin Johns, alternate with an account of Espinoza's subsequent relationship with Rebeca, a woman he has met at the craft market in Santa Teresa. A reader wondering what Norton has decided is in the grip of curiosity rather than suspense, but a reader familiar with Bolaño's "poetics of inconclusiveness" (SE viii) also knows that her curiosity may not be satisfied, so she is subject to a second-order suspense that relates not to the story but to the narrative discourse: will it eventually deliver the withheld information?

In this case, the answer is yes, but this is not a typical case. It is among the exceptions required for the effective operation of second-order suspense: if the withheld information were *never* revealed, the initiated reader would not be suspended between two live possibilities. Bolaño's work, as a whole, is loosely woven and abounds in loose ends: stories stop without concluding, and gaps within them are left unfilled. The anonymous critic who wrote of *2666* in *The New Yorker* that "the reader will be impressed by the range and power on display but might wish that the novel cohered, rather than merely concluding" understated the case, because the novel does not even conclude.[18] The critic also failed fully to grasp the range and power on display, for *2666* does cohere, not as a stand-alone unit but as the largest part of the whole that, as I argued in chapter 2, is constituted by Bolaño's fiction from *Nazi Literature in the Americas* onward.

The inconclusiveness of *2666* is particularly flagrant in "The Part About the Crimes." Anyone approaching this part of the novel with expectations shaped by genre fiction is bound to be disappointed. Ninety percent of the crimes are left unsolved or dubiously attributed (see appendix), and it would be misguided to assume that the unidentified murderers must be among the characters who feature in the narrative, for "The Part About the Crimes" is not a whodunit, however elliptical. Nor is it a narco-novel fascinated by the lifestyle of the drug bosses. Bolaño has decided to blank out the perpetrators and concentrate instead on surveying the damage done. Narrative tension in "The Part About the Crimes" depends less on curiosity about the identity of a putative serial killer or orchestrator of atrocities than on the more specific questions raised implicitly by the loosely interwoven stories of individuals affected in various ways by the crimes. One such story, which is typically inconclusive and illustrates the novel's centrifugal nature, relates Harry Magaña's private investigation of the murder of Lucy Anne Sander.

Lucy Anne Sander disappears one night while visiting Santa Teresa with Erica Delmore, a fellow factory worker from Huntsville, Arizona. The next day her body is found near the border fence (409). The Sheriff of Huntsville, Harry Magaña, promises Erica that he will make it his business to find out what happened (411). Some months later, Magaña returns to Santa Teresa, looking for a man called Miguel Montes, who may or may not be the Miguel (or Manuel) who tried to "hook up" with both women on the night of Lucy's disappearance (406). The search takes Magaña to Chucarit and Tijuana, then back to Santa Teresa, where, on entering a house where he hopes to find Montes or at least a clue to his whereabouts, he surprises a short man "pulling a bundle out from under a bed."

> With a sense of fatalism, Harry Magaña imagined that he was somewhere else, not a few minutes from downtown, at Francisco Díaz's house, which was like being at no one's house, but in the country, in the dust and brush, at a shack with a corral and a henhouse and woodstove, in the Santa Teresa desert or any other desert. He heard someone closing the front door and then steps in the living room. A voice calling the short man. And he heard the latter reply: I'm over here, with our friend. His rage grew. He wanted to bury his knife in the man's heart. He lunged at him, glancing desperately out of the corner of his eye at the two shadowy figures he had seen in the Rand Charger, coming down the hallway. (448)

The next we hear of Magaña is that he has disappeared and was last seen in Santa Teresa (453). He has presumably been killed. Presumably the bundle wrapped in plastic that he saw in the house of Francisco Díaz was a corpse. The text, however, obliges us to presume. As to the identities of the short man and the putative corpse, we have little basis for speculation. We know from letters found by Magaña that Montes was involved in at least five serious crimes and that he owed money to people who were not prepared to wait for more than three days (422). Among the photos that Magaña finds in Montes's house is one of "a little plane on a dirt landing strip, in the desert" (420). It seems likely that the plane is used to smuggle drugs.

The passage quoted above intensifies first-order suspense by slowing the pace of the discourse at a crucial moment, evoking the landscape that Magaña imagines just before he lunges at the short man. The whole story of Harry Magaña's investigation, broken into five separate fragments, produces second-order suspense by prompting the reader to wonder whether the text will yield answers to the curiosity questions: Is Miguel Montes a suspect or just a potential source of information? And what, exactly, happened to the sheriff? These questions, typically, go unanswered. Yet just as "The Part About the Crimes" depends for its narrative tension on the stories of particular individuals affected by the murders rather than on the search for an overall solution or the testing of conspiracy theories, so the story of Harry Magaña derives its interest largely from the diverse character portraits that it incorporates: Harry's Mexican friend Demetrio Águila, who tells him: "sometimes a stone wants to vanish. I've seen it. But God won't let it happen" (421); the Tijuana cop Raúl Ramírez Cerezo, who bores Magaña with gynophobic confidences (441); Chucho the pimp and his sentimental whores (443); and, most of all, Montes's "hometown girlfriend" and cousin in Chucarit, María del Mar, who shows Magaña the Montes family home:

> The first to leave was Miguel, said María del Mar in the darkness. Then his mother died and his father held on for a year here alone. One day he was gone. My mother says he killed himself. My father says he went north to look for Miguel. Didn't they have any other children? They did, said María del Mar, but they died when they were babies. Are you an only child too? asked Harry Magaña. No, it was the same in my family. All of my older brothers and sisters got sick and died before any of them were six. I'm sorry, said Harry Magaña. (439)

The undemonstrative sheriff is moved to tell Maria del Mar that Miguel Montes doesn't deserve her. "The girl smiled. She had small teeth. But I deserve him, she said. No, said Harry Magaña, you deserve much better" (439–440). María del Mar is at the margin of 2666. She has not seen Miguel Montes for years, and how Montes is linked to the murder of Lucy Anne Sander, one of 110 victims in "The Part About the Crimes," is never clarified. Nevertheless, this minor character is provided with a history—"She was sixteen and she had been in love with him since she was twelve" (438)—and an uncertain future: "Do you hope Miguel will come back someday? Harry Magaña asked her. I hope he comes back, but I don't know if he will. Where do you think he is now? I don't know, said María del Mar. In Santa Teresa? No, she said, if he was there you wouldn't have come to Chucarit, would you? True, said Harry Magaña" (439). María del Mar is not functional in the way that minor characters normally are in crime fiction: she does not provide any information to further Magaña's investigation, or even to lead him astray. It would be simple to edit her out of the novel, by removing her letter (422) and Magaña's visit to Chucarit. It could be argued that she brings out the compassionate side of the sheriff's character (after an interrogation scene that reveals his brutality [416]), but as well as deserving better than Miguel Montes, she deserves and plays a more than auxiliary role in the novel, contributing independently to the narrative tension in this strand of "The Part About the Crimes." What will happen to her? Will she go north to search for Miguel, as his father may have done? And if so, how will she survive? (She is just the kind of woman—a young, poor internal immigrant—who is at risk in Santa Teresa.) Bolaño does not oblige us to ask these questions, but he does provide enough detail and spend enough time with this marginal character for them to arise in the mind of an unhurried reader. In the end, *2666*, and especially "The Part About the Crimes," depends for its interest on the stories of ordinary people like this, who matter to the novel as individuals, however little space they occupy and even if they are not named, like the Salvadorean immigrant who finds the body of Anna Pachecho Martínez and is falsely accused of her murder:

> When he got out he was a broken man. A little later he crossed the border with a *pollero*. In Arizona he got lost in the desert and after walking for three days he made it to Patagonia, badly dehydrated, where a rancher beat him up for vomiting on his land. He was picked up by the sheriff and spent a day in jail and then he was sent to a hospital, where the only thing left for him to do was die in peace, which he did. (392)

REVELATIONS, SURPRISES, AND DRIFT

The investigations of Bolaño's detectives, whether literary or criminal, typically fail. As Patricia Espinosa puts it: "to search without finding is the ongoing game in Bolaño's narrative and poetic work."[19] When the detectives *do* occasionally manage to find their "targets," it comes as a surprise, disappearance being the norm, as suggested by the frequent variations on the formula "I/he/she never saw him/her/them again."[20] The findings are mysterious and fluky. In *Distant Star*, Romero returns to Barcelona and tells the narrator that he has tracked down Jules Defoe (that is, Carlos Wieder) in Lloret, not far away, but does not explain how (DS 136). In "Police Rat," Pepe the Cop, trusting to his "police instincts," guesses that one of a pair of rats coming down a tunnel toward him is the serial killer, and turns out to be right (IG 67). In *The Savage Detectives*, Belano, Lima, Madero, and Lupe end up in Villaviciosa more or less by accident (SD 568–569), ask about Cesárea Tinajero, and are sent to the washing troughs, where they find her. "Everything was much simpler than I ever imagined it would be, but I never imagined anything like this," writes Madero in his diary (569). Readers hoping for procedural detail or deductive solutions in the style of Arthur Conan Doyle or Agatha Christie will be disappointed. Bolaño's detectives owe more to Philip Marlowe than to Sherlock Holmes. Rather than detached champions of intelligence, out of danger by convention, they are agents engaged in the unfolding story, relying on instinct and skill, and their investigations place them in harm's way. The risks they run produce suspense, as in the thriller, whereas narrative tension in the whodunit depends primarily on curiosity.[21] Bolaño's fiction does of course raise curiosity questions, but as we saw in the previous section, they most often go unanswered.

Some readers are frustrated by this reticence, like Joachim in Antoni Casas Ros's novel *Enigma*, who feels compelled to destroy books that have failed to satisfy his curiosity and regards the ending of *Distant Star* as fundamentally enigmatic and cowardly on Bolaño's part: "no one will ever know whether the detective Romero killed him [Wieder] or not."[22] Perhaps no one will know for certain, but most readers would presume that Wieder has been killed. Why else would the narrator be so shaken and refuse to speak to Romero on the train back to Barcelona (DS 148)? Be that as it may, Joachim's excessive reaction does point up a general characteristic of Bolaño's fiction: it contains very few real, unequivocal revelations.

A surprise in narrative, as Meir Sternberg uses the term, is always a revelation: it is produced by closing an information gap of which the reader was previously unaware.[23] But as Raphaël Baroni has pointed out, narratives may also surprise simply by foiling a reader's expectations, whether these derive from familiarity with a genre or familiarity with the work of a particular author.[24] The scarcity of revelations in Bolaño's work does not mean that it holds few surprises in the broader sense of the word. On the contrary, its restless way of departing from both generic conventions and its own emergent regularities makes it especially unpredictable. In the second section of this chapter, I examined some ways Bolaño's short stories resist assimilation to a recognizable kind. This tendency is particularly marked in the posthumous collection *The Insufferable Gaucho*, where anomalous events and actions often simply bewilder rather than provoking the re-cognition or cognitive reassessment of the story so far that is, according to Raphaël Baroni, the normal effect of a surprise (300–303).

In the collection's title story, Manuel Pereda, a Buenos Aires lawyer, decides to retire to the family estate during the economic crisis in 2001. He notices that rabbits have multiplied alarmingly in the surrounding countryside. As Gustavo Faverón Patriau has shown, "The Insufferable Gaucho" not only parodies "The South" by Borges but also resonates with a range of other stories in the Argentine literary tradition, in three of which— Cortázar's "Letter to a Young Lady in Paris" (Cortázar 39–50), Wilcock's "Los conejos" ("The Rabbits"), and Di Benedetto's "Conejos"—rabbits figure significantly.[25] One day Pereda is out riding with one of his son's friends, a publisher named Ibarrola, who sets off at a gallop, heading for a group of ruined houses:

> Before he got there, a rabbit leaped up and bit him on the neck. The publisher's cry vanished at once into the vast open space.
>
> From where he was, all Pereda saw was a dark shape springing from the ground, tracing an arc toward the publisher's head, and then disappearing.

Dumb-ass Basque, he thought. He spurred José Bianco, and approaching Ibarrola, saw that he was holding his neck with one hand and covering his face with the other. Without saying a word, Pereda removed the hand from Ibarrola's neck. There was a bleeding scratch under his ear. (IG 30–31)

Up to this point, the story is broadly realistic. The rabbit that attacks Ibarrola, which seems to have sprung directly from *Monty Python and the Holy Grail* rather than the work of Cortázar, Wilcock, or Di Benedetto, does not, however, signal a shift into fantasy, for after this episode creatures and people behave once again in realistic if comic ways. The surprise is of the kind that Baroni calls "open": it disconcerts without proposing an alternative to the conventions it has violated.[26]

"Álvaro Rousselot's Journey" ends with an equally bewildering surprise. Álvaro Rousselot is an Argentine writer, some of whose books have, it seems, been plagiarized by a French filmmaker named Guy Morini. When Rousselot is invited to the Frankfurt Book Fair, he makes a side trip to Paris in order to elucidate "the mystery awaiting him there" (IG 85). Finally he tracks Morini down and confronts him in a hotel on the Normandy coast:

I am Álvaro Rousselot, he said, the author of *Solitude*, I mean the author of *Nights on the Pampas*.

It took a few seconds for Morini to react, but then he leaped to his feet, let out a cry of terror, and disappeared down a corridor into the hotel. Such a spectacular response was the last thing Rousselot had been expecting. His reaction was to remain seated. . . . Then he stood up and started calling Morini. Guy, he called, rather hesitantly, Guy, Guy, Guy.

Rousselot found him in an attic where the hotel's cleaning equipment was piled. Morini had opened the window and seemed to be hypnotized by the garden that surrounded the building, and by the neighboring garden, which belonged to a private house, and was visible, in part, through dark latticework. Rousselot walked over and patted him on the back. Morini seemed smaller and more fragile than before. For a while they both stood there looking at one garden, then the other. Then Rousselot wrote the address of his hotel in Paris and the address of the hotel where he was currently staying on a piece of paper and slipped it into the director's trouser pocket. (IG 98–99)

If Morini's delayed reaction is surprisingly dramatic, Rousselot's is surprisingly subdued and even tender. For years he has been suspecting Morini of stealing his narrative ideas, and now he seems to be overcome by pity, and loath to cause any further distress to "Guy," with whom he is mysteriously on first-name terms. The pair's silent and, it seems, coordinated contemplation of the gardens is a surprise without a "heuristic function."[27] Although it is tempting to speculate that Rousselot's curiosity is dissolved by communion with a doppelgänger, there is little in the story to warrant pressing it into that fantastic and specifically Borgesian mold. With its sinuous movement and the elusive psychology of its protagonist, "Álvaro Rousselot's Journey" is closer to the stories of Felisberto Hernández, which move from surprise to surprise without activating any "dynamics of re-cognition."[28]

As Rousselot walks away from the hotel, he considers killing himself, but instead he calls Simone, the woman with whom he has begun a relationship in Paris. She says she will come to fetch him, since he has completely run out of money: "For the rest of the day Rousselot felt that he really was an Argentine writer, something he had begun to doubt over the previous days, or perhaps the previous years, partly because he was unsure of himself, but also because he was unsure about the possibility of an Argentine literature" (IG 100). The protagonist's uncertainty is provisionally resolved as the reader's uncertainty deepens. Not only are the questions relating to Morini's films left open—Why did he *stop* plagiarizing Rousselot? How could he have had access to the manuscript of *Life of a Newly Wed* before its publication? (IG 84)—we are also left in doubt as to Rousselot's immediate future: Will he stay in Paris with Simone or return to his wife in Buenos Aires? Álvaro Rousselot is a man adrift, all the more so at the story's end, and the open surprise of his encounter with Morini serves to destructure the reader's anticipation, formerly oriented by the suspense question: Will he finally track down his opposite number? This is the effect that Mihály Dés refers to when he writes of Bolaño "diluting" or "deflating" the endings of his stories rather than simply leaving them open.[29]

As well as failing to provide answers to suspense and curiosity questions, the endings of Bolaño's stories often anticipate the beginning of a new phase in the protagonist's life. Simone's use of the word *chéri* on the telephone seems to foreshadow a durable intimacy with Rousselot (IG 99). At the end of "Cell Mates," as we saw in the second section of this chapter, Sofía seems to be on the way to recovery (R 68). "Sensini" closes with an opening: "Suddenly I realized that we were at peace, that for some mysterious reason the two of us had reached a state of peace, and that from now on, imperceptibly, things would begin to change. As if the world really was shifting" (LEE 17–18). In the final pages of "The Return," the ghost of a dead man embarks surprisingly on what promises to be a happy and lasting relationship with the necrophiliac who rented his body (R 149–151). And *2666* ends with the old Archimboldi setting off for Mexico, to discover what for him truly is a new world (893).

Bolaño's narrative texts do not neatly partition his fictional universe into separate event sequences, each with its beginning, middle, and end. His "poetics of inconclusiveness" is a poetics of continuity as well as of fragmentation, and the drift of his stories militates against any sense of a definitive ending. In "New Theses on the Story," Piglia notes that the experience of, or experimentation with, wandering and swerving in narrative is "based on the secret dream of a story that would have no end, the utopia of an order outside time where events would follow one another predictably, interminably, perpetually renewed."[30] The artful drifting of Bolaño's stories suggests a crucially different order or disorder, in which events would follow one another interminably and *un*predictably, renewed not just by endless variations on familiar and stable themes but by the metamorphosis of the themes themselves. This is the dream or utopia that we can glimpse when Bolaño's storytelling pivots on an open surprise and, rather than purging us of the "vulgar and idle curiosity to know 'what happens next,'" feeds that fundamental hunger while giving us no firm grounds for longer-term prediction.

4

AIMLESSNESS

THE DRIFTING OF Bolaño's stories, discussed at the end of the previous chapter, is not a purely formal feature of his writing. If his stories often drift, it is partly because many of his characters are drifters by choice, by nature, or by force of circumstance. When the narrator in "Sensini" says that the eponymous writer's stories are peopled by "brave and aimless characters" (LEE 5), he could be referring to the fiction of Bolaño. The characteristics of bravery and aimlessness are preeminently combined by Cesárea Tinajero in *The Savage Detectives*. In the final section of the next chapter I will argue that she exemplifies the active and passive courage to which Bolaño's fiction implicitly but insistently attaches value. I would like to open this chapter by stressing the way she lives without far-reaching projects or a strongly unified narrative account of her life.

In her youth, Cesárea Tinajero works as a secretary for General Carvajal, friend and patron of the stridentists, but the arrangement only lasts as long as it does because her personality and eccentricities are compatible with those of her employer. As Amadeo Salvatierra says: "she could never in her life have had a boss or what you might call a steady job" (SD 332). One day she decides to leave Mexico City and go to Sonora. Amadeo is shocked:

But why, Cesárea? I said. Don't you realize that if you leave now, you're going to give up your literary career? Do you have any idea what a wasteland Sonora is? What are you going to do there? . . . Look for a job and a place to live, said Cesárea. And is that all? I said. Is that all fate has in store for you, Cesárea, my love? I said, although I probably didn't say my love, I may just have thought it. And Cesárea gave me a look, a brief little sideways glance, and said that the search for a place to live and a place to work was the common fate of all mankind. Deep down you're a reactionary, Amadeo, she said (but she said it fondly). (434)

She is not only indifferent to the prospect of giving up her "literary career": the very idea of a literary career strikes her as reactionary, a falling away from the avant-garde ideal represented by the original visceral realism and already to some extent betrayed by stridentism (433). From 1930 to 1936, she holds a series of teaching positions in Sonora (560) before working in a canning factory (562), then selling medicinal herbs at a market stand (566). She finds places to live and work, but the drift of her life strips her of status and security, taking her to the margins of society. There is nothing in *The Savage Detectives* to suggest that she has formulated a project or a set of objectives, or that she regards her gradual social demotion as a failure.

My broad claim in this chapter is that Cesárea Tinajero is representative of a general tendency. The sympathetic characters in Bolaño's fiction tend to share her aimlessness, and are rarely inclined to fashion selves through storytelling or to live their lives in a narrative mode, as if they were—as they are in fact, seen from outside the worlds of the fiction—the protagonists of stories. There are exceptions, and not all of them are unsympathetic, but when it comes to writers, Bolaño is far from even-handed. Writers with well-formed career plans and well-honed accounts of their own development are systematically ridiculed. There is no simple correlation between aimlessness and ethical goodness, because Bolaño's most evil character, Carlos Wieder, is in his way an aimless drifter too, as I will show in the third section of chapter 6. But the satirical treatment of literary careerists does mark a preference: Bolaño's fiction values an improvising openness over concentrated striving to attain objectives and to "make something of one's life."

NARRATIVE IDENTITY

In arguing for these claims, I will be drawing on a number of interventions in the ongoing interdisciplinary debate over narrative identity. The expression "narrative identity" was coined by Paul Ricoeur in *Time and Narrative 3* (originally published in 1985), although he was by no means the first to think of personal identity as being narratively constituted, as he points out himself: "To answer the question 'Who?' as Hannah Arendt has so forcefully put it, is to tell the story of a life. The story told tells about the action of the 'who.' And the identity of this 'who' therefore itself must be a narrative identity."[1] Ricoeur is referring here to *The Human Condition* (1958), in which Arendt writes: "*Who* somebody is or was we can only know by knowing the story of which he is himself the hero—his biography, in other words; everything else we know of him, including the work he may have produced and left behind, tells us only *what* he is or was."[2] It is worth pointing out that what Arendt means here by "biography" is not a particular biographical or autobiographical account, but the sum of an individual's interactions with others over time:

> These stories may then be recorded in documents and monuments, they may be visible in use objects and artworks, they may be told and retold and worked into all kinds of material. They themselves, in their living reality, are of an altogether different nature than these reifications. They tell us more about their subjects, the "hero" in the center of each story, than any product of human hands ever tells us about the master who produced it, and yet they are not products, properly speaking. Although everybody started his life by inserting himself into the human world through action and speech, nobody is the author or producer of his own life story. In other words, the stories, the results of action and speech, reveal an agent, but this agent is not an author or producer. Somebody began it and is its subject in the twofold sense of the word, namely, its actor and sufferer, but nobody is its author. (184)

Arendt makes an important distinction here between living reality and reification, and her authorless biographies, which tell us who individuals are, belong to the first category. Consequently they are not prone to what Pierre Bourdieu calls "the biographical illusion": the belief—implicit in expressions such as "already," "always," and "from an early age," which recur frequently in life stories of all sorts—that a life is *in itself* a single, coherent set of events oriented toward a goal, which gives the events direction and meaning.[3] For Bourdieu, the *trajectory* of a life, as a sociologist might reconstruct it, inevitably simplifies but is less likely to betray the lived reality, because it takes into account the structuring of social space—what Arendt calls the "already existing web of human relationships"—and because the sociologist is, or should be, reflexively aware of the dangers of distortion and simplification associated with narrative genres like biography and autobiography.[4]

As opposed to Arendt and Bourdieu, some theorists of narrative identity play down or reject the distinction between lived reality and reification. Alasdair MacIntyre's rejection has been particularly influential. In chapter 15 of *After Virtue* (1981) he writes: "It is because we all live out narratives in our lives and because we understand our own lives in terms of the narratives that we live out that the form of narrative is appropriate for understanding the actions of others. Stories are lived before they are told—except in the case of fiction."[5] This has been denied, for example by Louis O. Mink, with whom MacIntyre argues in *After Virtue*, but also, among others, by Bernard Williams, in a talk given in the late 1980s (posthumously published in 2007) and recently by Peter Lamarque, who states flatly: "a story must be told, it is not found."[6] For Anthony Rudd, whose "In Defense of Narrative" specifically defends MacIntyre's account, Lamarque has succumbed to a version of "the myth of the 'Given'":

> Events do not exist in their own right, prior to and independently of their narration; and what counts as a distinct event in one narrative may not in another. We don't start with events as a sort of "Given" and then construct narratives around them, any more than we start with a pure sensory Given, which we then go on to conceptualize. We start with narratives and an event can only be understood as a segment cut out of a narrative.[7]

For some of the participants in the narrative identity debate, MacIntyre and Rudd among them, our lived reality is always already a narrative; for others, including Mink and Lamarque, life narratives are reifications of richer and messier primitive experience.[8] The positions adopted in this standoff may have psychological determinants, as suggested by the work of Galen Strawson, which I will discuss below. In any case, Lamarque's article is one manifestation of the "backlash" against narrative identity theories discerned by Rudd.[9] The theories themselves vary significantly in the scope of their claims, as Marya Schectman explains,[10] and they have been challenged in a variety of ways. Jane Forsey, for example, has pointed out that identity is often expressed and understood by mimetic (extralinguistic) rather than diegetic means, through gesture, posture, dance, clothing, décor, and so on.[11] Jeanette Bicknell has argued that narratives are always underdetermined by the events they connect, and that revisions of a narrative do not necessarily reflect greater self-knowledge or greater moral awareness.[12] John Christman has claimed that narrative unity, whether defined in causal, teleological, or thematic terms, does not characterize most human lives, and that unified personhood requires only reflective self-interpretation.[13]

In an article that has stimulated both debate and creative response, Galen Strawson has challenged the universal validity of what he calls the psychological Narrativity thesis ("one sees or lives or experiences one's life as a narrative or story of some sort, or at least as a collection of stories") and the ethical Narrativity thesis ("a richly Narrative outlook on one's life is essential to living well, to true or full personhood").[14] Strawson begins by distinguishing one's experience of oneself considered "principally as a human being taken as a whole" from self-experience, that is, experience of oneself considered "principally as an inner mental entity or 'self' of some sort" (190). Assuming that selves do not necessarily last as long as whole human beings, he goes on to distinguish between two kinds of self-experience:

> Diachronic [D]: one naturally figures oneself, considered as a self, as something that was there in the (further) past and will be there in the (further) future;
>
> Episodic [E]: one does not figure oneself, considered as a self, as something that was there in the (further) past and will be there in the (further) future. (190)

To this distinction he adds another, between "Narrative" and "non-Narrative." To be Narrative is "to see or live or experience one's life as a narrative or story of some sort, or at least as a collection of stories," and "to be non-Narrative is not to live one's life in this way" (210). Strawson believes that these "forms of self-experience" or "styles of temporal being" are not chosen so much as inherited: "I suspect that the fundamentals of temporal temperament are genetically determined, and that we have here to do with a deep 'individual difference variable'—to put it in the language of experimental psychology" (191). In order to live narratively, according to Strawson, one must have not only "some sort of relatively large-scale coherence-seeking, unity-seeking, pattern-seeking or most generally . . . *form-finding* tendency" (200) but also a "story-telling tendency," that is, "one must be disposed to apprehend or think of oneself and one's life as fitting the form of some recognized narrative genre" (201). Furthermore, form finding and storytelling may (but do not necessarily) involve revision or unconscious falsification (202).

Strawson's work in this area provides a set of conceptual tools that can be used to categorize the temporal temperaments of authors and fictional characters, by determining whether they are Diachronic or Episodic, Narrative or Non-Narrative. It also presents, as I said, a vigorous challenge to the psychological and ethical Narrativity theses, whose disquieting implications are made clear in Marya Schectman's *The Constitution of Selves*: "When a self-conception becomes wildly different in form from those standard in our culture—for example a self-conception that is not even narrative in form—the narrative self-constitution view does not consider it identity-constituting at all, nor those who organize their experience in this way persons."[15] Schechtman does say that, for her, nonpersons are not necessarily subpersons, but the fact remains that her theory takes no account of them (101–102). Strawson, by contrast, is concerned to show that the Episodic life is not an aberration that theorists can afford to set aside and that Narrativity is not a requisite for human flourishing. He insists that many people are naturally Episodic, but also suggests, in passing, that some may live episodically for historical or social reasons. "One can . . . imagine," he writes, "a Diachronic person who lives, by force of circumstance, an intensely picaresque and disjointed life, while having absolutely no tendency to seek unity or narrative-developmental pattern in it."[16] Wars, revolutions, military coups, and repressive regimes are among the circumstances that may force the formerly settled and sedate to lead picaresque and disjointed lives. Temporal temperament is only one of the factors that bear on a person's or a character's trajectory.

EPISODIC LIVES

I claimed at the beginning of this chapter that Bolaño's fiction is largely populated by aimless characters who are little inclined to see themselves as the protagonists of life stories. There are, I think, three interrelated reasons for this. The first is psychological: for Bolaño, as for Strawson, the Episodic life is not intrinsically inferior to the Diachronic life. It is equally worthy of fictional treatment, and there are many natural Episodics among Bolaño's characters. The second reason is historical: many of the stories that Bolaño tells are of lives uprooted or disoriented by history, picaresque by force of circumstance. And the third reason is literary or aesthetic: as we saw in chapter 3, Bolaño has a marked preference for drifting, discontinuous, and inconclusive narrative forms. This preference is partly motivated by the psychological and historical factors just mentioned; such forms are well fitted to the personal and collective experience of Bolaño's core characters: Latin Americans born in the 1950s, wanderers and exiles, restless or displaced.

In Bolaño's most detailed study of an Episodic, "Anne Moore's Life," we can see how the psychology of an individual, the historical period in which she lives, and a way of telling her story influenced by conversation and diary writing combine to produce a "life" (both an existence and a text, as in the medieval *vitae sanctorum* and Marcel Schwob's *Imaginary Lives*) that, while it would not qualify as the life of a person according to Marya Schechtman, is deeply affecting as a portrait and generates a paradoxical but highly effective narrative tension. Anne Moore's life is not thrown off course by political upheaval, but its aimlessness is no doubt fostered by the libertarian milieu in which she lives when she moves from Montana to California in the mid 1960s to attend college (LEE 76). Anne is a middle-class girl, a we know that neither Tony nor Bill can really be "the one," because proleptic allusions have alerted us to Anne's relationship with the narrator, which could have begun in Mexico, but began much later in Girona:

> They lived with Rubén's mother, in a suburb near La Villa, pretty close to where I was living at the time. If I'd seen you then, I would have fallen in love with you, I told Anne many years later. Who knows, said Anne. (84)

> During the days Anne spent in Mexico City, our paths might have crossed again; again I might have fallen in love with her, although Anne doubts it. (91)

No more than a moderate degree of sentimentality is required to suppose (on a first reading) that the opportunity repeated in Mexico will be repeated again, and finally seized. But Anne's relationship with the narrator, instead of being the one that closes the series and makes sense of it retrospectively, turns out to be just one more. Again love comes to an end, and the narrator, for his part, soon concludes that it was friendship, not love or sex, that really brought them together (99). Anne Moore drifts out of his life and he loses touch with her.

In its way of producing narrative tension, "Anne Moore's Life" is comparable to "Cell Mates," analyzed in chapter 3: the "secret story" in this case is, or promises to be, a love story, but when it seems finally to have surfaced, it is already sinking away again, although it does not entirely disappear: Anne goes to the United States with her Algerian lover, and the narrator imagines them there, together (103). A shadow of hope remains, and yet "Anne Moore's Life" is deeply sad. Is that because it is the life of an Episodic? Is it suggested that Episodics are condemned to repeat their mistakes and never learn? Does "Anne Moore's Life" support the "ethical Narrativity thesis"?

We have seen that Anne Moore does not like to tell the story of her past. Nor is she inclined to make long-term plans or commitments: "Bill suggested they buy a house and settle down in Seattle for good, but Anne didn't feel ready" (93); "One night, while they were making love, Bill suggested they have a child. Anne's reply was brief and calm, she simply said no,

doctor's daughter; her origins would seem to have prepared her for middle-American normality. Even her name is entirely unexceptional, shared by thousands. And yet she neither "finds her way" nor ends up leading a "normal" life. She does not complete her studies in San Francisco, and during the twenty years that follow, relationships, jobs, and trips succeed one another in an existence that seems to be perpetually starting over. Its phases are brought to an end by sudden ruptures, signaled in the text by temporal and logical connectors. The temporal connectors tend to be vague—"*Shortly afterward* they went back to San Francisco" (LEE 79); "*One day* she met a guy called Charles and they became lovers" (86); "*One day* Anne's love for Tony ran out and she left Seattle" (90)—and they are often combined with logical connectors marking an adversative relation:

> At first they lived off Anne's wages from the cafeteria and a scholarship that Paul had. *But then one day* they decided to travel to Mexico and Anne quit her job. (78)

> For some time, two or three months, Anne thought she was in love with Rubén and envisaged spending the rest of her life in Mexico. *But one day* she rang her parents, asked them for money to buy an air ticket, said good-bye to Rubén, and went back to San Francisco. (85)

> Bill said he really couldn't understand, but she could count on his support. *After a week, however,* things started going wrong again. (94)

These variations on "but one day . . ." signal but do nothing to explain the suddenness of the ruptures, which leave the reader, like Anne's lovers, wondering what happened. She does not seem to be anxious to test or impatient to exercise her powers of seduction; nor does she seem to be bored before deciding to break off the relationships. It is as if a switch has flipped in her psyche and she no longer feels constrained by the decisions and commitments of a former self.

The ruptures are especially painful when the lover has a strongly Diachronic temperament. In this regard, Charles and Anne form an especially ill-matched pair: "Charles liked to talk about his childhood and his adolescence, as if he sensed there was a secret there that he had overlooked. Anne, on the other hand, preferred to talk about what was happening to her at that precise moment in her life" (86). He not only tells the story of his past but also projects himself into the future: "Charles was very young, Anne remembers, and his fondest dream, apparently, was to have a whore" (88). He is determined to enter fully into the role: "Charles bought her a red dress and matching high-heeled shoes, and he bought himself a gun, because, as he said to Anne, no one respects a pimp without a gun" (86). Anne plays along briefly for reasons that are not entirely clear to her: "Maybe she accepted because at the time she was fond of him. Or because it seemed an exciting thing to try. Or because she thought it would bring on the catastrophe" (86). But the next day she tells Charles that she doesn't want to see him again. At this, the aspiring hard man, robbed of his story's continuation, nearly bursts into tears (88).

Mutual incomprehension leads to more tragic consequences in Anne's relationship with Tony. When Anne and Tony meet, they fall in love immediately and are married in Taiwan soon afterward. They come back to Seattle and set up a fruit store. For Tony, this is just the beginning of a story: the story of a happy married life. When Anne leaves, what drives Tony to despair is not being able to understand why: "Night after night he rang trying to find out why she had left him. Night after night Anne explained it to him: that was just the way things had turned out, love comes to an end, maybe it hadn't even been love that had brought them together in the first place, she needed a change" (90). These "explanations" explain nothing for Tony. Here we see Anne struggling to satisfy what Marya Schechtman, in her revised "narrative self-constitution view," calls "the articulation constraint":

> The articulation constraint requires that a person be able to articulate her narrative locally when appropriate, or at least to recognize the legitimacy of certain questions. Basically this constraint requires that confronted with questions like "how did you come to be in this place?" or "why did you choose that course of action?"... a person has something to say.[17]

Tony keeps calling and, significantly, rehearsing the beginning of [the] ken story, but refusing to talk about his life in the present: "W[hen Anne] asked about the fruit store, how the business was going, Tony [answered in] monosyllables and quickly changed the subject" (91). As Anne [points out,] he also tends to idealize the past, engaging in revision: "He lik[ed to talk] about their trip to Taiwan, their marriage, the things they had [done]. Sometimes he was sorry he hadn't gone to the Philippines wit[h Anne.] Anne had to remind him that she had wanted to go alone" (112). T[he breaking] up of the relationship breaks the narrative thread of Tony's life, [and after] repeated, futile attempts to understand, he finally kills himself at [age] twenty-two (91).

Anne Moore's relationships follow a repetitive pattern; so do [her affairs] and her trips. Her life, it seems, is more and more of the same. [Of people] in real life who resemble Anne Moore, it is often said that they th[at they never] learn or that they go on making the same mistakes. And that is [true. On one] occasion, she judges her own behavior: she laughs "at how naïve [she had] been with Rubén" (her Mexican lover), and she makes "what, fro[m a cer-] tain point of view at least, she considers a monumental error" in a[ccepting] Charles's proposal and working as a prostitute (86). But, from the[larger] point of view, it is worth asking whether her mistakes really are [mistakes,] because they can seem, provisionally at least, to be steps on the [way to a] vaguely intuited goal.

With Tony she finds peace, briefly: "Living with Tony, Anne rem[embers,] was like living in a protective cocoon. Outside, storms raged every d[ay, peo-] ple lived in constant fear of a private earthquake, everyone was talkin[g about] collective catharsis, but she and Tony had found a refuge where the[y could] be at peace. And we were, says Anne, though not for long" (89). [We have] already seen how their relationship ends. Bill, however, seems to offe[r a more] durable haven: "she thought of Bill and herself and felt that she ha[d finally] found something in life, her own private Alcoholics Anonymous, som[ething] solid, something she could hold on to, like a high branch she coul[d hang] from and balance on" (92). Yet, once again, the idyll breaks off abruptl[y. In this] way, Anne seems to be looking for the ultimate and definitive love th[at would] convert all her "errors" into trials or prefigurations. Even on a first r[eading,] she was still too young" (94). And yet she does not live in a happy-go-lucky manner, fully present in the present, since she regrets her errors and fears an imminent but unspecified catastrophe (86). What is happening "at that precise moment in her life" does not always suffice; sometimes the present moment is a void, as when she decides, for the first time, to leave Bill: "She spent five hours sitting there thinking about her life and her illness, and both seemed empty" (93). The drawings in her diary, showing "the paths a woman's life should follow, though hers had not" (100), suggest that, to some degree, her regrets, her fears, and her feelings of emptiness may be reactions to internalized social norms, which require a woman's life to conform to one of a number of familiar storylines. But the problem runs deeper than a conflict between social pressures and individual aspirations. Anne Moore also seems to exemplify a way of living episodically that is intrinsically dysphoric, just as some life stories are irremediably stories of tragedy and failure (a point that is rarely stressed by defenders of the ethical Narrativity thesis).

Strawson suggests a distinction between euphoric and dysphoric Episodic lives in "The Self"—"Some live intensely in the present, some are simply aimless. . . . Some go through life as if stunned"[18]—but in later papers he has left the simply aimless and the stunned aside, perhaps so as not to undermine his key assertion that Episodicity, in itself, is no bar to human flourishing. Since it is precisely failure to flourish that interests Bolaño as a storyteller, it is not surprising to find him exploring the unhappier varieties of Episodic experience. There can, however, be no doubting the serious and sympathetic nature of his portrait of Anne Moore: she may be lost, but in the narrator's eyes, she never entirely loses the aura of magnificence that she had when he first saw her in Girona with Bill: "They sat at the bar and I could hardly take my eyes off them. I hadn't seen such a beautiful man and woman for a long time. They were so sure of themselves. So distant and disconcerting. I thought all the other people in the bar should have knelt down before them" (LEE 98).

Anne Moore likes to speak about what is happening to her in the present. That oral commentary is accompanied by writing: she is an assiduous diarist. Near the end of the story, she returns from the United States to

Spain with "thirty-four notebooks . . . just under a hundred pages each, each page covered with small, hurried writing" (100). More than three thousand pages, more than half a page per day, on average: this intimate practice of writing has remained a constant in her otherwise disjointed life. Although the narrator provides little specific information about the contents of the diaries, he gives a richly figurative account of their effect on the reader:

> It was sometimes painful, plunging into that writing in the presence of the author (sometimes I wanted to throw the notebook aside and go and hug her), but mostly it was stimulating, although I couldn't say exactly what it stimulated. It was like a fever rising imperceptibly. It made you want to scream or shut your eyes, but Anne's handwriting had the power to sew your lips shut and prop your eyes open with matchsticks, so you had no choice but to go on reading. (101)

The narrator's verdict is, in his own words, "uninspired": "You should publish them, I said, and then I think I shrugged my shoulders" (101). But this reaction is not so much uninspired as inadequate, because a novice author cannot simply decide to publish such a text as it is. An entry into the literary field must be negotiated, as the narrator of this story is all too well aware, and the text must be shaped, in some measure, to meet the expectations of publishers and readers. Form-finding, as Strawson would say, is required, if not storytelling and revision. And it is the narrator who has taken on that shaping work, constructing a "life" from memories of what Anne said in conversations and what she wrote in her diaries, which he peruses systematically (100). He is fascinated not only by her "handwriting," her style, but also by the similarity between the experiences that she recounts and his own:

> Overall, her adventures were very similar to mine. Anne thought this was because the lives or the youths of any two individuals would always be fundamentally alike, in spite of the obvious or even glaring differences. I preferred to think that somehow she and I had both explored the same map, fought the same doomed campaigns, received a common sentimental education. (99)

There is, however, an important difference. The narrator's writing is a social practice—he publishes books—and is therefore, in a straightforward sense, transformative. A private diarist can repeat himself indefinitely and do so without realizing it, since he is never obliged to go back over what he has written. The public, published writer, however, runs the risk of losing that status if she does not tell a new story or employ a new way of telling. An obligation to vary, at least, if not to develop, is built into the social practice of writing.

This obligation is compatible with Episodic experience: the writer can accumulate practical knowledge without having to make a bildungsroman of her life. As Galen Strawson puts it: "The past can be alive—arguably more genuinely alive—in the present simply in so far as it has helped to shape the way one is in the present, just as musicians' playing can incorporate and body forth their past practice without being mediated by any explicit memory of it."[19] The past, in other words, can be present in the form of skills. If "Anne Moore's Life" leaves a deep impression of sadness, it is not just because she is socially maladapted or psychologically disposed to a dysphoric form of Episodic experience, but also because the potential power of her writing ("the power to sew your lips shut and prop your eyes open" [LEE 101]) is largely unrealized. In this respect it is interesting to contrast Anne with Gloria, who gives her a place to live when she arrives in Barcelona. Gloria, we are told, "had started studying music at the age of forty-something, and now she was playing with the Palma Symphony Orchestra, or something like that" (96). Because Anne's writing remains private, it lacks a social context that would require and support the development of skills, as the orchestra does in Gloria's case, so it does not provide a home where her past can live without need of memory.

Not all the Episodics in Bolaño's fiction live as disjointedly as Anne Moore. Liz Norton in 2666 and Auxilio Lacouture in Amulet, for example, lead lives that are unified to some degree by a practice. Liz Norton not only holds down an academic job but also joins the gang of critics who come to dominate Archimboldi studies (12–13). And yet, the narrator tells us:

> She didn't draw up long- or medium-term plans and throw herself whole-heartedly into their execution. . . . She was incapable of setting herself a

goal and striving steadily toward it. At least no goal was appealing or desirable enough for her to pursue it unreservedly. Used in a personal sense, the phrase "to achieve an end" seemed to her a small-minded snare. She preferred the word *life*, and, on rare occasions, *happiness*. (8)

Happiness for Norton seems to be a matter of fortuity, something that happens, that may be found but cannot be made. And striving to attain a personal goal is not noble, in her view, but somehow small-minded, a judgment that is perhaps akin to Galen Strawson's remark that Narrativity, in the sphere of ethics, "risks a strange commodification of life and time."[20]

Like Anne Moore, Auxilio Lacouture is a wanderer: "nobody drove me out of Montevideo; one day I simply decided to leave and go to Buenos Aires, and after a few months or maybe a year in Buenos Aires, I decided to keep traveling" (A 3). In Mexico City she drifts from one odd job to another and has no fixed address (40–41). Her life too leaves a strong impression of sadness, not because of her individual fate, but because of what it falls to her to witness and foresee: the sacrifice of a generation of idealists, represented at the end of the book, in a vision that combines the paintings of Remedios Varo and Marcel Schwob's *The Children's Crusade*, by an "interminable legion" of young people singing as they march toward an abyss (A 181–184). Auxilio lives episodically, and the sentences that signal the transitions from one phase of her life to the next recall Anne Moore's ruptures:

> I quit being the theater's official hanger-on. I went back to the poets and my life took a new turn, there's not much point explaining why. All I know for sure is that I gave up helping my director friend from '68, not because I thought his directing was bad, although it was, but because I was bored, I needed a change of air, a change of scene, my spirit was hungry for a different kind of restlessness. (48)

> Two weeks later I talked with his sister on the phone and she told me that Arturo was alive. I sighed. What a relief. But I had to keep going. I was the itinerant mother. The wanderer. Life drew me into other stories. (75–76)

The initiative is attributed not to a self with a plan, but to a restless spirit and simply to life, which might seem an evasive way of putting it, but the transitions in question do not have the destructive effects of Anne Moore's abrupt departures. If anything, Auxilio's friends are happy for her to move on and relieved when she does (41). She wanders from one lodging and job to another while responding faithfully to her vocation as "the mother of Mexican poetry" (11), which demands poverty and humility, but not chastity, and engages her in a series of paid and unpaid tasks: cleaning for the exiled Spanish poets Pedro Garfías and León Felipe, translating and typing in the Faculty of Philosophy and Letters at the UNAM, and providing moral support for the young poets, whom no one else takes seriously (171).

The poets come and go, but she remains, like an unofficial permanent secretary. She is the living archive of a generation. Her Episodic life may seem chaotic, but her unwavering commitment to Mexican poetry gives it a non-narrative coherence. And insofar as she realizes her potentials as carer and seer, it could even be called a flourishing life. She looks for herself in the words of the young poets:

> And there I was! Auxilio Lacouture, or fragments of Auxilio Lacouture: blue eyes, blond hair going gray, cut in a bob, long, thin face, lined forehead, and the fact of my selfhood sent a shiver down my spine, plunged me into a sea of doubts, made me anxious about the future, the days approaching at the pace of a cruise ship, although the vision also proved that I was living in and with my time, the time I had chosen, the time all around me, tremulous, changeable, teeming, happy. (21)

What she finds are fragments, but they belong together and compose a face; and she belongs to the time in which she has chosen to be fully present, rather than longing for a youth that is gone. Even at the culmination of this "horror story" (1), faced with the tragic vision that closes the novel, Auxilio does not give way to despair, but holds on to the song of the "ghost-children," or its echo, which is "barely audible" and yet has lasting powers: "that song is our amulet" (184).

DIACHRONIC LIVES

Bolaño's characters are not, of course, all Episodics. Anne Moore's lovers Charles and Tony, as we saw, have Diachronic temperaments. In this section I will examine two Diachronic characters who play more substantial roles and whose self-portraits contrast strongly: Azucena Esquivel Plata in *2666* and Sebastián Urrutia Lacroix in *By Night in Chile*. Both tell their life stories chronologically: in one, a self is defiantly affirmed; in the other, a self disintegrates.

In "The Part About the Crimes" in *2666*, the congresswoman Azucena Esquivel Plata summons the journalist Sergio González Rodríguez to her home in Mexico City (584). There she tells him about her childhood friendship with a woman named Kelly Rivera Parker. The point of her long monologue, broken into twelve sections, is to lead up to a request. Kelly Rivera Parker has gone missing in Santa Teresa, and Azucena Esquivel Plata wants Gónzalez Rodríguez, who has been investigating the murders of young women in that city, to write about Kelly's disappearance and "stir up the hive" (632). But Esquivel Plata also tells the story of her own life: her background in a grand conservative family whose fortunes have been declining since the demise of the Emperor Agustín de Iturbide in 1823, her studies, her brief marriage, and her careers as journalist and politician. This is a story of emancipation and self-realization, structured by two turning points. The first is the moment at which, insisting on a divorce in spite of her family's opposition, she is "overtaken by the demon of command or leadership, as it's called now" (601). This demon draws her away from her engagement in the "ineffectual left" (604) and toward the governing PRI. But Azucena Esquivel Plata is not motivated simply by a desire for power: "Of course I joined out of self-interest. But there are all kinds of self-interest, and I was tired of preaching in a vacuum. I wanted power, that I won't deny. I wanted free rein to change some things in this country. I won't deny that either. I wanted to improve public health and the public schools and do my bit to prepare Mexico to enter the twenty-first century" (609). She is lucid and frank about her motivations, and about the inertia of the party apparatus, which she discovers in her role as a congresswoman: "You think that doctor's daughter; her origins would seem to have prepared her for middle-American normality. Even her name is entirely unexceptional, shared by thousands. And yet she neither "finds her way" nor ends up leading a "normal" life. She does not complete her studies in San Francisco, and during the twenty years that follow, relationships, jobs, and trips succeed one another in an existence that seems to be perpetually starting over. Its phases are brought to an end by sudden ruptures, signaled in the text by temporal and logical connectors. The temporal connectors tend to be vague—"*Shortly afterward* they went back to San Francisco" (LEE 79); "*One day* she met a guy called Charles and they became lovers" (86); "*One day* Anne's love for Tony ran out and she left Seattle" (90)—and they are often combined with logical connectors marking an adversative relation:

At first they lived off Anne's wages from the cafeteria and a scholarship that Paul had. *But then one day* they decided to travel to Mexico and Anne quit her job. (78)

For some time, two or three months, Anne thought she was in love with Rubén and envisaged spending the rest of her life in Mexico. *But one day* she rang her parents, asked them for money to buy an air ticket, said good-bye to Rubén, and went back to San Francisco. (85)

Bill said he really couldn't understand, but she could count on his support. *After a week, however,* things started going wrong again. (94)

These variations on "but one day . . ." signal but do nothing to explain the suddenness of the ruptures, which leave the reader, like Anne's lovers, wondering what happened. She does not seem to be anxious to test or impatient to exercise her powers of seduction; nor does she seem to be bored before deciding to break off the relationships. It is as if a switch has flipped in her psyche and she no longer feels constrained by the decisions and commitments of a former self.

The ruptures are especially painful when the lover has a strongly Diachronic temperament. In this regard, Charles and Anne form an especially ill-matched pair: "Charles liked to talk about his childhood and his adolescence, as if he sensed there was a secret there that he had overlooked. Anne, on the other hand, preferred to talk about what was happening to her at that precise moment in her life" (86). He not only tells the story of his past but also projects himself into the future: "Charles was very young, Anne remembers, and his fondest dream, apparently, was to have a whore" (88). He is determined to enter fully into the role: "Charles bought her a red dress and matching high-heeled shoes, and he bought himself a gun, because, as he said to Anne, no one respects a pimp without a gun" (86). Anne plays along briefly for reasons that are not entirely clear to her: "Maybe she accepted because at the time she was fond of him. Or because it seemed an exciting thing to try. Or because she thought it would bring on the catastrophe" (86). But the next day she tells Charles that she doesn't want to see him again. At this, the aspiring hard man, robbed of his story's continuation, nearly bursts into tears (88).

Mutual incomprehension leads to more tragic consequences in Anne's relationship with Tony. When Anne and Tony meet, they fall in love immediately and are married in Taiwan soon afterward. They come back to Seattle and set up a fruit store. For Tony, this is just the beginning of a story: the story of a happy married life. When Anne leaves, what drives Tony to despair is not being able to understand why: "Night after night he rang trying to find out why she had left him. Night after night Anne explained it to him: that was just the way things had turned out, love comes to an end, maybe it hadn't even been love that had brought them together in the first place, she needed a change" (90). These "explanations" explain nothing for Tony. Here we see Anne struggling to satisfy what Marya Schechtman, in her revised "narrative self-constitution view," calls "the articulation constraint":

The articulation constraint requires that a person be able to articulate her narrative locally when appropriate, or at least to recognize the legitimacy of certain questions. Basically this constraint requires that confronted with questions like "how did you come to be in this place?" or "why did you choose that course of action?" . . . a person has something to say.[17]

Tony keeps calling and, significantly, rehearsing the beginning of their broken story, but refusing to talk about his life in the present: "When Anne asked about the fruit store, how the business was going, Tony replied in monosyllables and quickly changed the subject" (91). As Anne points out, he also tends to idealize the past, engaging in revision: "He liked talking about their trip to Taiwan, their marriage, the things they had seen; . . . Sometimes he was sorry he hadn't gone to the Philippines with her, and Anne had to remind him that she had wanted to go alone" (112). The breakup of the relationship breaks the narrative thread of Tony's life, and after repeated, futile attempts to understand, he finally kills himself at the age of twenty-two (91).

Anne Moore's relationships follow a repetitive pattern; so do her jobs and her trips. Her life, it seems, is more and more of the same. Of people in real life who resemble Anne Moore, it is often said that they they never learn or that they go on making the same mistakes. And that is how, on occasion, she judges her own behavior: she laughs "at how naïve she [has] been with Rubén" (her Mexican lover), and she makes "what, from a certain point of view at least, she considers a monumental error" in accepting Charles's proposal and working as a prostitute (86). But, from the reader's point of view, it is worth asking whether her mistakes really are the same, because they can seem, provisionally at least, to be steps on the way to a vaguely intuited goal.

With Tony she finds peace, briefly: "Living with Tony, Anne remembers, was like living in a protective cocoon. Outside, storms raged every day, people lived in constant fear of a private earthquake, everyone was talking about collective catharsis, but she and Tony had found a refuge where they could be at peace. And we were, says Anne, though not for long" (89). We have already seen how their relationship ends. Bill, however, seems to offer a more durable haven: "she thought of Bill and herself and felt that she had finally found something in life, her own private Alcoholics Anonymous, something solid, something she could hold on to, like a high branch she could swing from and balance on" (92). Yet, once again, the idyll breaks off abruptly. In her way, Anne seems to be looking for the ultimate and definitive love that will convert all her "errors" into trials or prefigurations. Even on a first reading, we know that neither Tony nor Bill can really be "the one," because proleptic allusions have alerted us to Anne's relationship with the narrator, which could have begun in Mexico, but began much later in Girona:

> They lived with Rubén's mother, in a suburb near La Villa, pretty close to where I was living at the time. If I'd seen you then, I would have fallen in love with you, I told Anne many years later. Who knows, said Anne. (84)

> During the days Anne spent in Mexico City, our paths might have crossed again; again I might have fallen in love with her, although Anne doubts it. (91)

No more than a moderate degree of sentimentality is required to suppose (on a first reading) that the opportunity repeated in Mexico will be repeated again, and finally seized. But Anne's relationship with the narrator, instead of being the one that closes the series and makes sense of it retrospectively, turns out to be just one more. Again love comes to an end, and the narrator, for his part, soon concludes that it was friendship, not love or sex, that really brought them together (99). Anne Moore drifts out of his life and he loses touch with her.

In its way of producing narrative tension, "Anne Moore's Life" is comparable to "Cell Mates," analyzed in chapter 3: the "secret story" in this case is, or promises to be, a love story, but when it seems finally to have surfaced, it is already sinking away again, although it does not entirely disappear: Anne goes to the United States with her Algerian lover, and the narrator imagines them there, together (103). A shadow of hope remains, and yet "Anne Moore's Life" is deeply sad. Is that because it is the life of an Episodic? Is it suggested that Episodics are condemned to repeat their mistakes and never learn? Does "Anne Moore's Life" support the "ethical Narrativity thesis"?

We have seen that Anne Moore does not like to tell the story of her past. Nor is she inclined to make long-term plans or commitments: "Bill suggested they buy a house and settle down in Seattle for good, but Anne didn't feel ready" (93); "One night, while they were making love, Bill suggested they have a child. Anne's reply was brief and calm, she simply said no, she was still too young" (94). And yet she does not live in a happy-go-lucky manner, fully present in the present, since she regrets her errors and fears an imminent but unspecified catastrophe (86). What is happening "at that precise moment in her life" does not always suffice; sometimes the present moment is a void, as when she decides, for the first time, to leave Bill: "She spent five hours sitting there thinking about her life and her illness, and both seemed empty" (93). The drawings in her diary, showing "the paths a woman's life should follow, though hers had not" (100), suggest that, to some degree, her regrets, her fears, and her feelings of emptiness may be reactions to internalized social norms, which require a woman's life to conform to one of a number of familiar storylines. But the problem runs deeper than a conflict between social pressures and individual aspirations. Anne Moore also seems to exemplify a way of living episodically that is intrinsically dysphoric, just as some life stories are irremediably stories of tragedy and failure (a point that is rarely stressed by defenders of the ethical Narrativity thesis).

Strawson suggests a distinction between euphoric and dysphoric Episodic lives in "The Self"—"Some live intensely in the present, some are simply aimless. . . . Some go through life as if stunned"[18]—but in later papers he has left the simply aimless and the stunned aside, perhaps so as not to undermine his key assertion that Episodicity, in itself, is no bar to human flourishing. Since it is precisely failure to flourish that interests Bolaño as a storyteller, it is not surprising to find him exploring the unhappier varieties of Episodic experience. There can, however, be no doubting the serious and sympathetic nature of his portrait of Anne Moore: she may be lost, but in the narrator's eyes, she never entirely loses the aura of magnificence that she had when he first saw her in Girona with Bill: "They sat at the bar and I could hardly take my eyes off them. I hadn't seen such a beautiful man and woman for a long time. They were so sure of themselves. So distant and disconcerting. I thought all the other people in the bar should have knelt down before them" (LEE 98).

Anne Moore likes to speak about what is happening to her in the present. That oral commentary is accompanied by writing: she is an assiduous diarist. Near the end of the story, she returns from the United States to

Spain with "thirty-four notebooks . . . just under a hundred pages each, each page covered with small, hurried writing" (100). More than three thousand pages, more than half a page per day, on average: this intimate practice of writing has remained a constant in her otherwise disjointed life. Although the narrator provides little specific information about the contents of the diaries, he gives a richly figurative account of their effect on the reader:

> It was sometimes painful, plunging into that writing in the presence of the author (sometimes I wanted to throw the notebook aside and go and hug her), but mostly it was stimulating, although I couldn't say exactly what it stimulated. It was like a fever rising imperceptibly. It made you want to scream or shut your eyes, but Anne's handwriting had the power to sew your lips shut and prop your eyes open with matchsticks, so you had no choice but to go on reading. (101)

The narrator's verdict is, in his own words, "uninspired": "You should publish them, I said, and then I think I shrugged my shoulders" (101). But this reaction is not so much uninspired as inadequate, because a novice author cannot simply decide to publish such a text as it is. An entry into the literary field must be negotiated, as the narrator of this story is all too well aware, and the text must be shaped, in some measure, to meet the expectations of publishers and readers. Form-finding, as Strawson would say, is required, if not storytelling and revision. And it is the narrator who has taken on that shaping work, constructing a "life" from memories of what Anne said in conversations and what she wrote in her diaries, which he peruses systematically (100). He is fascinated not only by her "handwriting," her style, but also by the similarity between the experiences that she recounts and his own:

> Overall, her adventures were very similar to mine. Anne thought this was because the lives or the youths of any two individuals would always be fundamentally alike, in spite of the obvious or even glaring differences. I preferred to think that somehow she and I had both explored the same map, fought the same doomed campaigns, received a common sentimental education. (99)

There is, however, an important difference. The narrator's writing is a social practice—he publishes books—and is therefore, in a straightforward sense, transformative. A private diarist can repeat himself indefinitely and do so without realizing it, since he is never obliged to go back over what he has written. The public, published writer, however, runs the risk of losing that status if she does not tell a new story or employ a new way of telling. An obligation to vary, at least, if not to develop, is built into the social practice of writing.

This obligation is compatible with Episodic experience: the writer can accumulate practical knowledge without having to make a bildungsroman of her life. As Galen Strawson puts it: "The past can be alive—arguably more genuinely alive—in the present simply in so far as it has helped to shape the way one is in the present, just as musicians' playing can incorporate and body forth their past practice without being mediated by any explicit memory of it."[19] The past, in other words, can be present in the form of skills. If "Anne Moore's Life" leaves a deep impression of sadness, it is not just because she is socially maladapted or psychologically disposed to a dysphoric form of Episodic experience, but also because the potential power of her writing ("the power to sew your lips shut and prop your eyes open" [LEE 101]) is largely unrealized. In this respect it is interesting to contrast Anne with Gloria, who gives her a place to live when she arrives in Barcelona. Gloria, we are told, "had started studying music at the age of forty-something, and now she was playing with the Palma Symphony Orchestra, or something like that" (96). Because Anne's writing remains private, it lacks a social context that would require and support the development of skills, as the orchestra does in Gloria's case, so it does not provide a home where her past can live without need of memory.

Not all the Episodics in Bolaño's fiction live as disjointedly as Anne Moore. Liz Norton in *2666* and Auxilio Lacouture in *Amulet*, for example, lead lives that are unified to some degree by a practice. Liz Norton not only holds down an academic job but also joins the gang of critics who come to dominate Archimboldi studies (12–13). And yet, the narrator tells us:

> She didn't draw up long- or medium-term plans and throw herself whole-heartedly into their execution. . . . She was incapable of setting herself a

goal and striving steadily toward it. At least no goal was appealing or desirable enough for her to pursue it unreservedly. Used in a personal sense, the phrase "to achieve an end" seemed to her a small-minded snare. She preferred the word *life*, and, on rare occasions, *happiness*. (8)

Happiness for Norton seems to be a matter of fortuity, something that happens, that may be found but cannot be made. And striving to attain a personal goal is not noble, in her view, but somehow small-minded, a judgment that is perhaps akin to Galen Strawson's remark that Narrativity, in the sphere of ethics, "risks a strange commodification of life and time."[20]

Like Anne Moore, Auxilio Lacouture is a wanderer: "nobody drove me out of Montevideo; one day I simply decided to leave and go to Buenos Aires, and after a few months or maybe a year in Buenos Aires, I decided to keep traveling" (A 3). In Mexico City she drifts from one odd job to another and has no fixed address (40–41). Her life too leaves a strong impression of sadness, not because of her individual fate, but because of what it falls to her to witness and foresee: the sacrifice of a generation of idealists, represented at the end of the book, in a vision that combines the paintings of Remedios Varo and Marcel Schwob's *The Children's Crusade*, by an "interminable legion" of young people singing as they march toward an abyss (A 181–184). Auxilio lives episodically, and the sentences that signal the transitions from one phase of her life to the next recall Anne Moore's ruptures:

> I quit being the theater's official hanger-on. I went back to the poets and my life took a new turn, there's not much point explaining why. All I know for sure is that I gave up helping my director friend from '68, not because I thought his directing was bad, although it was, but because I was bored, I needed a change of air, a change of scene, my spirit was hungry for a different kind of restlessness. (48)

> Two weeks later I talked with his sister on the phone and she told me that Arturo was alive. I sighed. What a relief. But I had to keep going. I was the itinerant mother. The wanderer. Life drew me into other stories. (75–76)

The initiative is attributed not to a self with a plan, but to a restless spirit and simply to life, which might seem an evasive way of putting it, but the transitions in question do not have the destructive effects of Anne Moore's abrupt departures. If anything, Auxilio's friends are happy for her to move on and relieved when she does (41). She wanders from one lodging and job to another while responding faithfully to her vocation as "the mother of Mexican poetry" (11), which demands poverty and humility, but not chastity, and engages her in a series of paid and unpaid tasks: cleaning for the exiled Spanish poets Pedro Garfías and León Felipe, translating and typing in the Faculty of Philosophy and Letters at the UNAM, and providing moral support for the young poets, whom no one else takes seriously (171).

The poets come and go, but she remains, like an unofficial permanent secretary. She is the living archive of a generation. Her Episodic life may seem chaotic, but her unwavering commitment to Mexican poetry gives it a non-narrative coherence. And insofar as she realizes her potentials as carer and seer, it could even be called a flourishing life. She looks for herself in the words of the young poets:

> And there I was! Auxilio Lacouture, or fragments of Auxilio Lacouture: blue eyes, blond hair going gray, cut in a bob, long, thin face, lined forehead, and the fact of my selfhood sent a shiver down my spine, plunged me into a sea of doubts, made me anxious about the future, the days approaching at the pace of a cruise ship, although the vision also proved that I was living in and with my time, the time I had chosen, the time all around me, tremulous, changeable, teeming, happy. (21)

What she finds are fragments, but they belong together and compose a face; and she belongs to the time in which she has chosen to be fully present, rather than longing for a youth that is gone. Even at the culmination of this "horror story" (1), faced with the tragic vision that closes the novel, Auxilio does not give way to despair, but holds on to the song of the "ghost-children," or its echo, which is "barely audible" and yet has lasting powers: "that song is our amulet" (184).

DIACHRONIC LIVES

Bolaño's characters are not, of course, all Episodics. Anne Moore's lovers Charles and Tony, as we saw, have Diachronic temperaments. In this section I will examine two Diachronic characters who play more substantial roles and whose self-portraits contrast strongly: Azucena Esquivel Plata in *2666* and Sebastián Urrutia Lacroix in *By Night in Chile*. Both tell their life stories chronologically: in one, a self is defiantly affirmed; in the other, a self disintegrates.

In "The Part About the Crimes" in *2666*, the congresswoman Azucena Esquivel Plata summons the journalist Sergio González Rodríguez to her home in Mexico City (584). There she tells him about her childhood friendship with a woman named Kelly Rivera Parker. The point of her long monologue, broken into twelve sections, is to lead up to a request. Kelly Rivera Parker has gone missing in Santa Teresa, and Azucena Esquivel Plata wants Gónzalez Rodríguez, who has been investigating the murders of young women in that city, to write about Kelly's disappearance and "stir up the hive" (632). But Esquivel Plata also tells the story of her own life: her background in a grand conservative family whose fortunes have been declining since the demise of the Emperor Agustín de Iturbide in 1823, her studies, her brief marriage, and her careers as journalist and politician. This is a story of emancipation and self-realization, structured by two turning points. The first is the moment at which, insisting on a divorce in spite of her family's opposition, she is "overtaken by the demon of command or leadership, as it's called now" (601). This demon draws her away from her engagement in the "ineffectual left" (604) and toward the governing PRI. But Azucena Esquivel Plata is not motivated simply by a desire for power: "Of course I joined out of self-interest. But there are all kinds of self-interest, and I was tired of preaching in a vacuum. I wanted power, that I won't deny. I wanted free rein to change some things in this country. I won't deny that either. I wanted to improve public health and the public schools and do my bit to prepare Mexico to enter the twenty-first century" (609). She is lucid and frank about her motivations, and about the inertia of the party apparatus, which she discovers in her role as a congresswoman: "You think that inside, at least, you'll have more freedom to act. Not true" (609). In fact, being inside seems to make only one real difference: it confers visibility and presence. "At the moment of truth . . . it makes just as much sense to be present and to err as to hunker down and wait" (609). In other words, since "there are things that can't be changed from outside or inside" (609), why not enjoy the compensations of fame and command? The insufficiency of these compensations, however, becomes apparent when Kelly Rivera Parker disappears and the investigation goes nowhere:

> I thought that anybody else would be afraid by now or beginning to be afraid, but all I felt, increasingly, was anger, an immense rage, all the rage the Esquivel Platas had stored up for decades or centuries, now suddenly lodged in my nervous system, and I also thought, with bitterness and remorse, that this anger or rage should have set in sooner, that it shouldn't have been driven, if that's the word, propelled by personal friendship . . . that it should have been triggered by so many other things I'd seen since I was old enough to take notice. (618)

This second turning point in the life story of Azucena Esquivel Plata is also a pivotal moment in the history of her family: the rage accumulated over centuries is about to be spent in action. Azucena's project of reversing the family's declining economic fortunes has been successful (612), but the difficulty of finding out what happened to her friend is of another order. She hires a detective, Luis Miguel Loya, who discovers, before dying of cancer, that Kelly was organizing orgies for a banker with connections to the drug trade and the PRI (629). Azucena then hands the dossier over to González Ródriguez, assuring him that he won't be alone: "I'll be with you always, though you can't see me, helping you every step of the way" (632). Loya's reaction to a similar assurance was, "I think you overestimate yourself," to which the congresswoman replied: "Fuck it all, of course I overestimate myself, if I didn't I wouldn't be where I am" (624).

This is a case of what Joshua Landy, in his reading of Proust, calls "lucid self-delusion," a paradox that he sums up as follows: "in order to become who we are, we must believe we are something else."[21] Landy traces this strategy for self-fashioning back to Nietzsche, who writes in *Untimely Meditations*: "Try for once to justify your existence as it were *a posteriori* by setting before yourself an aim, a goal, a 'to this end,' an exalted and noble 'to this end.' Perish in pursuit of this and only this—I know of no better aim of life than that of perishing, *animae magnae prodigus*, in pursuit of the great and the impossible."[22] Azucena Esquivel Plata's goal—"to uncover the truth" (2666 621)—is surely a noble one, but she is asking other people (Loya, González Rodríguez), who are not as well protected as she is, to risk perishing in pursuit of it. The rage lodged in her nervous system has not displaced the "demon of command."

Critics of narrative identity theories have argued that they express an unrealistic ideal of control in human life,[23] and that they may encourage the production of retrospective illusions through deception or self-deception.[24] Some have also pointed out a present or prospective danger, that of obtuseness or "missing the adventure," in Cora Diamond's words.[25] As John Lippitt puts it: "if we are not careful, our determination to follow our 'life-plans,' to pursue our 'goals,' threatens to lead to a kind of moral blindness, a lack of moral imagination."[26] Azucena Esquivel Plata is a strong Diachronic, and engages, compulsively it seems, in storytelling, but she knows at some level that in spite of her dominating nature, she is overestimating the control that she has over her life and how it will go. Because she makes admissions that are potentially damaging to her image and is critical of her past behavior ("I suppose I neglected my friends a little" [613]), she does not seem deceptive or self-deceived. And what she has done in the case of Kelly Rivera Parker is precisely *not* to "miss the adventure" but to allow the disappearance of her friend to broaden her ethical and political outlook.

Elsewhere, however, Bolaño illustrates the dangers pointed out by the critics of narrative identity theories, most forcefully in *By Night in Chile*, the delirious deathbed monologue of a Chilean priest, literary critic, and poet, Sebastián Urrutia Lacroix. The young Urrutia Lacroix has a clear plan for his literary career:

I felt I needed a pseudonym for the critical articles, so that I could retain my real name for my poetical efforts. So I adopted the name of H.

Ibacache. And little by little the reputation of H. Ibacache outstripped that of Sebastián Urrutia Lacroix, to my surprise, and to my satisfaction, since Urrutia Lacroix was preparing a body of poetic work for posterity, an oeuvre of canonical ambition, which would take shape gradually as the years went by . . . And Ibacache's purity—clothed as it was in the simple garments of critical prose, yet nonetheless admirable, since it was perfectly clear, whether reading between the lines or viewing the full sweep of the enterprise, that Ibacache was engaged in an ongoing exercise in dispassionate analysis and rationality, that is to say in civic virtue—Ibacache's purity would be able to illuminate far more powerfully than any other strategy the body of work taking shape verse by verse in the diamond-pure mind of his double: Urrutia Lacroix. (BNC 25)

This combination of critical productivity and creative parsimony, reminiscent of T. S. Eliot, aims to school the taste of the public and prepare it to receive the gradually matured poetic work. But Urrutia Lacroix is more Machiavellian, if less successful, than Eliot in that he uses a pseudonym and thus obscures the fact that his criticism is, at least in part, a form of aesthetic special pleading.

The start of Urrutia Lacroix's "brilliant career" (56) is followed by a period of boredom and exhaustion (58–59), during which he meets Mr. Raef and Mr. Etah, who commission him to study the preservation of churches in Europe. Mr. Etah asks Urrutia Lacroix to guess where his name comes from, and tells him that it is half-Finnish, half-Lithuanian (64), but the function of this exchange is to focus the reader's attention on the name's phonetic and orthographical oddness and prompt the realization that Etah and Raef are "hate" and "fear" in reverse (as Odeim and Oido correspond to the Spanish nouns *miedo* and *odio*). What these two men propose seems at first to be a junket: "to visit the churches at the forefront of the battle against dilapidation, to evaluate the various methods, to write a report and come home" (66). The most effective method turns out to be using birds of prey to kill the pigeons whose feces are the primary cause of deterioration. Urrutia Lacroix visits a succession of falconer-priests, whose hunting birds are named Turk, Othello, Xenophon, Ta Gueule ("Shut your face" in familiar French), Rodrigo, Ronnie, and

Fever. As the names suggest, this is a comic sequence, but after the introduction of Raef and Etah, with the coup d'état in Chile looming ahead, the use of falcons to kill pigeons—or hawks to kill doves—irresistibly takes on allegorical significance, whether, with Pablo Berchenko, we see the falcons and pigeons as standing for Catholic conservatives and liberation theologians or for military governments and civilian populations.[27]

Back in Chile, Urrutia Lacroix reacts to the election of Allende by plunging into a rereading of the Greek classics, which occupies him until the coup. It is only then that he is obliged, by Raef and Etah, to do his "patriotic duty" (89) by giving the members of the junta a crash course on the principles of Marxism. He continues to write poems but is dismayed to discover that his poetry is undergoing deep and unwelcome changes. First it veers "from the angelic to the demonic," from the Apollonian to the Dionysiac mode (84). Then he produces what seems to be the work of someone else: "I published a book of poems that struck even me as odd, I mean it was odd that I should have written them" (103). Meanwhile the "purity" of the critic Ibacache is compromised by mealy-mouthed reviewing—"Lafourcade published *White Dove*, and I gave it a good review, you might say I hailed it in glowing terms, although deep down I knew it wasn't much of a book" (81)—and his readiness to perform "various Chilean leg-ups of little consequence" (103).

Urrutia Lacroix, who embarked on his "brilliant career" with a clear and indeed Machiavellian plan, has seriously overestimated the degree of control that he can exercise over his life and its trajectory. He is co-opted by Raef and Etah for projects to which he is not personally committed, but whose fringe benefits (travel in Europe, proximity to the powerful) attract him. As semirealist characters, Raef and Etah are agents of state power, but as semiallegorical figures, they are able to control Urrutia Lacroix because of his susceptibility to fear and hate. His fearfulness is comically underlined when they approach him about tutoring the junta in Marxism: "Do you have any books about Marxism in your library? asked Mr. Etah. Heavens, it's not my library, it belongs to the community, there might be something, but only for reference, to be used as a source for philosophical essays aiming precisely to refute Marxism" (87). His susceptibility to hatred and contempt is apparent whenever he comes into contact with ordinary Chileans, as in his encounter with a farming family on Farewell's estate (10–11) and his visit to the Haiti café, which serves the best coffee in Santiago "according to the plebs": "A few men returned my gaze. In some of those countenances I felt I could read signs of an immense pain. Pigs suffer too, I said to myself" (63).

The self-deception that allows Urrutia Lacroix to go on believing that his life has been shaped by the resolute pursuit of a noble aim gradually gives way under the pressure exerted by a mysterious "wizened youth" who reappears throughout the novel, insulting and accusing the prostrate priest. The youth, who would have been five or six at the end of the fifties, by Urrutia Lacroix's reckoning (11), is the same age as Roberto Bolaño or very nearly so. Like Bolaño he comes from the south of Chile, "the rainy border lands, the banks of our nation's mightiest river, the fearsome Bío-Bío" (55), and has emigrated (37). After the return of democracy, he is "wandering around God knows where, in some black hole or other" (103). Urrutia Lacroix attempts to rid himself of the youth's importunate presence by arguing, by steering his bed away (in his delirium, he imagines it as a boat on a tropical river [57]), and by relegating his tormentor to the ranks of obscure poets whose only hope of survival is a word of recognition from the critic Ibacache (55–56). These strategies seem, at first, to succeed, but Urrutia Lacroix does not find peace. He is haunted by the youth's accusations and by what he has said, although not within the reader's hearing, about literature: "What has become of literature? I asked myself. Could the wizened youth be right? Could he be right after all? I wrote or tried to write a poem. In one line there was a boy with blue eyes looking through a window. Awful, ridiculous" (115–116). Something is troubling the poet's "diamond-pure mind"; here, as earlier, when he finds himself writing about "homosexuals and children lost in derelict railway stations" (84), it seems that the repressed is returning.

Even at this late stage, Urrutia Lacroix believes or wants to believe that history will vindicate his actions, words, and silences, and bear him away from his tormentor: "The wizened youth has always been alone and I have always been on history's side" (128). But then, in the novel's closing epiphany, it is revealed that the youth has not gone away at all but come closer:

And then I ask myself: Where is the wizened youth? Why has he gone away? And little by little the truth begins to rise like a dead body. A dead body rising from the bottom of the sea or from the bottom of a gully. I can see its shadow rising. Its flickering shadow. Its shadow rising as if it were climbing a hill on a fossil planet. And then, in the half-light of my sickness, I see his fierce, his gentle face, and I ask myself: Am I that wizened youth? Is that the true, the supreme terror, to discover that I am the wizened youth whose cries no one can hear? And that the poor wizened youth is me? (129)

So the man who adopted a pseudonym the more effectively to pursue his unitary, long-term project not only sees that project fail but also comes to realize that his self may really be inhabited by another.

The life of Urrutia Lacroix illustrates the three dangers that have been emphasized, as mentioned earlier in this section, by critics of narrative identity theories: an unrealistic ideal of control, self-deception, and "missing the adventure." The grand plan that, as a young man, Urrutia Lacroix lays out for his life and work with a confidence reminiscent of Stephen Dedalus is sabotaged by factors beyond his control: most obviously, his mediocrity (for which he attempts to compensate with a pretentiously redundant style), but also the turbulent history of Chile, from which he takes refuge in the classics, and his own unacknowledged motivations, particularly fear and hate, but also sexual desire. Yet he continues to deceive himself up until the last moment, believing in the purity of his mission—"more culture! more culture!" (104)—and maintaining that the years from 1973 to 1989 were a negligible hiccough: "Now we have a socialist president and life is exactly the same" (102). Through willful ignorance he has missed the terrible adventure of the dictatorship.

WRITING LIVES

Bolaño's fiction clearly contradicts the psychological Narrativity thesis by showing that not everyone sees or lives or experiences his or her life as a narrative or story of some sort. Whether or not it also contradicts the ethical Narrativity thesis, according to which "a richly Narrative outlook on one's life is essential to living well, to true or full personhood," depends on how one understands what it is to live well. Given the ethical minimalism implicit in Bolaño's fiction, which I will examine in chapter 7, an Episodic life like that of Auxilio Lacouture can qualify as well lived, although for a narrative identity theorist like MacIntyre it would be meaningless, because it lacks "any movement towards a definite climax or *telos*."[28] To contradict the ethical Narrativity thesis is only to enter a plea for diversity, not to argue against Narrativity in general. Yet it would not be accurate to claim that Bolaño's fiction maintains a strict neutrality with regard to temporal temperament (Diachronic or Episodic, Narrative or Non-Narrative), because among the characters who are writers, the strong Diachronics who have a career plan and want to get somewhere in particular by writing are systematically treated in a satirical way: Sebastián Urrutia Lacroix with his abortive "oeuvre of canonical ambition" (BNC 25); Pablo del Valle, who dreams of being elected to the Academy and plans to write an essay "taking its first sentence from Unamuno: Spain hurts me too" (SD 460–462); Marco Antonio Palacios, a rising star at twenty-four, with his well-considered advice on the exercise of "ingratiating charm" (SD 462–463); the world-renowned Hernando García León, who is commissioned by the Virgin Mary in a dream to write *The New Age and the Iberian Ladder* (SD 466); and the hapless Efraim Ivanov, who shoots to fame as the Cervantes of Soviet science fiction thanks to the ghostwriting of Boris Ansky and is killed in one of Stalin's purges in 1937 (2666 710–728).

None of the writers whom Bolaño's fiction allows us to take seriously thinks in terms of a literary career. Cesárea Tinajero, as we saw, regards the very notion as reactionary (SD 434), and seems unconvinced by Amadeo Salvatierra's instrumental approach to avant-garde art making: "Stridentism and visceral realism are just two masks to get us to where we really want to go. And where is that? she said. To modernity, Cesárea, I said, to goddamned modernity" (433). In any case, she is not dissuaded from her decision to leave the capital and go to the cultural "wasteland" of Sonora (433). When Perla Aviles asks the young Arturo Belano what he intends to do with his life, he replies that he has no idea and doesn't care (SD 148). Of Ulises Lima, Simone

Darrieux says, "Nothing he did ever seemed to be planned out" (SD 210). If Belano and Lima have a project in Mexico, it seems to be to alienate all the literary gatekeepers before disappearing from the national literary scene. Lima returns to Mexico, but not to resume any kind of career. When Clara Cabeza, Octavio Paz's secretary, draws up a list of more than five hundred young Mexican poets, it does not include Lima's name (SD 480). Belano, it is true, begins to worry at one point about the reception of his books in Spain— "I must be getting bourgeois," he says (SD 446)—but then he becomes a war reporter and disappears in Liberia. The prodigy Boris Ansky, in *2666*, unconcerned by semblances (2666 722) and immune to self-pity (729), makes no effort to publish under his own name before disappearing from his village in German-occupied Ukraine.

Archimboldi would seem to be the exception to this rule. Inspired by Ansky's notebook, he publishes steadily and eventually becomes a famous writer, rumored to be among the candidates for the Nobel Prize. Insofar as his books succeed, he does have a career. And he does not lay claim to avant-garde purity:

> Archimboldi had a view of literature (though the word "view" is too grand) as something divided into three compartments, each connected only tenuously to the others: in the first were the books he read and reread and considered magnificent and sometimes monstrous, like the fiction of Döblin, who was still one of his favorite authors, or Kafka's complete works. In the second compartment were the books of the epigones and authors he called the Horde, whom he essentially saw as his enemies. In the third compartment were his own books and his plans for future books, which he saw as a game and also a business, a game insofar as he derived pleasure from writing, a pleasure similar to that of the detective on the heels of the killer, and a business insofar as the publication of his books helped to augment, however modestly, his doorman's pay. (817)

If Archimboldi can be said to use writing, he uses it to arrive at a state of autonomy rather than an elevated social position. The earnings of the business buy him more time to play a game in which the key stake is his own pleasure. After the death of his wife, Ingeborg, he leads the life of a "vanished writer," to the irritation of his publisher, the Baroness Von Zumpe (864), declining to capitalize on his slowly growing fame, working as a gardener in Venice, then roaming through southern Europe and North Africa before disappearing (provisionally, at least) in Mexico.

Archimboldi's approach to writing and to life allies him with Tinajero, Belano, Lima, and Ansky rather than with Urrutia Lacroix, Pablo del Valle, Marco Antonio Palacios, Hernando García León, and Efraim Ivanov. He seems to make no long-term plans. His wandering life is like his fiction, which his sister Lotte discovers by accident near the end of the novel: "The writing was clear and sometimes even transparent, but the way the stories followed one after another didn't lead anywhere" (887). If meaning is conferred on a life by "movement toward a climax or *telos*," Archimboldi's life lacks meaning. Yet in the world of *2666*, and in the context of Bolaño's work as a whole, it is none the worse for that lack. For Archimboldi it is important to go on making literary works, but what he has made of his life, what overall shape it has, is a question that seems not to trouble him at all, as it does not occupy Galen Strawson:

> I'm completely uninterested in the answer to the question "What has GS made of his life?" or "What have I made of my life?" I'm living it and this sort of thinking about it is no part of it. This does not mean that I am in any way irresponsible. It is just that what I care about, insofar as I care about myself and my life, is how I am now.[29]

The narrator of *2666* tells us that, as a soldier, Archimboldi "felt no need or perhaps wasn't able to think seriously about the future" (673), and there is no reason to suppose that he later undergoes a deep change in temporal temperament. Like Anne Moore and Liz Norton, he seems to be an Episodic, but unlike them, he has found a practice or a discipline in which he can lose himself, the practice of writing fiction for publication, which is at once social and solitary. As opposed to the arrivistes systematically satirized in Bolaño's work, he does not subordinate writing to the achievement of a socially prized end, and when his sister asks him if he will "take care of it all," that is, of her son's predicament in Santa Teresa, he does not miss the adventure, although by this stage he is over eighty. His first reaction is to ask for a beer (891), but on the novel's last page he sets off for Mexico, just as Arturo Belano, in "The Days of Chaos," sets off for Berlin, where his son has disappeared (SE 144).

At the end of a brilliantly intricate analysis of self-creation in Proust, Joshua Landy concludes: "Not everyone has to be an artist; but anyone who wishes to possess a unified Self must be an artist of life."[30] Bolaño's fiction suggests that not everyone wishes or should wish to possess a Self with a capital S, unified in the Nietzschean fashion that Landy recommends:

> At any given moment in our life . . . we should not be asking what we are—for we will always only be a tangle of unfulfilled possibilities—but wondering instead what we will have been. To think autobiographically is, in fact, to conjure up an idealized future self and to account for one's current constitution in terms of it. Thus an autobiographical text, or even a life lived in the autobiographical mode, is part of a narrative continuum that extends beyond the present moment, tracing the various lines of one's development toward their point of convergence at infinity, an ideal telos from which one projects, "as it were a posteriori," consistency and indeed purpose into a life of chaos and contingency. One manages to speak as it were from beyond the grave, to write one's own epitaph; but always in the awareness that this is a fantasy, and a transitional one at that. (125)

Since, according to Proust, each of us has a diachronically stable "true self," a unique perspective or temperament (112–113), as well as a more or less durable "sense of self," the Nietzschean total Self, as described above, might seem a luxury. "With Oscar Wilde," argues Landy, "Proust may well have claimed to have put only talent into his written works, reserving all his genius for the mode of being he practiced" (126). But in *Finding Time Again* the narrator's priority is the elaboration of the work, since he senses that his time is short: "for the duty to write my book took precedence over that of being polite or even good-natured."[31] Or, one might add, over the desire to cut a striking figure. Proust's narrator, at this late stage, is too busy doing the work to give much thought to being a work. Even the young and healthy may wonder whether a total Self is worth possessing, given that it is, by necessity, a partly fictional artifact, made as well as found, and the making may require a considerable investment of time and energy if the result is to be unique and memorable. Anyone, artists included, may fail or decline to engage in such a project without abdicating full humanity.[32]

One may grant that the total Self is a luxury option and still be bothered by the fact that some people have a very short-lived sense of self. Talk of the Episodic life may seem, especially to people of a Diachronic temperament, like a sophisticated way of justifying both the failure to honor past commitments (since the self who made them, the Episodic may say, no longer exists) and the avoidance of promises (since the present self will be gone when the time to fulfill them comes). The self-declared Episodic can appear to be irresponsible or in bad faith. For Kathleen V. Wilkes, to be Episodic is to be morally disabled:

> Morality is a matter of planning future actions, calculating consequences, experiencing remorse and contrition, accepting responsibility, accepting praise and blame; such mental phenomena are both forward- and backward-looking. Essentially. . . . The Episodic life could not be richly moral and emotional; we must have a life, or self, with duration. We are, and must consider ourselves as, relatively stable intentional systems. Essentially.[33]

Responding to Wilkes, Galen Strawson has offered a detailed argument to the effect that "there is no significant positive or negative correlation between either Diachronicity or Episodicity and responsible behavior."[34] His fundamental point is straightforward: we *do* have a life with duration, but the agent engaged by commitments and promises, whether one is Diachronic or Episodic, is not an inner mental entity or self but the human being considered as a whole (220).

This debate, like the disagreement about whether or not stories are lived before they are told, is unlikely to be settled soon by a universally persuasive intervention, and fiction is of limited use to philosophy here, since fictional characters are under no obligation to represent the way people generally behave: their behavior may be, and often is, both credible and exceptional with respect to real lives. Yet the terms of the philosophical debate might help to clarify how ways of living in time are related to ways of treating others in Bolaño's fiction. To return to the case of Anne Moore, not only does her life fail to flourish, as I noted above, it also damages some of the lives with which it is entangled, partly because of her temporal temperament. It would make no sense to claim that she acts responsibly in suddenly leaving her lovers Tony and Bill. Yet she is not entirely indifferent to the people whom she has known and loved in the further past, as the end of the story shows. The narrator visits an old Russian man named Alexei in the apartment building where Anne used to live, who shows him three postcards from his ex-neighbor:

> The third postcard was from Berkeley: a quiet street in Bohemian Berkeley, read the caption. I'm seeing old friends and making new ones, said Anne's clear handwriting. And it ended like the first card, advising dear Alexei to look after himself and eat every day, if only a little.
>
> Sadly, curiously, I looked at the Russian. He looked back at me kindly. Have you been following her advice? I asked. Of course, he replied. I always follow a lady's advice. (LEE 105)

Anne's erratic but genuine concern for her old friends contrasts with the behavior of the strongly Diachronic Pablo del Valle in *The Savage Detectives* who, as soon as a literary prize makes him financially independent, leaves the girlfriend who has supported him for years (SD 460–461). If Anne Moore is irresponsible in leaving Tony and Bill for reasons that she cannot articulate, so is Pablo del Valle when he "upgrades" from a postal worker to an intellectual for reasons that are perfectly clear, however euphemistically expressed:

> I told her we weren't right for each other and that I didn't want to hurt her and that I wished her the best and that she knew she could always count on me if she ever needed anything. . . . I can't remember which great writer said it, but love smiles on a winner. It wasn't long before I was living with another woman and renting an apartment in Lavapiés.

. . . My current girlfriend is studying English literature and writes poetry. We spend a lot of time talking about books. And sometimes she has great ideas. I think we make a wonderful couple: people look at us and nod their heads. We embody optimism and the future in a certain way, a way that's pragmatic and thoughtful too. (SD 460–461)

Del Valle has no trouble satisfying Schechtman's "articulation constraint."[35] He can respond to the question, "Why did you choose that course of action?" His response coheres with an ambitious life plan, but his monologue goes on to show that mere articulation can guarantee only a superficial kind of responsibility. When he is haunted by the sound of his ex-girlfriend's steps and thinks he can hear her delivering mail at night, he knows how to find relief: he makes love to his new girlfriend, then sleeps and dreams that he is being inducted into the Academy (or sometimes that he is being inducted into Hell). "I pay for my relationship with the mailwoman with a few nightmares. It could be worse. I can handle it. If I were less sensitive, I'm sure I wouldn't even remember her anymore" (461). The end of the monologue reveals, however, that, as in the case of Sebastián Urrutia Lacroix, the guilt has not been gradually paid off but simply repressed: "Everything that begins as a comedy ends as a horror movie" (462).

Although Bolaño is not engaged in a systematic defense of the Episodic life, Diachronics in his work appear to be just as prone as Episodics to the kinds of irresponsibility that damage the lives of other individuals. Furthermore, his stories repeatedly illustrate a point that Strawson makes in response to Wilkes: "the heart of moral responsibility, considered as a psychological phenomenon, is just a sort of instinctive *responsiveness* to things, a responsiveness in the present whose strength or weakness in particular individuals has nothing to do with how Episodic or Diachronic or Narrative or non-Narrative they are."[36] In Bolaño's fiction this sort of responsiveness is tested in critical situations that involve facing danger and violence, and in those situations his Episodic characters respond quickly, surely, and effectively. While Anne Moore leaves emotional damage in her wake, her fellow Episodics Arturo Belano, Cesárea Tinajero, and Auxilio Lacouture fulfill, at great personal risk, a duty to protect and rescue, as we shall see in the next chapter.

5

DUELS AND BRAWLS

Borges and Bolaño

THE POET'S COURAGE AND THE DUTY TO RESCUE

MONG THE AUTHORS he admired, Roberto Bolaño reserved a special place for Jorge Luis Borges. "Borges," he wrote, "is or should be at the center of our canon" (BP 337). Perhaps surprisingly for readers in the English-speaking world, what Bolaño particularly valued was not the conceptual brilliance of the thought experiments that made Borges famous in Europe and North America from the early 1960s on, but the Argentine writer's humor and courage. In an interview, Bolaño described his tutelary elder as "possibly the best humorist we've had" (B 77), alluding to a comic vein that is evident in Borges's erudite hoaxes, his parodic collaborations with Adolfo Bioy Casares (such as *Chronicles of Bustos Domecq*), and his satirical portraits of ridiculous characters like Carlos Argentino Daneri in "The Aleph." Bolaño too was a hoaxer, a parodist, and a satirist, especially in *Nazi Literature in the Americas*, a book whose debt to Borges's *A Universal History of Infamy* he signaled explicitly (B 42).

As for courage, the title of Bolaño's essay "The Brave Librarian" (BP 311) does not, I think, reflect an admiration for particular acts in Borges's life, such as submitting the implicitly anti-Peronist text "The Dagger" for publication in *La Nación* in 1953 or suggesting to four young men who had interrupted one of his lectures at the University of Buenos Aires in 1962 that they "go out on the street and have it out," much less the decision, in 1976, to travel to Chile and accept a decoration from Pinochet, against the advice of friends who warned that he was ruining his chances of winning the Nobel Prize.[1] Why then was Borges a "brave librarian" for Bolaño? Perhaps because Borges repeatedly celebrated courage in his fiction and his poetry, as in these lapidary and questionable lines from "Milonga for Jacinto Chiclana": "Having shown courage is one thing/You never have to regret."[2] This celebration was driven by a persistent feeling of unworthiness in relation to the military heroes among his ancestors: "As most of my people had been soldiers . . . and I knew I would never be, I felt ashamed, quite early, to be a bookish kind of person and not a man of action."[3] Another reason for calling Borges brave is that as a poet he was, in Bolaño's eyes, endowed with a special kind of courage. In "The Best Gang," Bolaño writes: "If I had to hold up the most heavily guarded bank in Europe and I could choose my partners in crime, I'd take a gang of five poets, no question about it. Five real poets, Apollonian or Dionysian, but always real, ready to live and die like poets. No one in the world is as brave as a poet. No one in the world faces disaster with more dignity and understanding" (BP 117). Anyone with a reasonably detailed knowledge of more than a few poets' lives will have to admit that the final claims are unwarranted generalizations. Poets, like all other kinds of people, have been known to panic in the face of disaster and to react to it in petulant and self-regarding ways. Perhaps more than other kinds of people, they have also been known to court disaster and bring harm on themselves and those around them in the search for stimulating intensities of experience. These common-sense objections aside, the scenario evoked in "The Best Gang" clearly reveals the hard rhetorical work that Bolaño demands of poets and poetry in general. In chapter 7, I will be showing how he expands the concept of poetry so that it comes to stand for a general attitude or stance of openness. Here I want to stress Bolaño's identification of poetry with the specific virtue of courage. A personified poetry might be called courageous because it has persisted against a widely shared estimate of the odds against it. The death of poetry has been predicted, announced, or called for repeatedly since the time of Hegel at least,[4] and yet the art goes on refusing to die altogether, even producing "late" flowerings of bewildering diversity. "Poetry is braver than anyone," as Bolaño puts it in his poem "The Worm" (UU 653). More contentiously, he attributes this transpersonal endurance to the individuals who collectively make it happen, and who need not be especially dauntless themselves. For example, at the beginning of the story "Enrique Martín," he shifts the stress from the poet's active bravery in a dangerous enterprise such as a bank heist to his or her passive capacity to withstand hardship: "A poet can endure anything. Which amounts to saying that a human being can endure anything. Except that it's not true: there are obviously limits to what a human being can endure. Really endure. A poet on the other hand, *can* endure anything. We grew up with this conviction" (LEE 26). I doubt that many of Bolaño's readers could sincerely include themselves in that "we." Few people today would credit poets with exceptional capacities in any domain other than poetic composition, such as brave action, endurance of hardship, prophecy, or legislative authority, albeit unacknowledged, as at the end of Shelley's "Defense of Poetry."[5] Bolaño, however, seems to be one of the few. His attitude here, as in "The Best Gang," might seem romantic. It is. Rodrigo Fresán has written that "Bolaño is one of the most romantic writers in the best sense of the word."[6] In this chapter I will argue that Fresán's "best sense" is a historical sense, in that Bolaño's fiction revives a romantic ideal of the poet's courage, which found memorable expression in a pair of poems by Hölderlin, "Timidity" ("Blödigkeit") and "The Poet's Courage" ("Dichtermut"), written in 1800 and 1803–1804 respectively. Courage, in those poems, is a matter of decision and willpower but also of trust, acceptance, and openness:

> Well, then, travel defenseless
> On through life and fear nothing there!

> All that happens there be welcome, be blessed to you!
> Be an adept in joy, or is there anything
> That could harm you there, heart, that
> Could offend you, where you must go?[7]

In an "aesthetic commentary," Walter Benjamin offers the following gloss on the earlier poem: "'Timidity' has now become the authentic stance of the poet. Transposed into the middle of life, he has nothing remaining to him except motionless existence [*das reglose Dasein*], complete passivity, which is the essence of the courageous man—nothing except to surrender himself wholly to relation [*Beziehung*]."[8] Benjamin's difficult and variously interpreted interpretation of Hölderlin may seem a far cry from Bolaño's bank-robbing gang, but the courage implicitly celebrated in Bolaño's fiction and often exemplified there by poets is, I will argue, close to the spirit of "Timidity" and "The Poet's Courage" in that it is manifested not only by decisions and actions but also by "surrender to relation" and being there, motionlessly, in dangerous and difficult places.[9]

The real poet's courage, as opposed to the ineffectual rhetoric of the poetaster, is illustrated in part II, chapter 20 of *The Savage Detectives* by Xosé Lendoiro's story about a boy who fell into a chasm called "The Devil's Mouth" near Castroverde in Galicia. Lendoiro is a lawyer and poet, but also claims to be a "man of action" (SD 404). Nevertheless, when no one seconds his proposal to lower the thinnest man present into the chasm on a makeshift rope of belts, he retreats to the role of bystander. A young man is eventually lowered on a proper rope, but after "superhuman howls" are heard from the chasm, he is hauled back up, terrified and speechless (405):

> What did you see? his relatives asked him. He wouldn't answer and covered his face with his hands. That was when I should have taken charge and stepped in, but my position as a spectator kept me, how shall I say, bewitched by the play of shadows and useless gestures. . . . This young fellow was clearly a weak character. . . . What did you see? the group repeated. The young man replied: I saw the devil. (405)

Had Lendoiro not been "bewitched," he might have interrupted this interview and organized further action; as it is, the rescue group is paralyzed by superstitious fear until the watchman from a nearby campground, who is none other than Arturo Belano, goes down into the chasm and saves the boy. While Belano is underground, Lendoiro realizes that what is happening bears "an extraordinary resemblance" to a story by Pío Baroja called "The Abyss" ("La Sima"). In Baroja's story, a shepherd boy falls into a chasm while trying to retrieve a stray goat with his grandfather, who then calls on his fellow shepherds for help. A would-be rescuer returns to the surface claiming to have seen the devil "all ruddy, all ruddy,"[10] after which no one else dares to make another attempt. The ruddy "devil" may well have been the goat or the boy, injured and smeared with blood. At the story's close the shepherds' superstitious fear is ratified by a priest who performs the last rites at the mouth of the chasm while a "mysterious complaint" can be heard from underground (314).

Both Baroja's story and Bolaño's rewriting of it are parabolic and specifically related to the parable of the Good Samaritan. In *The Savage Detectives*, as in the gospel according to Saint Luke, it is the outsider—the Chilean in Spain, the Samaritan in Judaea—who proves to be the true neighbor. One of the problems raised by "Good Samaritan laws," which aim to make the conduct of the priest and of the Levite in the parable legally actionable, is how to formulate a "convenience limitation" so that the rescuer is not obliged to expose herself to an unreasonable risk.[11] Xosé Lendoiro's story shows that however such a limitation is formulated, there are situations in which it is impossible to know, before acting, whether or not it applies. The blackness of the chasm figures that impossibility. Although, for Belano, the metaphysical threat of the devil's presence is no doubt groundless, the chasm may harbor real physical dangers, which cannot be precisely gauged without confronting them. From the point of view of normative ethics, what Belano does may be supererogatory, beyond the call of duty, praiseworthy but not required. After all, the Guardia Civil has been called and is presumably on its way (405). But in Bolaño's fiction, standing by, as Lendoiro does, is clearly a failing.

Throughout the chapter, the behavior of Lendoiro and Belano is contrasted, and it is significant that both of them are poets, or have at least published verse. As Belano is preparing for his descent, Lendoiro goes over to congratulate him: "Xosé Lendoiro, lawyer and poet, I said as I shook his hand effusively. He looked at me and smiled as if we'd met before" (406). Later it becomes clear that Belano smiles not because he recognizes Lendoiro, but because, under the circumstances, the lawyer's pompous self-introduction reveals what kind of poet he must be:

"I realized what Arturo Belano had known from the moment he saw me: I was a terrible poet" (417). Descending into the chasm, Belano goes where he must without fear, as Hölderlin would have his "genius" do in "Timidity." This is a decision and an action, but also a "surrender to relation," as Benjamin puts it in his commentary on Hölderlin's poem. It is a surrender rather than a negotiation because Belano cannot measure the risk that he is taking in attempting to restore the relation between the child and the community to which he is provisionally lost. Lendoiro may have published verse, but he is not the sort of "real poet" whom Bolaño would enlist in his bank-robbing gang. And in the end, he knows it. Having contracted a fatal illness, he tries to secure the City of Barcelona Award in order, as he says, to die as himself, "not as an ear on the edge of a chasm" (419). But this attempt to erase the shame of his inaction fails, and the giant for which he took himself in an access of deluded grandiosity returns to "say or whisper: save the boy" (421). In Bolaño's fictional universe, as in Vermont, Minnesota, and Rhode Island, there is a duty to rescue, and there is no getting away from it.

This duty to rescue motivates many of the confrontations in Bolaño's fiction, as we shall see. I claimed above that the courage implicitly celebrated by Bolaño is characterized by "motionless existence" and "surrender to relation" as well as by decisions and actions—in other words, that it has a passive as well as an active aspect—but this claim is unlikely to command immediate assent, because in Bolaño's work, as in that of Borges, courage is often tested in potentially or actually violent conflict. In the work of both writers, moreover, knives are objects of fascination and carry a special symbolic weight. On a first impression, Bolaño would seem to have inherited Borges's nostalgia for the warrior ethic and the honor code, a nostalgia that has been condemned by progressive Latin American critics since the 1960s, and with particular force by Ariel Dorfman in "Borges and American Violence," originally published in 1968. Is that first impression sound? Is it true to say that Bolaño is a faithful if undisciplined disciple of the Argentine master, "infinitely wilder," as he said himself (B 98), but a follower nonetheless? If so, to what degree is his work open to the kind of critique formulated by Dorfman?

BORGES AND AMERICAN VIOLENCE

As a first step toward answering these questions, I will outline the main points of Dorfman's article. He begins by comparing Borges to "a great prestidigitator" who makes a rabbit disappear. Distracted by the performer's "tricky hands"—that is, by Borges's intellectual agility—we, the audience, forget about the vanished animal, which in this little allegory stands for violence. Dorfman reproaches Borges for his retrograde celebration of violent conflict between individuals and for turning his back on the collective struggles for liberation under way in the 1960s. Analyzing a series of stories from *Fictions* (1944) and *The Aleph* (1949), he discerns a repeated pattern of traits in the narration of violent episodes. His findings can be summarized as follows:

1. For Borges's characters, as opposed to characters in European fiction, violence is *inevitable*;[12]

2. The imminence of violent death brings about an *epiphany* or revelation, allowing the protagonist to understand the meaning of his or her "own selfhood or of reality" (27);

3. The epiphany or revelation is *teleological*: it is a culminating moment, which makes sense of the protagonist's whole life retrospectively (27); as such, it is an end in itself, and it often brings the story to an end;

4. Curiously, the violence is *personal* and intimate; it takes the form of a duel, but the opponent turns out to be a mere instrument or even an aspect of the protagonist (31–33). An observation made by Martín Kohan is relevant here: Borges's combats are always conceived as *singular*, one against one. Even when Cruz decides to fight alongside Martín Fierro in "A Biography of Tadeo Isidoro Cruz," the duality of this fighting pair is reduced by a "lightning flash of final identification."[13]

And I would add one further trait:

5. Once the fight has begun, it is experienced as a liberation, and produces a *neutralization of affect*.

Not all of the characteristics enumerated above appear in each of the stories of violent conflict, but Dorfman convincingly constructs an "ideal type" whose most complete realizations are to be found in "The South" and "A Biography of Tadeo Isidoro Cruz." In "The South," Juan Dahlmann, who lives in Buenos Aires, goes to his ranch to convalesce after an operation. He is insulted by some laborers in a bar, and one of them challenges him to a fight. An old gaucho throws Dahlmann a dagger, and from that point on, violence seems *inevitable*: "It was as though the South itself had decided that Dahlmann should accept the challenge."[14] He experiences a *neutralization of affect*: "while there was no hope in Dahlmann, there was no fear, either" (179). By accepting the challenge and his probable defeat, he corrects his humiliating, passive "death" in the sanatorium (which he has perhaps never left: like "The Other Death," this is the story of a "forking in time").[15] Dahlmann's probable death is a *personal* affair because it is the dignified end that he would have "dreamed or chosen" for his life. The "young thug" is a mere instrument:

> As he crossed the threshold, he felt that on that first night in the sanatorium, when they'd stuck that needle in him, dying in a knife fight under the open sky, grappling with his adversary, would have been a liberation, a joy and a fiesta. He sensed that had he been able to choose or dream his death that night, this is the death he would have dreamed or chosen. (179)

In "A Biography of Tadeo Isidoro Cruz," Borges provides the clearest and most explicit formulation of his idea of the fight as a teleological epiphany. Tadeo Isidoro Cruz is the police sergeant who changes sides to join forces with the outlaw Martín Fierro in Hernández's epic *El Gaucho Martín Fierro*: "Cruz . . . cried that he was not going to be party to killing a brave man, and he began to fight against the soldiers, alongside the deserter Martín Fierro" (214). At that culminating moment, Cruz discovers his destiny:

> In the future, secretly awaiting him, was one lucid, fundamental night—the night when he was finally to see his own face, the night when he was finally to hear his own true name. . . . Any life, however long and complicated it may be, actually consists of a single moment—the moment when a man knows forevermore who he is. (213)

For Alan Pauls, this is the prototype of the "significant moment" in the work of Borges: "that decisive, punctual event which defines the meaning of a life once and for all."[16] It is surely significant that the prototype should be a moment of violence, rather than, say, a moment at which a character notices or fails to notice that someone else needs a quieter kind of help. But is it really true, even in the fiction of Borges, that any life actually consists of a single moment? In another story from *The Aleph*, we find precisely the opposite assertion: "To die for a religion is simpler than living that religion fully; battling savage beasts in Ephesus is less difficult (thousands of obscure martyrs did it) than being Paul, the servant of Jesus Christ; a single act is less [*menos*] than all the hours of a man."[17] Now this statement should be treated with caution, because it is made by Otto Dietrich zur Linde in "Deutsches Requiem," who conducts experiments with prisoners in a concentration camp and also says "what matters is that violence, not servile acts of Christian timidity, now rules" (234). Nevertheless, the idea is not entirely alien to Borges, whose late poem "The Speck" ("El Ápice") concludes: "You are made of time, which never ceases./You are every solitary instant."[18] It is sometimes tempting but always hazardous to forget Borges's propensity to contradict himself and change his mind. In his work, the extreme valorization of significant moments, which, to borrow an expression from Simon Critchley's reflections on the political thought of Alain Badiou, might be termed "a heroism of the decision,"[19] cohabits with a quieter heroism of endurance, whose domain of application comprises all the hours of a life and every solitary instant.

BOLAÑO'S BRAWLS

What of Bolaño? How faithfully does he follow Borges in the representation of fighting? Various scenes in his work that dramatize potentially or actually violent conflict and function as tests of courage particularly invite comparison with the stories analyzed in Dorfman's article. In what follows, I will concentrate on the following nine: the face-off between the German campers in *The Skating Rink* (SR 164–167); Diego Soto's attempt to defend a homeless woman from her skinhead attackers in *Distant Star* (DS 71); the bar brawl at the end of "Last Evenings on Earth" (LEE 156–157); Mauricio "The Eye" Silva's intervention to save a child from ritual castration in India (LEE 115–117); the duel between Arturo Belano and Iñaki Echavarne in *The Savage Detectives* (SD 441–442); the fight in the final pages of the same novel, in which Belano, Lima, and Cesárea Tinajero take on Alberto and the policeman (SD 571–572); the confrontation between Belano and the King of the Rent Boys in *Amulet* (A 92–102); the scrap in which Manuel Pereda wounds the pseudo-adolescent writer near the end of "The Insufferable Gaucho" (IG 39–40); and the shoot-out in which Lalo Cura defends the wife of his employer, Pedro Rengifo, in *2666* (394–396). Do the five characteristics of violence in the fiction of Borges, as formulated above, also characterize these scenes in Bolaño? The short, broad answer is no. A longer and more convincing answer requires consideration of each characteristic in turn.

1. In the fiction of Bolaño, physical violence is frequent but not inevitable. Sometimes, although it appears to be imminent, it does not eventuate. In *The Skating Rink*, two German campers are about to come to blows, and "the few spectators sheltering behind trees and cars" anticipate "an outbreak of murderous violence" (SR 164). But the caretaker, Remo Morán, succeeds in defusing the situation, with some help, as we shall see in a moment. In *Amulet*, Ernesto San Epifanio has slept with the King of the Rent Boys, who now considers the young poet to be his subject. Belano, however, secures San Epifanio's freedom without having to fight (A 100–101). And in *The Savage Detectives*, the duel between Belano and the critic Iñaki Echavarne ends in a game (SD 455).

Although the narrator of "Mauricio ("The Eye") Silva" says that "violence, real violence, is unavoidable, at least for those of us who were born in Latin America during the fifties, and were about twenty years old at the time of Salvador Allende's death" (LEE 106), what is actually unavoidable for such characters in Bolaño's fiction is the *risk* of violence: not a certain kind of act but a certain kind of situation from which it may not be possible to extricate oneself without inflicting or suffering physical harm. In some of these situations, the Latin American protagonist prevails; in others, he or she is defeated. The first alternative is illustrated by the story of Mauricio Silva, a gentle Chilean photographer, who, on assignment in India, visits a brothel where he finds a boy about to be castrated in a religious ceremony and manages to rescue him along with a young eunuch:

> What happened next is all too familiar: the violence from which there is no escape. The lot [*destino*] of Latin Americans born in the fifties. Naturally, The Eye tried to negotiate, bribe and threaten, without much hope of success. All I know for certain is that there was violence and soon he was out of there. (LEE 117; PA 22)

The second alternative is exemplified by the death of Diego Soto in *Distant Star*. Soto, an exiled Chilean living comfortably as a professor in France, seems to have left violence behind in Latin America: "He thought he had escaped the curse (or we thought he had, anyway; Soto, I suspect, never believed in curses)" (DS 69). But on the way back from an academic conference, he sees three neo-Nazis beating a homeless woman:

> Perhaps his eyes filled with tears, tears of self-pity, because something told him he had met his destiny. Now he wouldn't have to choose between Tel Quel and the Oulipo. For him, life had chosen the crime reports. In any case, he dropped his bag and books at the door and approached the youths. Before the fight began he insulted them in Spanish. The harsh Spanish of southern Chile. The youths stabbed Soto and ran away. (DS 71)

The appeal to destiny both here and in "Mauricio ('The Eye') Silva" recalls Borges, whose Tadeo Isidoro Cruz realizes his "deep-rooted destiny as a wolf, not a gregarious dog" (1998: 214). Yet in the passages from Bolaño, what cannot be avoided or escaped is not the performance of a violent act but risky intervention to prevent or stop violence that is imminent or under way. Neither Mauricio Silva nor Diego Soto considers alerting the relevant authorities; there would not be time for them to protect the homeless woman, and the Indian boy is firmly under the control of a religious institution. Neither Silva nor Soto "owes it to himself" to fight; both owe their actions to a person incapable of fighting. What they cannot do is abandon the helpless or ignore the duty to rescue. In both cases bodily harm is done, but the similar case of Belano's confrontation with the King of the Rent Boys shows that intervening effectively in such a situation does not necessarily involve or occasion violence.

2. In Bolaño's fiction, confrontations and fights test courage but do not generally lead to an epiphany or give access to special knowledge. In most of the scenes that I am considering here, no account is given of what the characters think as they face the threat of violence or engage in combat. The reasons for this are partly technical: some of the incidents are seen through the eyes of characters who are not directly engaged in the conflict. The duel between Arturo Belano and Iñaki Echavarne in *The Savage Detectives* is observed from a distance by Belano's ex-lover, Susana Puig, and by Echavarne's second, Jaume Planells (SD 441–442, 451–455). Juan García Madero watches the brawl at the end of the novel from Quim Font's Impala, where he and Lupe have taken refuge (SD 571–572). And Belano's confrontation with the King of the Rent Boys in *Amulet* is witnessed by Auxilio Lacouture, who has followed Belano and San Epifanio to the hotel where the King holds court. Even when the focal character is at the front line, so to speak, Bolaño gives little indication of what he or she is thinking. Remo Moran in *The Skating Rink* is wary of projecting later thoughts back onto a moment dominated by emotion: "I sensed that something was going to happen (or maybe that's just how it seems to me now, maybe then I was just a bit afraid)" (165). When two gunmen come to kill the wife of Lalo Cura's employer in *2666*, the young bodyguard's mind is entirely occupied by the problem of which man to shoot at first (396). By contrast, when Diego Soto goes to the defense of the homeless woman in *Distant Star*, he may have time to reach a realization: "Perhaps his eyes filled with tears, tears of self-pity, because something told him he had met his destiny" (DS 71). But note that the content of this Borgesian epiphany is bracketed by expressions of uncertainty: "Perhaps. . . . In any case" (71).

3. The confrontations related by Bolaño are not teleological. First, they do not conclude the stories or novels in which they occur, with the exception of the bar brawl in "Last Evenings on Earth," and even in that case,

B anticipates the following day in the last sentence of the story: "Tomorrow we'll leave, tomorrow we'll go back to Mexico City, thinks B joyfully. And then the fight begins" (LEE 157). Second, the confrontations are not culminating moments in the lives of the characters, not ends in themselves, but obstacles to be overcome. In "The Insufferable Gaucho," Manuel Pereda, who is explicitly identified as a parodic heir to Juan Dahlmann in Borges's "The South" (IG 22), encounters a cocaine-addled writer, who picks a fight with him in the street for no good reason. Pereda pricks the writer in the groin with his knife and continues on his way, wondering whether to stay in Buenos Aires and "become a champion of justice, or go back to the pampas . . . and try to do something useful" (IG 40–41). In "Last Evenings on Earth," B's father, who has been playing cards, decides to call it a night, but cannot take his winnings away without engaging in a fight. Remo Morán's objective when he steps in to prevent "an outbreak of murderous violence" in *The Skating Rink* is to restore peace among the campers, but he can do this only by putting himself in harm's way. In *2666*, Lalo Cura performs professionally, guarding the body of his employer's wife, unlike his two colleagues, who run away as soon as they see the gunmen approaching.

At the end of *The Savage Detectives*, in *Amulet*, and in "Mauricio ("The Eye") Silva," the confrontations are necessitated by threats to the freedom of third parties. In *The Savage Detectives*, Belano, Lima, and Cesárea Tinajero fight to stop Lupe being captured by Alberto, her ex-pimp. In *Amulet*, the explicit goal is the liberation of a symbolic captive: the King of the Rent Boys regards Ernesto San Epifanio as his subject and his slave (94). But there is another objective, which Belano, San Epifanio, and Auxilio Lacouture discover retrospectively. In the King's hotel room they find a young man who has been effectively reduced to slavery: Juan de Dios Montes. Belano insists on taking him away. Months later, at a party, San Epifanio and Auxilio agree that their "hidden purpose had been to stop him [that is, Juan] being killed" (A 103). Mauricio "The Eye" Silva frees two boys, the oldest of whom "couldn't have been more than ten years old" (LEE 115), from a brothel where they would otherwise have grown up as prostitutes.

As I pointed out in chapter 2, the duel between Belano and Iñaki Echavarne in *The Savage Detectives* is a curious anomaly. The motive for challenging

Echavarne to a duel is slim and dubious: Belano *assumes* that the critic is going to write a bad review of his latest book (SD 447). Moreover, as a way of responding to a perceived, or in this case anticipated, insult, a duel with sabers and seconds is, of course, anachronistic. Belano does not, as far as we know, go in for historical reconstructions. One thing, however, is certain: this confrontation is not a culminating moment or an end in itself. In fact, it seems to mark a beginning:

> Then I saw Iñaki's sword raised higher than prudence or musketeer mov-
> ies would advise and I saw his opponent's sword advance until its point
> was a fraction of an inch from Iñaki's heart, and I think, though it can't be,
> that I saw Iñaki turn pale . . . and then the other guy abruptly drew back
> the point of his sword and Iñaki stepped forward and struck him with the
> flat of his blade on the shoulder, in revenge for the fright he'd given him,
> I think, and Quima sighed and I sighed and blew smoke rings into the
> tainted air of that hideous beach and the wind whipped the rings away
> instantly, before there was time for anything, and Iñaki and his opponent
> kept going at it like two stupid children. (SD 455)

What began in earnest, at least from Belano's point of view, ends in play. And it seems that the duelers' hidden purpose, discernible in retrospect, was to initiate a friendship. When Belano tells Jacobo Urenda in Rwanda that Echavarne has sent him medicine from Barcelona, it is clear that the friendship between writer and critic is lasting (500).

With respect to teleology, Diego Soto's defense of the homeless woman is, again, something of an exception. Soto's confrontation with the neo-Nazis ends his life and marks his destiny as specifically Latin American, in line with the opening of "Mauricio ('The Eye') Silva." He *seems* to have become a European intellectual engaged in purely symbolic conflict of the kind that opposed the Tel Quel group and the Oulipo, but life chooses otherwise and obliges him to engage in a confrontation that is fatally physical.[20] Facing his killers, he affirms his origins linguistically: "Before the fight began he insulted them in Spanish. The harsh Spanish of southern Chile" (DS 71). And his obscure death in exile—"there was a brief article in the

Catalonian newspapers" (71)—links him with his old friend and rival from Concepción, Juan Stein, who, according to Bibiano O'Ryan, was killed in the FMLN's final offensive in El Salvador (60).

4. Whereas combat in the fiction of Borges is singular, one against one, as Martín Kohan has pointed out, this is unequivocally the case in only two of the nine scenes under consideration here: Belano and Echavarne's duel, and Manuel Pereda's scrap with the pseudo-adolescent writer (what Mauricio Silva has to do to escape from the brothel with the boys remains unclear: "All I know for certain is that there was violence and soon he was out of there" [LEE 117]). Bolaño's fights are generally brawls, involving three or more people, rather than duels. And even when only two are involved, the adversary is not an instrument at the service of the protagonist's self-understanding: Echavarne becomes a friend to Belano, and the pseudo-adolescent writer is a mere nuisance to Manuel Pereda. In Bolaño's fiction, violence is an interpersonal rather than a personal affair. In six of the nine scenes, it is risked in order to protect or rescue other characters who are themselves at risk: the drunken campers in *The Skating Rink*; the homeless woman in *Distant Star*; the Indian boys in "Mauricio ("The Eye") Silva"; Lupe in *The Savage Detectives*; Ernesto San Epifanio and Juan de Dios Montes in *Amulet*; and Pedro Rengifo's wife in *2666*. And in three of those six cases, the characters who face conflict in response to an ethical demand are actively accompanied. In *The Skating Rink*, Remo Morán owes his sudden fame as a fearless peacemaker to the intervention of his girlfriend, Caridad, who appears at the crucial moment with a knife and displays it to the drunken German campers, "as if displaying one of her breasts" (SR 166). Similarly, in *Amulet*, when words and rhetoric (or "literature," as Auxilio Lacouture says) prove insufficient to persuade the King of the Rent Boys to relent, Belano turns and says to Auxilio, "Give it to me," at which point she places her open jackknife on the palm of his right hand (A 98). True to her name (*auxilio* means help), she has followed "the two heroes" without being asked, and although she describes herself as an "invisible witness" (92), her action is no less heroic (and more disinterested) than that of Ernesto San Epifanio. The heroic trio at the end of *The Savage Detectives* is similarly composed of two men and a woman: Belano, Lima,

and Cesárea Tinajero. Again the woman's intervention is decisive. Cesárea saves Lima's life by throwing herself at the policeman who is aiming a gun at his head (SD 572).

5. The neutralization of affect that occurs when Borges's heroes face their violent fates is not experienced by Bolaño's characters. The fights are not in themselves liberating, although they may result in liberation or the preservation of liberty. When the emotional state of the protagonist is indicated, it is sometimes a state of fear. Remo Morán says: "To tell the truth I was pretty nervous" (SR 166). In *Amulet*, Auxilio notices Ernesto San Epifanio's lower lip trembling (A 95), and there is a moment at which Belano seems to be "losing his nerve" (96). Diego Soto, for his part, is "perhaps" affected by "self-pity" (DS 71), while Mauricio Silva runs a gamut of emotions from fear to rage to exaltation (LEE 116–117).

To sum up, with the exceptions noted above, violent combat in Bolaño's fiction, as opposed to that of Borges, is frequent but not inevitable, nonepiphanic, nonteleological, interpersonal, and it does not produce a neutralization of affect.

It is hardly surprising that the two writers should have represented fighting differently, given the very different lives they led. In the prologue to *Evaristo Carriego*, Borges writes: "For years I believed I had grown up in a suburb of Buenos Aires, a suburb of dangerous streets and showy sunsets. The truth is that I grew up in a garden, behind a fence of iron palings, and in a library of endless English books."[21] The Palermo of the knife and the guitar was out there (so the young Borges was assured) on the street corners, but all his time was spent with characters from fiction. Looking back, he wonders what was happening beyond the fence, and explains that his book about Carriego, less a document than an exercise of the imagination, is an attempt to satisfy that curiosity. By his own admission, Borges's knife fighters are imaginary creatures. Bolaño, on the other hand, had a closer acquaintance with "dangerous streets" and the characters who claim them as their territory. He pursued his truant education by reading stolen books in Mexico City's Alameda (B 104; LEE 60–64). His father did not provide him with a library, but taught him to box (LEE 212). As he said in an interview: "I'm driven by something infinitely wilder than Borges was" (B 98).

Reading biographically, it is tempting to suppose that the fights in Bolaño's work are more realistic and less idealized than those in the fiction of Borges, and that the resemblances are merely superficial. But that would be to over-simplify the relationship between the two writers.

So far I have been comparing Bolaño's fights with similar scenes in the stories analyzed by Dorfman, which are drawn from *Fictions* and *The Aleph*, both published in the 1940s. These stories belong to one phase in the long career of Jorge Luis Borges, albeit the phase often regarded as the most important.[22] If we look at the later fiction we will discover a significant shift in the narrative handling of violent confrontation. In this respect, "The Duel" and "The Other Duel" from *Doctor Brodie's Report* (*El informe de Brodie*, 1970), are particularly telling. As the titles suggest, the two stories form an antithetical pair. "The Duel" relates a symbolic rivalry between two paint-ers, Clara Glencairn and Marta Pizarro, who wholly sublimate their aggres-sion. It is an "intimate" and "delicate duel," in which the women engage "with perfect loyalty."[23] When Clara dies, Marta realizes that her life now lacks meaning: "she exhibited in the National Gallery a sober portrait of Clara after the manner of those English masters whom the two women had so admired. Some judged it her finest work. She was never to paint again" (37). By contrast, the conflict between men in "The Other Duel" is brutal in the extreme. Two gauchos, Manuel Cardoso and Carmen Silveira, have come to hate each other. Unlike the enmity that opposes Aureliano and Juan de Panonia in "The Theologians" (which ends with the revelation that "in the eyes of the unfathomable deity [they] were a single person"),[24] their conflict is not woven into the fabric of the universe. Its roots are obscure but trivial. It converts each into the slave of the other.[25] When both men are taken prisoner, a captain in the opposing army sends for them and says:

> I already know that you can't stand the sight of each other and that for some time now you've been looking for a chance to have it out. I have good news for you. Before sundown, the two of you are going to have that chance to show who's the better man. I'm going to stand you up and have your throats cut, and then you'll run a race. God knows who'll win. (41–42)

The race is duly run, with the soldiers' fellow captives, who will all have their throats cut too in due course, looking on and laying bets. "Cardoso, as he fell, stretched out his arms. Perhaps never aware of it, he had won" (43). The duel leads not to a revelation, but to the humiliation of both men.

Borges abjures the notion of the epiphanic duel with a somewhat lighter touch in "The Congress" (originally published in 1971). At one point in the story, the narrator, Alejandro Ferri, and his associate, Eguren, are challenged by a man with a knife:

> On leaving the establishment, we ran into a huge specimen of a man. Eguren, who may have been a bit drunk, gave him a shove. The stranger quickly barred our way and told us, "Whoever wants to leave is going to have to pass by this knife."
>
> I remember the glint of the blade in the darkness of the long entrance-way. Eguren drew back, visibly afraid. I wasn't too sure of myself, but my hatred got the best of my fright. I reached into my armpit, as if to draw out a weapon, and said in a firm voice, "We'll settle this out on the street."
>
> The stranger answered—with another voice now, "That's the sort of man I like. I wanted to test you, friend." Then he began to laugh in a cordial way.
>
> "As to 'friend,'" I answered him, "that's what you think." The three of us made our way past him.[26]

Here physical violence is faced down, as in *The Skating Rink* and *Amulet*. There is no neutralization of affect: hatred dominates. What the situation reveals is simply Eguren's faint heart and Ferri's hot head. It is a test of courage but not an epiphany. And rather than a culminating moment or a *telos*, the confrontation is a mere obstacle. The "huge specimen of a man" blocks the way, but Ferri and his companions eventually get past him and are able to continue toward the story's true epiphany, the revelation that "The Congress of the World," a kind of secret society to which they belong, has become the world itself (33).

At the beginning of the story, Ferri makes fun of a writer who strongly resembles the author, Borges: "The library's new director, I am told, is a literary man who dedicates himself to the study of ancient languages (as if modern ones were not sufficiently rudimentary) and to the demagogic exaltation of an imaginary Buenos Aires of knife fighters. I have never cared to meet him" (16). Here we can see a facet of Borges's humor that I did not mention at the beginning of this chapter: not Borges the hoaxer, the parodist, or the satirist, making fun of others, but an expert in subtle self-derision. Ferri's remark is a way of distancing a former self and its illusions, and is just one of many such rhetorical moves that Borges made from the mid 1960s on, as Edwin Williamson has shown in a persuasive chapter of his biography.[27]

If we take the whole of Borges into account, and not just the famous stories of the 1940s, the differences between his representations of violent conflict and those of Bolaño begin to lose their neat clarity, and it becomes more difficult to claim that the resemblances are merely superficial. Where fighting is concerned, Bolaño has more in common with the later Borges than with the author of *Fictions* and *The Aleph*.

HEROISM AND TIME

In the previous section we saw that Dorfman's critique of Borges cannot be simply transposed to the significantly dissimilar case of Bolaño. But that, of course, does not exempt Bolaño's brawls from critique. Of the nine scenes that I analyzed, two in particular, from *The Savage Detectives*, in both of which Arturo Belano initiates combat, raise ethical questions about the exercise of courage. When Belano challenges Echavarne to a duel, he is, as I explained in chapter 2, prey to a persecutory delusion, but he also exemplifies the more common case of a man looking for a fight. As Amélie Oksenberg Rorty points out, courage can be expansive, creating occasions for its own use, not just because courageous dispositions are often socially rewarded, but also because "the uncertainties and risks associated with traditional courage are often addictively intense and exciting."[28] Another factor contributing to the addictiveness of courage may be the euphoric effect of domination sometimes experienced by victors, even when their victory could not be described as courageous, like Espinoza and Pelletier's beating of the Pakistani taxi driver in *2666* (74). Expansive, addictive courage can lead to avoidable violence, as it almost does in Belano and Echavarne's duel, making the world more dangerous overall.

Belano has no just cause for challenging Echavarne. When he comes face to face with Alberto at the end of *The Savage Detectives*, however, Lupe's freedom is at stake, and perhaps her life as well. As Alberto walks past him, holding a gun, heading for the car where Lupe and García Madero are cowering, Belano grabs his gun arm and stabs him fatally in the chest (SD 572). Is this a justifiable homicide? To answer yes unreflectively would be not only to favor a form of vigilantism but also, I will argue, to misread the character of Arturo Belano. A comparison with Lalo Cura's shooting of the gunmen helps to clarify the case. Lalo responds to an imminent and deadly threat to his employer's wife and to himself: "The gunmen shoved the maids aside. One was carrying an Uzi submachine gun. . . . The other was carrying a pistol . . . and he looked like a professional. Just as the maids were pushed aside to clear the line of fire, Pedro Rengifo's wife felt someone tugging on her suit and pulling her to the ground" (395). Lalo may be working for a criminal, but he acts in legitimate defense. Belano's case is murkier. Alberto's intent is not entirely clear—"Maybe then Cesárea said that they were going to kill us. The policeman laughed and said no, they only wanted the little slut" (SD 571)—but it is reasonable to suppose that he is planning to kidnap Lupe. The imminence of the threat, however, and the necessity of the response are both disputable. Although kidnapping is an offense that may be legitimately defended against by using deadly force in many U.S. jurisdictions, Belano's killing of Alberto, unlike Lalo Cura's killing of the gunmen, is not presented as unequivocally justifiable, let alone lawful.[29]

This should not surprise us. Belano and Cura are very different creatures. Like all the native sons of the mythical town of Villaviciosa, Cura is a born killer, fearless and unflinching (LEE 70–71; SD 576; 2666 556), but it turns out that he is also pure of heart. Uncorrupted by his time in the employment of the drug boss Pedro Rengifo, he becomes an incorruptible policeman who spends his spare time studying criminology textbooks

(2666 437–438, 554) and remains immune to the climate of brutal misogyny in which he works. At one point his colleagues are discussing the case of a woman murdered and raped by her husband:

> How could Llanos rape her, one of them asked, if he was her husband? The others laughed, but Lalo Cura took the question seriously. He raped her because he forced her, because he made her do something she didn't want to do, he said. Otherwise, it wouldn't be rape. One of the young cops asked if he planned to go to law school. Do you want to be a lawyer, man? No, said Lalo Cura. (438)

He does, however, want to enforce the law and ensure that justice is done. Arturo Belano, by contrast, is an occasional outlaw, dealing drugs with Ulises Lima to finance the publication of the visceral realist magazine *Lee Harvey Oswald* and to raise money for his trip to Europe (SD 21, 103, 307). Justice is not a high priority in his life as a literary gang leader. Consider his taste for expelling members of the visceral realist group (SD 86, 89, 94–95, 159): even if this is done as a joke, as Ulises Lima says to García Madero, the members concerned are not aware of that (SD 101). Remembering the effects of Belano's scorn, Perla Aviles illustrates his cruel streak with macabre similes:

> he looked at me as if the flesh had been stripped from my face and it was just a skull, he looked at me with a smile and said: don't be corny, Perla. That was all. I turned pale and flinched, only managing to move a little bit away, and I tried to get up, but I couldn't, and all that time he sat there motionless, looking at me and smiling, as if all the skin, muscles, fat, and blood had slid off my face, leaving only the yellow or white bone. (SD 151)

The Savage Detectives does not construct Belano and Lima as positive heroes. They are mysterious and fascinating but also somewhat disquieting figures (Lima becomes a mugger with Heimito Künst in Vienna [SD 287–290]).

Belano is courageous, certainly, but the justice of his action at the end of the novel is open to doubt: perhaps he goes too far too quickly, spurred by a fear to which Lalo Cura seems immune. Bolaño is careful to show that Belano is putting on a brave face in the days leading up to the fight. When Juan García Madero expresses his anxiety about the inevitable showdown with Alberto, Belano plays it cool: "It's no big deal, said Belano, to put an end to the discussion. After all, there are twice as many of us as there are of them. . . . They're armed, said Lupe. So am I, said Belano" (580). Nevertheless he is visibly nervous (560), and when García Madero asks him for a cigarette, he notices Belano's hands shaking (561), unlike the hands of Colonel Guadalupe Sánchez, who, according to a story that Madero and his friends hear in Agua Prieta, smoked a cigar in front of the firing squad so calmly that the ash did not fall (551).

The qualifications noted in the previous paragraphs do not apply to Cesárea Tinajero, whose intervention in the climactic brawl is unequivocally just and unaccompanied by posturing. The threat to Lima's life is immediate: the policeman is aiming a gun at his head (572). Cesárea is unarmed and she steps in without hesitation to protect a man whom she has known for a matter of hours. She is the purest incarnation of the sacrificial ideal of heroism that Bolaño formulated in an interview:

> A hero is someone who, at a given moment, is capable of sublimating or scorning his or her life and giving it up without asking for anything in return. . . . One of the things that attracts me to people like this is their indolence, that kind of slow-motion luxury, and also their conception of time, which, in a way, is another kind of luxury, a conception of time marked by the absolute, in which a second can be equivalent to ten years, for example. (B 122)

The hero, for Bolaño, is indolent as well as decisive, passive as well as active, and seems to live in time more freely than others, as if he or she could stretch or dilate it, and so have more time in which to act, or not, as the case may be. An alternative description of this dilatory power is provided in a poem on the "strange gratuitous occupation" of writing poetry, where Bolaño suggests that the only way to overcome fear may be to "settle into" it "like one inhabiting slowness" (UU 13). This is what Cesárea Tinajero seems to be doing, even in the last moments of her life. While Belano's precipitate attack is recounted in the preterite, as a sequence of punctual actions ("he seized [*retuvo*] Alberto's gun arm. His other hand shot out [*salió*] of his pocket" [SD 572; LDS 604]), Césarea's movements are described in the imperfect tense, as ongoing processes: "I saw the huge bulk of Cesárea Tinajero, who could [*podía*] hardly run, but was running [*corría*], toppling [*derrumbándose*] onto them" (SD 572; LDS 604). Her capacity for unhesitating self-sacrifice is coupled with a "slow-motion luxury."

Hans Reiter, better known as Benno Von Archimboldi, exhibits a courageous indolence in *2666* when he infuriates three German paratroopers with whom he has done a black market deal by insulting their hero, General Udet, who killed himself because of slander spread by Göring. To Reiter, this is an abject reason for suicide, at a time when respectable reasons are not scarce:

> So this Udet killed himself because of Göring's salon intrigues? . . . So he didn't kill himself because of the death camps or the slaughter on the front lines or the cities in flames, but because Göring called him an incompetent. . . . Maybe Göring was right. . . . Maybe the man was essentially incompetent. (799)

The prudent thing to do at this point would be to take his pay and leave, but while the paratroopers remain "silent, as if contemplating whether to kill him or settle for beating him to a pulp" (799), he asks, instead, for another whiskey: "Archimboldi drank slowly, savoring the liquor" (799). Even in potentially violent situations like this one, passivity and patience may serve courage. Reiter's bravery consists not only in deciding to speak his mind but also, after having done so, in taking his time to leave. As Alain Badiou has written, "What demands courage is holding on, in a different duration from that imposed by the law of the world. The raw material of courage is time."[30]

The capacity to endure and inhabit a different duration is eminently exercised by Auxilio Lacouture in *The Savage Detectives* and *Amulet*. When the student demonstrations at the National Autonomous University of Mexico (UNAM) are repressed in September 1968 and the campus is occupied by the armed forces, Auxilio holds out in a bathroom for twelve days without food (A 114): "I knew that I had to resist. I sat down on the tiles of the women's bathroom and, before the last rays of sunlight faded, read three more of Pedro Garfías's poems, then shut the book and shut my eyes and said: Auxilio Lacouture, citizen of Uruguay, Latin American, poet and traveler, resist" (32). Poetry is crucial to this feat of resistance: Auxilio continues to read the book by Garfías that she happened to be reading in the bathroom when the soldiers came to evacuate the building, and she transcribes poems from memory onto toilet paper (173–174). Referring to her transcriptions, she says, "Because I wrote, I endured" (175), echoing Enrique Lihn's stirring declaration of faith, "Because I Wrote."[31] In her redoubt, where nothing is left to her but "motionless existence" and "complete passivity," Auxilio comes to signify, in another phrase from Walter Benjamin's commentary on "The Poet's Courage" and "Timidity," "the untouchable center of all relation."[32] In utter isolation, she connects scattered fragments of experience just as she knows and connects all the poets of Mexico City. Some of those fragments belong to a parallel past (106) or, paradoxically, to the future:

> I don't know why I remember that afternoon. That afternoon of 1971 or 1972. And the strangest thing is that I remember it prospectively, from 1968. From my watchtower, my bloody subway carriage, from my gigantic rainy day. From the women's bathroom on the fourth floor of the Faculty of Philosophy and Literature, the timeship from which I can observe the entire life and times of Auxilio Lacouture, such as they are. (56)

Indeed, the oracular Auxilio sees further still into the future, glimpsing a cemetery in the year 2666 in her "memory" of going to provide backup for Belano and San Epifanio in 1974 (79, 86). Auxilio's twelve days of resistance, hunger, and delirium enfold and concentrate a whole life devoted to poetry—not to her personal status in the poetry world, where she is widely regarded as a sad case, but to poetry itself. Whether venturing with her knife into the "royal bedchamber" of the King of the Rent Boys or defending the autonomy of the National Autonomous University of Mexico in her bathroom stall (30), she, like Arturo Belano and especially Cesárea Tinajero, embodies an ideal of the poet's courage that has romantic and specifically Hölderlinian roots: active and passive, decisive and enduring, at the service of relation rather than personal honor.

In this chapter I have examined situations in which the risk of violence emerges when individuals or small groups come into conflict. I have concentrated on how those emergencies test the courage of characters who respond to an unspoken ethical demand, often a demand to protect or rescue. In the next chapter I will turn to the question of why it is that such situations arise so often in Bolaño's fiction and broaden the focus to take in violence perpetrated by political and criminal organizations.

6

EVIL AGENCIES

I T WOULD BE hyperbolic to use the category of evil in discussing much contemporary fiction, but not in Bolaño's case. His fictional universe accommodates ethical extremes: it is not full of heroes and villains, but as I argued in the previous chapter, it is home to at least one exemplar of heroism (Cesárea Tinajero). In this chapter I will be substantiating the unsurprising claim that it is also inhabited and haunted by a small number of genuinely villainous characters, intent not just on dominating the lives of others but also on destroying them. If we adopt Claudia Card's definition of evils as "reasonably foreseeable intolerable harms produced by inexcusable wrongs,"[1] many of the occurrences narrated by Bolaño will fall into that category. But not all of them can be explained in the secular, rational terms of Card's analysis.

THE ACCOMPLICE

In Bolaño's fiction, four kinds of agents are principally involved in the perpetration of evils: the accomplice, the dictator, the sociopath, and the administrator. Three of these appear in *By Night in Chile*. The novel's narrator, Sebastián Urrutia Lacroix, manages to avert his gaze from the crimes of

Chile's military regime until he discovers that he has attended parties in a house whose basement was being used to torture political prisoners: "Why didn't anyone say anything at the time? The answer was simple: Because they were afraid. I was not afraid. I would have been able to speak out, but I didn't see anything. I didn't know until it was too late. Why go stirring up things that have gradually settled down over the years?" (122). The question is rhetorical, but can of course be answered, as it has been, for example, by Carlos Santiago Nino in *Radical Evil on Trial*, and we may doubt that Urrutia Lacroix, ruled as he clearly was by fear, would have spoken out had he known. He did not stumble into the torture chamber, unlike the "theorist of the new avant-garde scene" who promptly returned to the party and said not a word (120), but he did notice signs that might have alerted him and he failed to draw the uncomfortable conclusion: "I thought how odd it was that, with all the racket and the lights, the house was never visited by a military or police patrol" (116).

This is not an entirely fictional situation. María Canales and her husband Jimmy Thompson are based on Mariana Callejas and Michael Townley. Mariana Callejas really did hold parties in a house (at 4925 Vía Naranja in the Lo Curro district of Santiago) whose basement really was used by her husband, Michael Townley, for torture and interrogation. Townley, a U.S. citizen, was convicted of the murder, in Miami, of Allende's ex-ambassador to the United States, Orlando Letellier, and his secretary, Ronni Moffit (1976). He has also confessed to carrying out the assassination of the Chilean general Carlos Prats and his wife, Sofia Cuthbert, in Buenos Aires (1974), and to having organized the attempted assassination of the former vice-president and Christian Democrat leader Bernardo Leighton and his wife, Anita Fresno, in Rome (1975). He is currently living in the United States with a new identity under the terms of the federal witness protection program.[2]

When Townley was extradited to the United States in 1978 to be tried for the murders of Letellier and Moffit, a number of Chilean artists and intellectuals discovered "too late," like Urrutia Lacroix, the nature of their host's professional activities. This placed them in an awkward position, because a person who has associated with criminals and repeatedly spent time in close proximity to a crime scene is liable to be suspected of complicity, or at least of ignoring the signs that something was amiss. Such a suspicion is expressed in Pedro Lemebel's *crónica* "The Black Orchids of Mariana Callejas, or The DINA's Cultural Centre":

> It is possible to believe that many of those guests did not really know where they were, although almost everyone in the country was acquainted with the vulture flap of the unregistered cars. Those DINA taxis that picked up fares during the curfew. All of Chile knew and kept quiet: something had been said, somewhere, some gossip over a cocktail, some story told by a painter who had fallen foul of the censors. Everyone saw but preferred not to look, not to know, not to hear about those horrors leaked in the foreign press.[3]

Urrutia Lacroix is not legally complicit. He did not encourage or aid Jimmy Thompson in the commission of his crimes.[4] And there is no reason to doubt his claim that he "didn't know until it was too late," but it seems that he also preferred not to know. If his behavior, as Stefano Brugnolo and Laura Luche write, falls into what Primo Levi calls "the gray zone"—"the space which separates . . . the victims from the persecutors"[5]—it belongs to that zone's lighter fringe. In the section of *By Night in Chile* devoted to María Canales's salon, as in the descriptions of Urrutia Lacroix's short course on Marxism (to be discussed in the next section), Bolaño is not concerned to expose the priest's degree of complicity so much as the servile way he is attracted to the powerful and the socially distinguished.

The case of María Canales is altogether different. After the return of democracy and the revelation of Jimmy Thompson's crimes, Urrutia Lacroix visits her and asks: "Did you know about everything Jimmy was doing? Yes, Father. And do you repent? Like everyone else, Father" (125). When she tells Urrutia Lacroix that she is about to be evicted, we discover that she is resistant to the idea of starting her life anew under an assumed identity:

> I looked at her sadly and said perhaps that was for the best, she was still young, she wasn't involved in any criminal proceedings, she could start

over, with her children, somewhere else. And what about my literary career? she said with a defiant look. Use a *nom de plume*, a pseudonym, a nickname, for God's sake. She looked at me as if I had insulted her. (125)

To start over would be to abandon the symbolic capital that she has accumulated under the name "María Canales." When she refers to her career, she cannot be considering her chances of publishing again, which would surely be increased by the use of a pseudonym. She must be thinking of her public life as a writer, which pseudonymous publication would not allow her to pursue.

When Bolaño wrote *By Night in Chile*, Mariana Callejas, the model for María Canales, was not involved in any criminal proceedings. In 2003 she was charged with direct participation in the double homicide of General Carlos Prats and Sofía Cuthbert. Although she was initially found guilty, the Chilean Supreme Court overturned the verdict, and in 2010 Callejas received a suspended five-year sentence for complicity in the crime.[6] Like María Canales, Mariana Callejas is aggrieved by the failure of her literary career, which began under promising auspices: Enrique Lafourcade, whose fiction-writing workshop she attended, called her a "chemically pure writer."[7] She feels that she has suffered from discrimination, which might have two implications: either she believes that she acted patriotically in abetting the assassination of Prats and Cuthbert, or she holds that literary judgments should be in no way affected by the general ideas, political positions, or criminal record of the author concerned, a separation that Louis-Ferdinand Céline advocated simplistically when he wrote: "nothing is more vulgar than ideas . . . I'm not a man of ideas. I'm a man of style."[8] She may indeed be both an unrepentant accomplice and a radical aesthete.

The attitude of the fictional character Canales is similarly ambivalent. She offers to show Urrutia Lacroix the basement where the torture and the killings took place, then bursts out laughing uncontrollably (although Urrutia Lacroix admits that he may have imagined the laughter) (125–126). If she repents at all, it is "like everyone else" (125), which is to say, not very much. Aestheticism emerges in her parting remark to Urrutia Lacroix— "That's how literature is made" (126)—to which the priest attributes a general validity: "That is how literature is made in Chile, but not just in Chile, in Argentina and Mexico too, in Guatemala and Uruguay, in Spain and France and Germany, in green England and carefree Italy. That is how literature is made. Or at least what we call literature, to keep ourselves from falling into the rubbish dump" (127). The meaning of the initial "that" is not immediately clear, but Canales seems to be referring to her soirées: literature is made in an elevated space, above and separate from the base world of political conflict; it is made by turning a blind eye to cruelty and injustice. For someone who adheres to this aestheticism, the expression "a chemically pure writer" is pleonastic: all genuine writers, as writers, are pure of social concerns and political commitments. They are pure as Ernst Jünger was, according to Salvador Reyes, quoted by Urrutia Lacroix: "Don Salvador said that one of the purest men he had met in Europe was the German writer Ernst Jünger" (26).[9] Just as the wizened youth mouths an inaudible "no" in response to Urrutia Lacroix's statement of this position (128), so Bolaño's work is opposed to radical aestheticism. *By Night in Chile*, in particular, implies that absolute separations between the basement and the salon, between politics and culture, between the grossly material and the purely spiritual are condemned to fail eventually, unleashing a "storm of shit" (130).[10]

THE DICTATOR

Urrutia Lacroix's conscience is troubled not only by his association with the Canales-Thompson couple but also by a special assignment that he took on at the menacing behest of Mr. Etah and Mr. Raef: explaining the principles of Marxism to the members of Chile's military junta. The section of *By Night in Chile* devoted to Urrutia Lacroix's classes is Bolaño's satirical footnote to the Latin American dictator novel: Pinochet, Merino, Mendoza, and Leigh are portrayed as ignorant, undisciplined, and prurient. Their attendance is very irregular, and both Pinochet and Mendoza fall asleep (92). When the discussion begins to flag, they talk about Marta Harnecker, and are clearly more interested in her looks and sex life than her *Basic Elements of Historical Materialism*: "General Leigh said that the young woman in question was intimately acquainted with a pair of Cubans. The admiral confirmed this report. Is that possible, said General Pinochet. Can that be possible? Are we talking about a woman or a bitch?" (94).

In a conversation before one of the classes, Pinochet reveals his frustrated desire to be recognized as a writer. He belittles the intellectual merits of former presidents Allende, Frei, and Alessandri: "They didn't read, they didn't write. They pretended to be cultured, but not one of them was a reader or a writer. Maybe they knew something about the press, but they knew nothing about books. . . . How many books do you think I've written?" (99). For all Pinochet's insistence on his intellectual industry and breadth of view (he has read *White Dove* by Lafourcade: "very much a book for the younger generation, but . . . I enjoyed it" [100]), his political thought begins and ends with the belief that communism is evil. He has power over life and death, but cannot dictate his reputation, and longs for a superiority beyond his reach.

Urrutia Lacroix's portrait of Pinochet and the other members of the junta is unintentionally ironic: when in their presence, he is intimidated and enthralled by men whom the reader cannot help seeing as utterly banal and petty. The quasi-magical effects that power has on him are illustrated by his description of the garden in which he takes a moonlit stroll with Pinochet: "Let's take a walk, said the general. As if he were a magician, as soon as we stepped through the window frame and entered the enchanted gardens, lights came on, exquisitely scattered here and there among the plants" (93). But these effects are dependent on physical proximity. When Urrutia Lacroix's mentor, the critic Farewell, envious of his protégé's brief access to the summit of real as opposed to literary power, asks him what Pinochet is like ("A man like that, he must have something that makes him stand out" [97]), Urrutia Lacroix shrugs, not coyly, but because in hindsight and at a distance he really cannot think of a distinguishing characteristic. It is then that he remembers the general's tirade against Allende, Frei, and Alessandri, but what that memory reveals is a very common craving for recognition.

The Pinochet whom Urrutia Lacroix has encountered is distinguished only by what Mary Midgely, in a reflection on Hitler, calls "absolute concentration on the main chance":

> Influential psychopaths and related types, in fact, get their power not from originality, but from a perception of just what unacknowledged motives lie waiting to be exploited, and just what aspects of the world currently provide a suitable patch of darkness onto which they can be projected.... To gain great popular power, you must either be a genuinely creative genius, able to communicate new ideas very widely, or you must manage to give a great multitude permission for things which it already wants.... In order to find these things, and to handle skillfully the process of permitting the unthinkable, absolute concentration on the main chance is required, and this seems only possible to those without serious, positive aims of their own.[11]

Pinochet's aim in learning about Marxism is entirely negative: "to understand Chile's enemies, to find out how they think, to get an idea of how far they are prepared to go" (100). And when he adds, "I know how far I am prepared to go myself, I assure you" (100), he does not have a specific distance in mind: he will go as far as necessary.

In order to perceive unacknowledged motives in the population, an influential psychopath needs a certain sensitivity, and if Midgely is right, there may, disturbingly, be an element of truth in the dictator's typical claim to be the incarnation of a people's spirit. The poet, jurist, and veteran "Pinochet watcher" Armando Uribe Arce admits this in Freudian terms: "For us Pinochet is 'unheimlich' or 'uncanny'; he provokes a disturbing feeling of strangeness, but at the same time he corresponds to something deeply ours from way back; we perceive this darkly, with ambiguous distaste and pleasure. He is a mystery of the Chilean psyche."[12] It was the responsiveness of Pinochet's political unconscious, Uribe Arce conjectures, that enabled him to remain in power longer than any other government since independence (27). This kind of sensitivity distinguishes the dictator from the sociopaths often employed by repressive states to eliminate opposition and propagate fear.

THE SOCIOPATH

"Sociopaths," writes Adam Morton, "primarily lack certain emotions: sympathetic pleasure at another's happiness, dismay at another's sorrow, remorse at having brought trouble to another."[13] They are not always socially dysfunctional, because they may learn to interact with others in a way that mimics unfelt emotions, but they have difficulty understanding that many human acts are performed either for the sake of the interaction itself, or in order to benefit others (49–51).

In *By Night in Chile* a probable sociopath is marginally present. Urrutia Lacroix glimpses Jimmy Thompson at his wife's parties: "he was generally to be seen listening to one of the duller guests with infinite patience" (108). In *Distant Star* a clearly sociopathic character, Carlos Wieder, is central. Bolaño described the novel's project, in "Self Portrait," as "a very modest approximation of absolute evil" (BP 16). His choice of words is noteworthy: an approximation is only an approach, not a grasping or an analysis. Like the star of the book's title, Wieder remains distant. Women introduced to him after the coup in Chile are struck "by his coldness, by something remote in his gaze. As Pía Valle put it, there seemed to be another pair of eyes behind his eyes" (DS 77). The guests at his photographic exhibition have a similar impression: "his eyes somehow separate from his body, as if they were watching from another planet" (84). Like Cesárea Tinajero and Arturo Belano in *The Savage Detectives*, Wieder is a poet who disappears, but there is a sense in which he was already gone from the start or never fully there: as the narrator says, "in fact, he had *always* been an absent figure" (104).

Wieder remains an enigma for the other characters in *Distant Star*, and for the novel's readers. Yet we can say either that he is not consistently motivated by self-interest or that, like many sociopaths, he suffers from what Gary Watson calls a "prudential deficit," that is, an incapacity to further his own interests by means of rational planning.[14] Just when he has come to prominence as a multimedia performer under the protection and patronage of the new military regime, he sabotages his artistic career by transgressing limits of two kinds, set by standards of taste and by confidentiality requirements. From the point of view of the guests at his exhibition, who are all sympathetic to the regime, when Wieder shows photographs of women whom he has mutilated and killed, he not only oversteps the bounds of what is permissible in art but also violates the protocol of the armed forces. That is why Military Intelligence agents are called in and confiscate the photographs (DS 91). Wieder is not in the least surprised or perturbed by the possible consequences. After the agents have left, when everyone else is pale and exhausted, he stands "at the window, showing no sign of fatigue, with a glass of whiskey in his perfectly steady hand, contemplating the dark cityscape" (DS 93).

The scene of the exhibition shows that the "absolute evil" represented by Wieder is not simply what Kant called "radical" evil, which prioritizes self-interest over duty,[15] because it would clearly be in Wieder's interests not to risk arrest and expulsion from the air force. By exhibiting images of his victims, he is reducing his chances of perpetrating similar atrocities in the future. So what kind of evil are we faced with in this case? Because of Wieder's near-perfect opacity, it is difficult to say.[16] One might construe what he does in preparing the exhibition as "evil for evil's sake," which Kant took to be diabolical rather than human.[17] Claudia Card has argued that diabolical evil *is* to be found among humans and should be understood in a secular way not as a kind of evil done simply for its own sake, but as "doing one evil for the sake of another."[18] This conception applies to the creation of "gray zones," in which "some victims of evil become perpetrators of the very evils they suffer" (56), for example the prisoners in death camps who became *Kapos* and members of the *Sonderkommandos* charged with operating the gas chambers.[19] For Card, using prisoners in this way qualifies as diabolically evil because one intolerable harm is used to produce another: "Gray zones destroyed or undermined capacities for moral agency in many of their victims (a morally inexcusable intolerable harm) as a means toward the end of exterminating the Jewish people (another morally inexcusable intolerable harm)."[20]

Wieder's artwork might be understood as using one harm to produce another: he uses real murder and torture to horrify and nauseate the viewers of the photographs (Tatiana von Beck Iraola vomits in the passage before she can reach the bathroom; a cadet starts crying and swearing and has to be dragged from the room [DS 87–88]). In this case, however, the means are far more atrocious than the end. What Wieder has done to his victims is clearly intolerable and inexcusable and therefore qualifies as evil on Card's terms, but what he does to the viewers is a lesser harm, and its excusability depends on intentions and longer-term effects. Imagine that the photographs had been found and exhibited by an artist or human rights activist opposed to the regime: in such a case, the potential harms of horror and nausea may well be excusable, given the intention to make the viewers aware of an atrocity and so to contribute to the prevention of similar occurrences in the future. Now there is nothing in *Distant Star* to suggest that Wieder has any such intention, or that his exhibition is an act of repentance; on the contrary, throughout the evening he seems particularly pleased with himself.[21] But the nature of his motivation remains mysterious.

Discussing serial-killer fiction, Adam Morton writes: "Characters have to make some kind of sense, and the danger is that the criminal will turn out to be a force of nature rather than a motivated character."[22] This is a danger that Bolaño courts deliberately. Wieder is repeatedly associated with the destructive forces of nature. He is said to have looked "as if he had just come through a storm" (34). The critic Ibacache recalls that his voice on the other end of the telephone "sounded like wind and rain" (106). According to an officer who accompanied him on several missions in Santiago, Wieder "believed that nature intervenes actively in history, shaping it, buffeting our lives" (110). And for Jules Defoe, one of Wieder's pseudonyms, literature is "a hurricane, seen far off in an immensity of open space" (135). These associations implicitly naturalize Wieder's evil by suggesting that it is comparable to a natural disaster like a hurricane or an earthquake. Such disasters can cause intolerable harm, but outside a theist framework it makes no sense to ask if they are excusable or inexcusable wrongs, and we cannot (yet) stop them happening, only protect ourselves as best we can. Perhaps Wieder is simply a freak event in human life: unusual but inevitable and natural. Perhaps he exemplifies the possibility of random evil, envisaged by Romero when he reappears in *The Savage Detectives*:

the heart of the matter is knowing whether evil (or sin or crime or whatever you want to call it) is random or purposeful [*casual o causal*]. If it's purposeful, we can fight it, it's hard to defeat, but we have a chance, like two boxers in the same weight class, more or less. If it's random, on the other hand, we're fucked, and we'll just have to hope that God, if He exists, has mercy on us. (SD 373; LDS 397)

Casual and *causal*, the Spanish words translated by "random" and "purposeful," are anagrams of each other, and their similarity here suggests the difficulty of knowing which one indicates the truth.

Even if Wieder is an incarnation of random evil, even if his killings are "explosions of chance," as Bolaño's paradigmatic paranoid reader, Graham Greenwood, might say, it is one thing to explain his behavior in this way and another to justify it.[23] Wieder's supporters use naturalizing associations in attempting to exonerate their hero, but he could be seen both as a thoroughly natural freak of nature and as thoroughly evil. The private detective Romero, for whom Wieder is one more target, may indeed see him in that way, but for the narrator, Bibiano O'Ryan, and Marta Posadas, Wieder has a sinister, supernatural aura, and although I have been considering him, so far, as a realistic character, *Distant Star* is not a strictly realist novel. As we saw in chapter 3, it has strong affinities with horror cinema and fiction. Bibiano compares Ruiz-Tagle's apartment to that of Roman and Minnie Castavet in *Rosemary's Baby* (DS 7). When Ruiz-Tagle reappears as the aviator-poet Carlos Wieder, he moves from remembered daily life into a realm of mystery and fantastic speculation. At certain moments Wieder seems to have stepped out of a war film: his die-hard fans, for example, "imagine him wearing a black greatcoat and a monocle, smoking a long pipe made from an elephant's tusk" (94, see also 82). When the narrator identifies him at the end of the novel, he has aged prematurely, seems to be going through a rough patch, and doesn't look like an infamous killer (145), but the encounter is disturbing enough to produce a hallucination that incorporates the figure of the storm employed by Wieder's admirers: "the letters on the pages I was turning . . . were no longer beetles but eyes, the eyes of Bruno Schulz, opening and closing . . . in the midst of total darkness. No, not total, in the midst of a milky darkness, like the inside of a storm cloud" (144).

The disturbance is moral as well as sensory and emotional:

> He seemed *adult*. But he wasn't adult, I knew that straight away. He
> seemed self-possessed. And in his own way, on his own terms, whatever
> they were, he was more self-possessed than the rest of us in that sleepy
> bar, or most of the people walking by the beach or invisibly at work, get-
> ting ready for the imminent tourist season. (145)

He is not more self-possessed than *all* the people in the vicinity of that
bar, because somewhere outside is Romero, in whom he will soon meet his
match. Nevertheless, the narrator is impressed. Wieder's sociopathic indifference to others immunizes him against attraction to institutional power
and prestige, which is a genuine vice in Bolaño's fiction, as I will argue in
chapter 7. This gives him the aura of the man who walks alone and suffices
to create a passing impression of adulthood. But he is not truly adult, for the
terms of his self-possession are purely egotistical. He cares for no one and
seems to enjoy causing the most grievous harm.

Having confirmed his target's identity, Romero leaves the narrator in a park,
goes to Wieder's apartment, and presumably kills him there. Presumably, because
Romero gives no account of what actually happened. When he returns with a
bulging folder under his arm, breathing easily, all he will say is that it was "difficult . . . like these things always are" (DS 148). The narrator is troubled by his collaboration in what Jean Franco has rightly called an act of "private vengeance":[24]

> Nothing like this has ever happened to me, I confessed. That's not true,
> said Romero very gently. Worse things have happened to us, think about
> it. You could be right, I admitted, but this really has been a dreadful busi-
> ness [*un asunto espantoso*]. Dreadful, repeated Romero, as if he were savor-
> ing the word. Then he laughed quietly, grinning like a rabbit, and said,
> Well, what else could it have been? I wasn't in a laughing mood, but I
> laughed all the same. (DS 149; ED 157)

He feels a blend of disquiet and relief. On a personal level, the danger of acting as Romero has presumably done is that there are no longer

institutional checks against being corrupted by criminality or indeed by something darker. And Bolaño does not exclude the possibility that this has happened to some degree. Romero's laugh and rabbitlike grin, and his savoring repetition of the word "dreadful" [*espantoso*], as if to bring out the "dread" [*espanto*], are absent from the shorter version of the story in *Nazi Literature in the Americas* (NLA 204), and these details have been added, I think, to stop the reader relaxing, to provoke an uncomfortable twinge at the end. This is an attenuated version of the classic horror-film reversal, in which a character supposedly saved from zombies or vampires turns out to have been bitten and rounds on his or her savior.

The mention of Romero's rabbitlike grin connects with an earlier animalizing description: "he had a smile like a weasel or a field mouse" (118). Like many Chilean emigrants, he is hoping to return to his country, and he has a business plan, which is to become a funeral director: "the profit on the coffins can be as much as three hundred percent," he remarks (139). Romero is on the right side, as the narrator says of Marta Posadas (14), but there is something uncanny about him. And it cannot be coincidental that the Chilean detective shares his surname with George Romero, director of *Night of the Living Dead.* The ending of *Distant Star* is haunted by the faint suggestion that the "absolute evil" embodied by Wieder may not be simply an isolated freak of nature, an extreme form of sociopathy, but a metaphysical disease that has already spread by contagion, a kind of evil that is diabolical in the archaic sense of the word, not in the technical, secular sense defined by Claudia Card.

THE ADMINISTRATOR

In *2666*, Bolaño portrays a fourth kind of person involved in the perpetration of evils: the administrator or bureaucrat. In a prison camp at the end of the Second World War, Hans Reiter, later known as Benno Von Archimboldi, hears the confession of a troubled fellow prisoner, Leo Sammer, who, before his arrest, had been in charge of supplying workers to the Reich's

factories in Poland. One day a train carrying five hundred Jewish prisoners from Greece and destined for Auschwitz arrived by mistake in the city
where Sammer was posted. He tried unsuccessfully to send the prisoners
to work in factories, then to send them on to the extermination camp at
Chelmno, before being instructed by the Office of Jewish Affairs in Warsaw
to "dispose of them" (759).

Sammer might be seen as an incarnation of the "sheer thoughtlessness"
that characterized Adolf Eichmann according to Hannah Arendt,[25] but
given the ambiguity of Arendt's formulation, it is important to specify the
sense in which he can be said to be thoughtless. For Arendt, Eichmann
had an "almost total inability ever to look at anything from the other fellow's point of view" (48), but as Isabelle Delpla has pointed out, had he been
unable to understand and take into account other points of view, he would
not have been able to deceive his interlocutors, as he did on many occasions,
nor would he have been such a successful administrator and negotiator.[26]
The deficiency in his case was not cognitive but affective: he was insensitive
to the suffering of others. If by "thoughtless" we mean lacking in empathy, the adjective applies to both Eichmann and Sammer. But Arendt also
meant that Eichmann was incapable of thinking for himself, that he could
only implement policies and carry out orders coming down from his superiors, and this is a more controversial claim.[27] Sammer, as we shall see, is not
really thoughtless in this way.

Neither in the case of the historical person Eichmann nor in that of the
fictional character Sammer was the lack of empathy absolute from the very
start. In 1941 Eichmann sent a group of German Jews to the ghetto in Lodz
rather than to Russian territory, where he knew that they would have been
shot immediately. Arendt comments: "yes, he had a conscience, and his conscience functioned in the expected way for about four weeks, whereupon
it began to function the other way around."[28] Similarly, Sammer provides
minimal food for the prisoners in his charge: "I told one of my employees
to go to the bakery and buy all the bread available to distribute to the Jews.
Have them charge it to me" (753). On visiting the tannery that is being used
as a detention center, he tells his secretary to bring blankets for the guards
and the prisoners (758). When he sees some Polish boys speaking to a group

of Jews who have been put to work sweeping the streets, he calls a policeman and says: "If any of those little bastards insults my workers, shoot him" (755).

This last order betrays a brutal insensitivity that is evident even before Sammer begins to "dispose of" the Jews, although he claims that it isn't in his nature to be tough (761). He makes no allowance for the serious illness of the mayor, Mr. Tippelkirsch. When Tippelkirsch explains his lateness for a meeting by saying that he is running a temperature of 104 degrees, Sammer replies, "Let's not exaggerate" (756). During the meeting Tippelkirsch faints (757), and shortly after the end of the war he dies of pneumonia (767). Even when Sammer is providing food and blankets for the Jewish prisoners, he has no real sense of what they have already undergone. He is surprised by the deaths among them: "Two dead Jews? I repeated, dazed. But they all got off the train on their own two feet!" (755). Although briefly dazed, he is impatient to return to "the main business of the day": "Several factories in the Reich wanted at least two thousand workers and I had missives from the General Government requesting available labor. I made a few phone calls: I said I had five hundred Jews available, but they wanted Poles or Italian prisoners of war" (753). Aware of the practical absurdity of this situation—"Italian prisoners of war? I'd never seen an Italian prisoner of war!" (753)—Sammer finds himself trapped in a bureaucratic dead end when no authority will take responsibility for the misdirected prisoners. But a nonbureaucratic solution is suggested by the mayor:

"And what if, as a temporary measure, we lent a pair of Jews to each peasant in the region, wouldn't that be a good idea?" asked Mr. Tippelkirsch. "At least until we decide what to do with them."

I looked him in the eye and lowered my voice:

"That's against the law and you know it," I said.

"Yes," he said, "I know it, you know it, but our situation is grim and we could use the help. I don't think the peasants will complain."

"No, absolutely unthinkable," I said. (756)

In the end, Sammer does adopt this "illegal," "unthinkable" measure, allowing some prisoners to do farm work (766), but only after more than three hundred of them have been killed on his orders.

Sammer is neither totally impervious to the suffering of others nor totally incapable of breaking a rule (as Eichmann claimed to be, invoking Kant),[29] but his compassion is soon extinguished and his disobedience comes too late. Once he has decided to have the prisoners executed, he reserves all his compassion for the executioners. He does not blame them for getting drunk; he understands their weariness (2666 762–763). He engages in a mental maneuver perfected by Himmler and analyzed by Hannah Arendt. The trick consists of directing the spontaneous pity normally felt in the presence of physical suffering toward the self, "so that instead of saying: What horrible things I did to people! the murderers would be able to say: What horrible things I had to watch in the pursuance of my duties, how heavily the task weighed upon my shoulders!"[30]

Sammer organizes a squad of policemen and volunteers to shoot and bury groups of prisoners in the forest. At first there are adult volunteers— policemen and local farmers—but soon their ranks thin, and, judging their progress unsatisfactory, Sammer recruits and trains alcoholic Polish boys, promising them wine and food. Although the boys "put their hearts into it" at the start, they too slow down in their killing, as they debilitate themselves with drink and begin to fall ill (764–765). Finally, running out of manpower and burial places, Sammer simply gives up: "The work was too much for us. Man wasn't made to bear some tasks for very long" (765–766). For him, as for Major Wilhelm Trapp, commander of Reserve Police Battalion 101, "the problem," as Christopher R. Browning writes, "was not the ethically and politically grounded opposition of a few but the broad demoralization shared both by those who shot to the end and those who had not been able to continue. It was above all a reaction to the sheer horror of the killing process itself."[31]

Sammer does not witness the actual killings, but he chooses the site (761) and visits it when one of his secretaries tells him that there is no more room for bodies (764). He is not merely a desk criminal, nor is he merely following an order when he organizes the shooting. What the "distinctly adolescent voice" from the Office of Jewish Affairs says to him is this: "I've talked to my superiors and we're in agreement that the easiest and best thing would be for you to dispose of them [*que usted mismo se deshaga de ellos*]" (2666 759; 2666s 948). That the sense of this agreement is not self-evidently clear is shown by what Sammer goes on to say: "That night I couldn't sleep. I understood that what they were asking me to do was to eliminate the Greek Jews myself and at my own risk" (759). An understanding is required to transform the ambiguous "dispose of" (*deshacerse de* can also be translated as "to get rid of" or "to part with") into "eliminate." "The easiest and best thing" implies a contrast between options, but there too is an ambiguity. Is the contrast between eliminating the Jews and keeping them in detention or between Sammer himself (*usted mismo*) taking charge of the problem and his handing it over to another authority? I am not claiming that Sammer contravenes the spirit of the order, only that its enunciation leaves a margin for interpretation. As David Cesarani and Isabelle Delpla have argued, the Nazi bureaucracy, with its internal conflicts among competing agencies, rarely addressed commands to high-level officials that were unequivocal and explicit enough to be carried out with a thoughtless obedience.[32]

At the end of his confession, Sammer says: "Anyone else in my place . . . would have killed all the Jews with his own hands" (767), which is patently false: the mayor, for example, would have sent them to work on farms, and few of the initial volunteers for the firing squads were able to withstand the horror for long. Shortly after unburdening himself, Sammer is found strangled in the prison camp (767). Reiter later tells his lover, Ingeborg, that he was the killer (775). Perhaps the bureaucrat's belief that his guilt was mitigated by physical distance from the crimes that he organized provoked Reiter into getting his own hands dirty. Or perhaps the killing was a way to escape from "the swamps of nauseating meaninglessness" into which, according to Isabelle Delpla (who speaks from personal experience), we are led by the self-justifications of war criminals.[33] These are mere speculations, however, since Bolaño deliberately leaves Reiter's motivation in this instance, as in many others, completely blank.

THE SECRET OF EVIL

In Bolaño's fiction, the accomplice, the dictator, the sociopath, and the administrator are distinct types and are treated in contrasting ways. The dictator Pinochet and the sociopath Wieder are portrayed, in satirical and fantastic modes respectively, through the eyes of other characters, while the administrator Sammer and the accomplices Urrutia Lacroix and María Canales speak for themselves and are steadily condemned by their attempts at self-justification. Pinochet remains convinced that he has done his patriotic duty and Canales seems to believe that she is a victim of bad luck, while Urrutia Lacroix, whose complicity is relatively slight, must face a "storm of shit" when his system of self-deception fails (BNC 130). Wieder is (presumably) killed by a private detective, and Sammer is similarly executed outside the law.

As well as differentiating kinds of agents who contribute to the perpetration of evils, Bolaño is concerned to show how they can enter into "symbiotic" relationships, producing relatively stable configurations of power that sponsor and systematize violent crime.[34] In *By Night in Chile*, Pinochet and the junta rely on the willing brutality of men like Jimmy Thompson, as well as the willful ignorance and complicity of Urrutia Lacroix and his kind. In *2666*, the local implementation of the final solution dictated by Hitler depends on Sammer's administrative zeal and respect for "the law," but also on his active interpretation of instructions. By exposing these interrelations, and showing how normal human desires and fears can lead people to participate in atrocities, Bolaño's fiction anatomizes evil and advances toward a post-theological understanding of its causes. But this movement is limited by two factors, one diegetic and the other discursive. The diegetic factor, internal to Bolaño's fictional universe, is the urgency of preventing further evils. As Romero says to the narrator in *Distant Star* before going to confront Wieder: "as to whether he'll do any more harm, all I can say is: we don't know; we can't know; you're not God and nor am I; we're only doing what we can, that's all" (DS 147). It is not a priority for Romero to discover whether the "absolute evil" that Wieder embodies is natural or supernatural, random or purposeful. He has a task to complete, for which he has been handsomely paid. Fulfilling his contract ensures that Wieder will do no more harm, but also that his motivations will remain mysterious.

The second factor that limits the understanding of evil is discursive: getting to the bottom of it would diminish the unresolved suspense that is a hallmark of Bolaño's storytelling and would work against his method of using gaps in earlier texts to stimulate ongoing invention. This factor operates in *2666*, where the perpetrators of the serial murders in Santa Teresa are systematically occulted. Before discussing the occultation as a writerly strategy, however, I would like to consider briefly two other ways of understanding it, neither of which seems to me entirely adequate.

First, the decision not to make the serial killers characters in the novel might be seen as contributing to its realism. Most of the real crimes that Bolaño used as models, committed in and around Ciudad Juárez from 1995 to 1998, remain unsolved: only the people who are implicated know for certain who the culprits are and how they operated, although the courageous investigative journalism of Sergio González Rodríguez, Diana Washington Valdez, and others points to a durable system of complicity and mutual protection among drug traffickers, state and federal police officers, and politicians. *2666*, however, is not a documentary novel, and in "The Part About the Crimes" Bolaño freely imagines the lives of the victims, and of police officers and journalists investigating the killings, so why did he not complete the picture?

It might be suggested, secondly, that the decision not to represent the commission of the serial murders is a principled refusal. Perhaps, like J. M. Coetzee's fictional novelist Elizabeth Costello, Bolaño felt that some places should remain forbidden to fiction because they are like bottles inhabited by genies: "When the storyteller opens the bottle, the genie is released into the world, and it costs all hell to get him back in again."[35] The *narcorranchos* seen in the distance near the end of "The Part About the Crimes" (627–628) may be such places. There are limits to the horror of *2666*: what the serial killers do to the women—the process of torture and rape—is not narrated, although the results are abundantly described, with forensic precision and realistic repetitiveness (see appendix). And Bolaño's self-imposed limits allow for a formidable range of horrors. When the murders of women have been solved—usually in cases of domestic violence—an account is sometimes given of the crime itself (418–419, 511–512, 515). And the Santa Teresa jail, where we are shown the rape and torture of men, is not a forbidden place (485, 487, 521–522). Reading "The Part About the Crimes," one may feel like the aging Elizabeth Costello, appalled and gripped by Paul West's *The Very Rich Hours of Count von Stauffenberg*: "*Let me not look. . . . Do not make me go through with it!*" (179). But as Costello ruefully admits, she once had no qualms about "rubbing people's faces" in horror (179). Bolaño is more like the younger Costello, and it is not self-evident that he limits his representation of evils in *2666* for purely ethical reasons, especially since the occultation of the serial killers coheres with a discursive strategy that he used extensively in other works: opening information gaps and holding them open.

At the end of "The Part About Fate," Oscar Fate remembers mysterious words: "No one pays attention to these killings, but the secret of the world is hidden in them. Did Guadalupe Roncal say that, or was it Rosa? . . . The suspected killer said it, thought Fate. The giant fucking albino who appeared along with the black cloud" (*2666* 348). It is significant that Fate is provisionally unsure about the source of these words: the three characters whom he mentions represent three distinct perspectives, which nevertheless converge. Guadalupe Roncal is a journalist investigating the crimes; Rosa Amalfitano is a young woman at risk, a potential victim; and the "albino giant" Klaus Haas is a suspect. If the words might have been spoken by any one of these three characters, they would seem to have the weight of a shared opinion, but the actual speaker, although he may well have been wrongly imprisoned, is hardly a reliable source of information. And what could the words mean? If the secret of the world is hidden in the crimes, would it be revealed by judging the criminals in courts of law? Would such trials reveal a worldwide criminal conspiracy? Or do the crimes conceal a secret facet of human nature that might emerge in judicial or psychological examination of the criminals, as the "banality of evil" was disclosed by Eichmann's self-defense, according to Hannah Arendt?[36] Perhaps what Haas means is that the crimes constitute a message emitted by some evil power operating *through* the perpetrators. If this third hypothesis were founded, it would not be enough to try or examine the criminals; one would also have to be able to read the crimes, in the paranoid manner recommended by Graham Greenwood (DS 102), or at least allegorically, as José Ramón Ruisánchez suggests.[37] In any case, Klaus Haas seems to hold out as little hope for this world as the author of the book of Revelation, who saw seven angels pouring out the vials of the wrath of God upon the earth and a beast with two horns whose number was 666 (13:18).

It would be relatively simple to dismiss Haas's words as delusional if not for a pair of details and a paratextual note whose effect is to keep the suspicion of something supernatural alive. At the craft market in Santa Teresa, Pelletier buys a clay figurine from a vendor with a curious abnormality: "The man was blond and two little devil horns sprouted from his forehead" (2666 125). Later, Oscar Fate's attention is caught by a foosball table: "the strangest thing, though, is that the players on the red team had tiny horns on their foreheads" (305). These man-made protuberances are no more than strange in themselves, but they echo the vendor's horns, mentioned in passing, and make it slightly more difficult for the attentive (or paranoid) reader to interpret the feature noticed by Pelletier as a natural deformation of the skull.

In his "Note to the First Edition," Ignacio Echevarría writes: "In one of his many notes for 2666, Bolaño indicates the existence in the work of a 'hidden center [centro oculto],' concealed beneath what might be considered the novel's 'physical center.' There is reason to think that this physical center is the city of Santa Teresa" (2666 896–897; 2666s 1123). This is particularly tantalizing. What lies at the hidden center? Is the "secret of the world" somehow encrypted there? These are questions that the novel and its paratexts, including the author's recently published sketches of its "tubular structure,"[38] raise, but do no more than raise. To answer them would be to shut down a motor of writerly invention and dry up a source of readerly curiosity.

A posthumous fragment entitled "The Secret of Evil" makes this especially clear (SE 11–13). The title promises the key to the unsolved mysteries of 2666. In the text, a North American journalist in Paris receives a phone call from a stranger who claims to have important information to communicate. They arrange a rendezvous on a bridge. The mysterious informant has the look of someone who has spent a long time in a prison or a mental hospital. Before he delivers his information, the text breaks off—unsurprisingly, since it was announced in the second sentence that the story was unfinished, "because this kind of story doesn't have an end" (SE 11).

"Story" is ambivalent here. "This kind of story" could mean both this kind of event sequence or this kind of text. Read in the first way, the sentence would suggest that revealing and therefore dispelling the secret of evil is a task that can never be completed. This is Paul Ricoeur's position when he speaks of "the shadowy, never completely demythologized background that makes evil a unique enigma."[39] For some thinkers, even attempting to overcome this limit to our understanding would be an error. Considering Jean Améry's account of the intellectual at Auschwitz, Susan Neiman writes: "where events call the value of reason itself into question, we should be wary of the urge to comprehension. Even Kant found the idea of theodicy to be noxious: *solving* the problem of evil would be a moral mistake."[40] Bolaño may have agreed, but he was above all an imaginative writer, and it is more persuasive to read "this kind of story doesn't have an end" not as a philosophical thesis but as a metafictional comment: narratives of this kind stop without concluding. "This kind of story," as we saw in chapters 2 and 3, is the kind that Bolaño prefers, partly because it leaves a gap that another story may come to fill in part.

Twentieth-century atrocities renewed the urgency of attempts under way since the Enlightenment to extract the problem of evil from the theological context in which it had been traditionally discussed and to solve it naturalistically, but they also produced new obstacles to this project, because evil seemed to assume new forms, under Nazism in particular. Up to a point, Bolaño's fiction participates in the drive to understand: it anatomizes evil, distinguishing its agents and showing how they interact. But there is a central gap in the anatomy, corresponding to the perpetrators of the serial killings in Santa Teresa. This is perhaps a merciful omission, and it can be argued that such characters and their actions are both properly obscene, to be kept "off stage," and improper objects of rational inquiry. But the gap is narratively effective as well: it promises a revelation that can be indefinitely deferred and it marks out a space for future invention. Like the other gaps in Bolaño's work, discussed in chapter 2, this one plays a part in sustaining the operation of his fiction-making system. And here a fundamental difference appears between fictional responses to atrocity and the work of investigative journalists and political activists. Journalism and activism strive in principle for complete transparency in the hope that justice may finally be done. While fiction is by no means politically or morally inert, and may in some cases bring to light formerly hidden aspects of a real situation, the deployment of what Stephen Greenblatt, in a reading of *Hamlet*, has called "strategic opacity" is also one of its most powerful and characteristic resources.[41] As Bolaño and the narrator agree in Oswaldo Zavala's *Siembra de nubes* (*A Scattering of Clouds*), a story needs to know how to construct and keep a secret.[42]

7

A SENSE OF WHAT MATTERS

COMPLEXITY OF CHARACTER
AND MINIMALIST ETHICS

ONE OF THE reasons Bolaño's fiction matters to so many readers is that it is underpinned by a strong, distinctive, and relatively simple sense of what matters in life. His characters live in ethically and politically oriented worlds. This does not go without saying. Since Western literatures began strongly to affirm and defend their autonomy with respect to political and religious institutions in the mid-nineteenth century, many critics and writers have campaigned to purge literature of didacticism, and some have gone further and argued that literature should be ethically and politically neutral. It is worth distinguishing these two objectives, because only the first is really attainable.[1] Whether or not it is really desirable depends on the way "didacticism" is defined. If the term is used very broadly to cover all authorial generalization and any kind of invitation to judge the actions of fictional characters, Bolaño is a didactic writer, for he does occasionally generalize from an authorial point of view (see, for example, the beginnings of "Enrique Martín" and "Mauricio ['The Eye'] Silva" [LEE 26, 106]), and his fiction often prompts us in more or less subtle ways to identify some acts as good and others as bad, some characters as admirable and others as reprehensible. How the prompting is effected and the nature of the good and the bad in Bolaño's fictional universe are the subjects of this chapter.

Sometimes the tone of the narration guides our responses. While certain characters can be taken seriously, satire ensures that others cannot. Satire, however, is applied selectively to the reprehensible. It is not reserved for the relatively harmless, like the accomplice Urrutia Lacroix, but extended also to the dictator Pinochet and the rest of the Chilean junta. The administrator Sammer and the sociopath Wieder, by contrast, are treated seriously. This difference in treatment is related to the fictional status of the characters involved. Wieder and Sammer, who are invented, execute or organize massacres of innocents. To hold them up to ridicule would be, indirectly, to make light of their crimes and so to reduce the ethical depth of *Distant Star* and *2666*. Pinochet, Merino, Mendoza, and Leigh were real people ultimately responsible for crimes whose seriousness can hardly be cast into doubt by satirical portraits in fiction. In *By Night in Chile* the satire works against a background of widely known facts, and denunciation can be taken as read.

As we saw in chapters 5 and 6, the ethical spectrum of Bolaño's fiction is very broad indeed. Cesárea Tinajero's heroic intervention in the fight with Alberto and the policeman stands at one end, Carlos Wieder's evil "performances" at the other. These characters, who are polar opposites in ethical terms, representing sacrificial altruism and sadistic egotism, are similar in other ways: both are avant-garde poets, both disappear for years before being tracked down by amateur or professional detectives, and both are aimless Episodics. This need not be disturbing; all it shows is that the oppositions between avant-garde and traditional aesthetics, low and high public profiles, and Episodic and Diachronic temperaments do not map neatly onto the opposition between good and evil. A further trait these characters share is that they remain remote and sketchy, partly because they disappear and are therefore largely absent from the narratives structured by the quests to find them, but also because they stand for an ideal and its opposite, and this almost allegorical function imposes a certain abstraction.

Bolaño's fictional universe, then, has clearly marked ethical poles, but it is not Manichaean in that term's common, pejorative sense. The characters do not divide neatly into the good and the bad, and most are a long way from the extremes. Bolaño's major characters combine more and less admirable traits that are sequentially revealed, so our global impressions of them are subject to revision. As E. M. Forster showed, "round" characters are necessarily dynamic and surprising.[2] The first manifestation of a trait, however, may be interpreted as a change in character, rather than the revelation of an aspect that has not been salient hitherto. This is how Jean Franco reads the behavior of Oscar Fate and Rosa Amalfitano: "In *2666*, 'good' people like Rosa Amalfitano and Fate can easily slip over the edge. No one is safe."[3] Franco sees the world of the novel as one in which there are no robust character traits, that is, traits that are both stable and consistent across a broad and diverse range of situations.[4] The real world is much more like that than we are generally willing to believe, according to Gilbert Harman and John Doris, who base their arguments on empirical research in social psychology, including Milgram's famous obedience experiments and Zimbardo's prison experiment.[5] In such a world, people can only be provisionally "good" because under certain circumstances they are bound to slip over the edge into "badness."

But in what sense are Rosa and Fate "good"? And how do they slip over the edge? Both are broadly sympathetic characters, partly because both have recently lost their mothers and are outsiders in Santa Teresa. Fate is a somewhat weary but still idealistic African American journalist from New York. Personal ambition does not seem to enter into his reasons for wanting to write about the killings (2666 294). Rosa is a seventeen-year-old college student from Barcelona who wants to have a good time. When Franco writes of Rosa and Fate slipping over the edge, she must be referring to what happens in the course of their last night in Santa Teresa. Since I will be disagreeing with her interpretation of those events, I offer a summary account of them in the following paragraph.

At the fight between Count Pickett and Merolino Fernández, which Fate has been sent to cover, he is introduced to Rosa Amalfitano by a local journalist, Chucho Flores. Fate goes to dinner with a group of Chucho and Rosa's friends, two of whom he has already met: Charly Cruz and Rosa Méndez. The sixth member of the party is a man called Juan Corona. After dinner they visit various clubs. At the fourth place, Fate finds Rosa in a room with Chucho and a man wearing a checkered shirt. Chucho says, "We're doing some business here." Rosa is sitting in an armchair, with her legs crossed, smoking. She seems to be high (317). At some point, the group is joined by a mysterious man with a mustache who smiles and says nothing. They all end up at Charly Cruz's house, where Charly shows Fate a pornographic film supposedly made by Robert Rodríguez. Then Fate looks for Rosa and, with a sense of déjà vu, finds her in a room with Juan Corona and Chucho Flores, who have been arguing. She is sitting in an armchair, with her legs crossed, snorting cocaine (323). Fate takes Rosa by the hand and says, "Let's go."

> As they left the room he felt Corona grab his arm and saw him lift his free
> hand, which seemed to be holding a blunt instrument. He turned around
> and dealt Corona an uppercut to the chin, in the style of Count Pickett.
> Like Merolino Fernández earlier, Corona dropped to the floor without a
> sound. Only then did Fate realize Corona was holding a gun. (324)

Fate takes the gun and beats a hasty retreat with Rosa and Chucho Flores. Having dropped Chucho off at a bus stop, thrown the gun away, and driven around Santa Teresa for a while, he returns to his motel with Rosa. While she is sleeping, the clerk at reception warns him that the police (or someone pretending to be the police) called to ask if he was there. Fate then drives Rosa home, where she tells her father, Oscar Amalfitano, what has happened. Amalfitano asks Fate to take Rosa across the border and put her on a plane to Barcelona, which he agrees to do, but first he keeps a promise to accompany his Mexican colleague Guadalupe Roncal when she goes to interview Klaus Haas in prison.

In Charly Cruz's house, Fate and Rosa find themselves in circumstances that are not only "sordid" (323), as the narrator puts it, adopting Fate's point of view, but also dangerous. Asked later by Fate if he thinks that Chucho Flores is mixed up in the killings, Oscar Amalfitano says, "They're all mixed up in it" (343). That is no doubt an exaggeration, but a number of details suggest that Juan Corona, Charly Cruz, and the nameless man with the mustache are involved, and that they have specifically targeted Rosa Amalfitano.

First there is the fact that Corona pulls a gun on Fate when he attempts to leave with Rosa. Furthermore, the man with the mustache, who seems to be subordinate to Cruz, is anxious to keep an eye on Fate (322) and reacts with alarm to his departure with Chucho Flores and Rosa (325), as if he had been sent to make sure that no one left the premises. The way he keeps checking his watch (319) implies that he is expecting an imminent arrival, perhaps that of his masters in crime.

Are Fate and Rosa corrupted by the sordid and dangerous circumstances in which they find themselves? Do they "slip over the edge"? Both later admit that they acted imprudently: "'I think I've been an idiot,' said Fate. 'I was the idiot,' said Rosa" (325). But they intuit the danger and manage to escape in time. Rather than corrupting Fate's character, the circumstances test and prove a courage of which he is not sure himself until the decisive moment: "Now I have to try to be what I am, thought Fate, a black guy from Harlem, a terrifying Harlem motherfucker. Almost immediately he realized that neither of the Mexicans was impressed" (323). His uppercut is delivered, it turns out, in self-defense and is instrumental in fulfilling the duty to rescue that, as we saw in chapter 5, is implicit in Bolaño's fiction. Perhaps Fate is not entirely disinterested, since he is strongly attracted to Rosa, but although we may initially suppose that they have made love in the ellipsis on page 339 we later learn that they have not: "He saw his room at the motel again and wondered whether or not they'd made love. Of course not, he said to himself" (346). The events of Fate and Rosa's long night show that they are not models of wholesome living, but there is nothing to suggest that they were ever "good" in that way. What the night does *not* show is that there are no robust character traits in the world of *2666*. Character, in the ethical sense of the word, is not blank or nonexistent in Bolaño's novels and stories. It is, however, often complex. Our global impressions of his characters are subject to revision simply because we cannot see all of their aspects at once.

We are free to disapprove of Rosa and Fate consuming drugs and pornography respectively at Charly Cruz's house, but the narrative does not shape such reactions, as opposed to the way it prompts us to judge Urrutia Lacroix and Pinochet (by making them ridiculous) or Sammer and Wieder (by insisting on the harm that they have done to others). Throughout Bolaño's fiction, drug use, pornography, prostitution, and "deviant" but consensual sexual practices are presented in a nonjudgmental, libertarian way that is consistent with contemporary liberal interpretations of John Stuart Mill's "Harm Principle": "The only part of the conduct of anyone which is amenable to society is that which concerns others. In the part which merely concerns himself, his independence is of right absolute. Over himself, over his own body and mind, the individual is sovereign."[6] Or, in a vernacular translation: "As long as I'm not harming anyone else, it's no one else's business." Many, of course, disagree, believing with Kant that we are bound by duties to the self.[7] And, in any case, it is no simple matter to draw a line between the part of conduct that concerns others and the part that concerns the self.[8] As David Dyzenhaus has shown, much depends on how narrowly or broadly "harm" is conceived,[9] and many feel that a narrow conception, excluding the harm done by prostitution and pornography in contributing to a regime of inequality, is simply unrealistic.[10] Indeed, Bolaño's fiction acknowledges this indirectly in the story of the young prostitute Lupe in *The Savage Detectives*. Lupe presents herself to Juan García Madero as a free woman (SD 36), who lucidly prefers Alberto, her pimp, because he is a real man (40), who does literally what all men do metaphorically: "All these stupid men are always measuring their dicks. Mine does it for real. And with a knife" (39). A few weeks later, when Lupe says that she wants to study contemporary dance in the afternoons instead of working, Alberto tries to kill her, and she runs away (85). In the last part of the novel, when she is traveling in Sonora with Belano, Lima, and García Madero, a Pápago woman asks her, "Which of these men is yours?" to which she replies: "None of them." "She didn't have a man either," says the Pápago woman, referring to Cesárea Tinajero, whose real freedom Lupe has approached in fleeing Mexico City and Alberto (558). Approached, but not yet attained, for she is still dependent on the protection of her three male companions and Cesárea herself.

My aim here is not to intervene in the philosophical debates about the validity of duties to the self or about how best to conceptualize harm, but to point out that Mill is more congenial than Kant to Bolaño's outlook. More congenial still is Ruwen Ogien, who, in his ongoing campaign against moral paternalism, is constructing a "minimalist ethics," which rests on just three principles: the moral indifference of the relationship to the self; not harming others; and equal consideration for all.[11] This minimalism narrows the scope of morality so that it covers only what we owe to each other as individuals, not what we owe to ourselves, or to abstract entities like the needs of society or symbolic entities like the flag of the nation.[12] This is not a purely theoretical or apolitical program, as Ogien's recent work shows. His defense of a negative conception of political liberty underwrites vigorous opposition to a range of state policies, for example on the treatment of asylum seekers and other "undesirables."[13]

In this section I have been attempting to forestall simplifying descriptions of Bolaño's fiction as either Manichaean or ethically blank, by insisting on the complexity of his major characters and the way their various traits are sequentially revealed. There is, however, a sense in which what really matters in his fictional universe is relatively simple: the personal qualities that we, as readers, are invited to judge positively or negatively—the fiction's specific virtues and vices, so to speak—are clearly identifiable and few in number.

GENEROSITY, COURAGE, ANARCHISM

For the crusading children of Auxilio Lacouture's vision at the end of *Amulet*, courage and erotic love are what really matter: the young people marching toward the abyss are "united only by their generosity and courage" (181); their song is one of "war and love" (184). Thirty years later, for a survivor of that generation, the single parent Oscar Amalfitano, *eros* has been replaced by *philia*,[14] as we see when he argues with a disembodied voice that finally identifies itself as belonging to the spirit of his father (2666 210):

Calm is the one thing that will never let us down. And Amalfitano said: everything else lets us down? And the voice: yes, that's right, it's hard to admit, I mean it's hard to have to admit it to you, but that's the honest-to-God truth. Ethics lets us down? The sense of duty lets us down? Honesty lets us down? Curiosity lets us down? Love lets us down? Bravery lets us down? Art lets us down? That's right, said the voice, everything lets us down, everything . . . except calm, calm is the one thing that never lets us down, though that's no guarantee of anything, I have to tell you. You're wrong, said Amalfitano, bravery never lets us down. And neither does our love for our children. Oh no? said the voice. No, said Amalfitano, suddenly feeling calm. (208)

According to Jean Franco, Amalfitano "is a man who trusts nothing and for whom everything disintegrates into a nightmare of disillusion,"[15] but here we see him finding ethical bedrock and rejecting his father's nihilism. Not everything disintegrates or lets us down. While the objects of love have changed in the transition from Auxilio's vision to Amalfitano's argument, courage has remained a fixture. It is a stable virtue in Bolaño's fiction, but not the most fundamental. That courage on its own cannot make a character good is shown very clearly by the case of Carlos Wieder, who is capable of daring feats ("No challenge was too great for him" [DS 33]) and patient endurance ("He had the face of a man who knows how to wait without losing his nerve or letting his imagination run wild" [145]), but incapable, it seems, of any kind of love or generosity. Courage in Bolaño's fiction is an "executive" virtue in that, unlike generosity, it does not itself yield a characteristic motive but is, in the words of Bernard Williams, "necessary for that relation to oneself and the world which enables one to act from desirable motives in desirable ways."[16] If one agrees with G. H. von Wright that courage is a "self-regarding" virtue,[17] it should be added that the "desirable motives and desirable ways" may be so for the courageous person alone, as in the case of Carlos Wieder.[18]

In her essay "Questions for Bolaño," Jean Franco suggests that in limiting the salient virtues in his fiction to courage and generosity, Bolaño may have been too restrictive. Those virtues can ground a "personal morality," she grants, but that is not enough to give the marchers in Auxilio's vision a direction: "my final question is whether in this voluntaristic universe there is no alternative but to march heroically on towards nowhere."[19] Contrasting

Bolaño's treatment of the Juárez murders with essays by Rosa Linda Fregoso and Marilena Chauí, she writes:

> Both critics support the view that action to right wrongs can be meaningful. In contrast, Bolaño often sounds like a romantic anarchist. The ending of *Amuleto* has the young people marching towards the abyss. The narrator knew that "although they were walking together, they did not constitute what is commonly known as a mass: their destinies were not oriented by a common idea" [translation inserted (A 181)]. In other words, they are without a common goal. Can this be the exodus? Or do that generosity and valor belong to an earlier age? It is Shelley and Mary that I see marching along and perhaps dragging Byron reluctantly behind. (216)

The brawl at the end of *The Savage Detectives* is also problematic for Franco. It "prompts the reader to ask whether there is anything, in the author's view, between the totalitarian state and anarchy, or between the criminal and the outraged citizen" (213).

The passages that I have quoted from Franco's essay raise three important questions, which I will address in the remainder of this chapter, concentrating on *2666* in responding to the first two: Can action to right wrongs be meaningful in Bolaño's fiction? Are his worlds socially atomized? Is he a romantic anarchist?

To begin with the first question, action to right wrongs in Bolaño's fiction is largely unsuccessful but by no means nonexistent. It is undertaken in *2666*, for example, by the congresswoman Azucena Esquivel Plata, the journalists Sergio González Rodríguez and Guadalupe Roncal, and the police officer Juan de Dios Martínez, who all seek justice for the victims of the crimes with a courageous determination. Does their lack of success make their action meaningless? Susan Wolf has argued that for a life to be meaningful it must be "actively and . . . somewhat successfully engaged in projects of independent worth,"[20] but her requirement of success in some degree has been persuasively challenged by Robert Adams, who argues that "a life can derive meaning of the greatest value from a project that has failed."[21] He gives the example of Claus von Stauffenberg's attempt to overthrow

Hitler in 1944. Bolaño not only falls in with this view in his fiction and in interviews but also uses it to define literature itself: "To be brave, knowing beforehand that you'll be defeated, and to go out and fight: that's literature" (B 90). This, of course, is pessimistic in that it anticipates failure, but at the same time it is more optimistic about opportunities for meaningfulness than Wolf's initial formulation.[22]

In *2666*, action to right wrongs is not meaningless according to the view defended by Adams, nor is it limited to individual initiatives. Between the criminal and the outraged citizen there are feminist organizations, the judicial and municipal police forces, and the press. Activists from Women of Sonora for Democracy and Peace (WSDP) and Women in Action (WA) make television appearances denouncing the "endless trickle of deaths in Santa Teresa" and the "climate of impunity" (512, 505). WSDP also organizes a women's march from the university to city hall (607). *2666* does not document the work of activists, unlike the essays with which it is contrasted by Franco, but it does imagine in detail the daily lives of police officers and journalists investigating the crimes.

Although the police forces are deeply and scandalously dysfunctional, certain of their members are honest, diligent, and brave, notably Juan de Dios Martínez and Lalo Cura. Their resistance to the ambient corruption is signaled not only by scrupulous investigations (see 392, 451, 526) but also by conflicts with their colleagues. When Juan de Dios Martínez goes to Serafino's to arrest Officer Jaime Sánchez for the murder of Ema Contreras, he finds Inspector Ortiz Rebolledo among the spectators at a poker table:

> I've come to make an arrest, said Juan de Dios, and Ortiz Rebolledo stared at him, smiling broadly. You and these two? he asked. And then: Don't be a dick, why don't you go suck cock somewhere else? Juan de Dios Martínez looked at him as if he didn't know him, shook him off, and went over to Jaime Sánchez. From there he could see that Ortiz Rebolledo had hold of the arm of one of the two policemen, who was talking his ear off. He must be telling him who I'm here to arrest, thought Juan de Dios. (499)

Ortiz Rebolledo initially presumes that Juan de Dios Martínez has come for him, and not by mistake.

Lalo Cura, for his part, challenges a fellow officer named González (554). Although the reason for the challenge is not specified, it can be supposed, since González has just run through an exasperating catalogue of misogynous jokes (552–553). Lalo and González, accompanied by a group of other officers, drive to a secluded spot to settle their score. The fight itself is not narrated; five pages later we find Lalo returning in a patrol car with Epifanio Galindo at the wheel, reflecting on the similarity between the Sonora desert and the sea (559). Lalo may be naïve, as his friend and mentor Epifanio says (472), but a reader who remembers how he conducted himself when gunmen attempted to assassinate the wife of his former employer (394–396) will presume that he held his own against González.

If the police forces in *2666* are not entirely dishonored, it is not just because of a few individuals who resist corruption but also because of the solidarity that emerges between them as they discover that they have a common goal. We see this happening in an exchange that momentarily casts Epifanio Galindo's probity into doubt:

> When Epifanio asked why he'd gone to the Podestá ravine, Lalo Cura answered that it was because he was a cop. You little shit, Epifanio said, don't go where you're not called, do you hear me? . . . Don't you know, you snot-nosed bastard, that there is no such thing as modern criminal investigation? You're not even twenty years old yet, are you? Or am I wrong? You aren't wrong, Epifanio, said Lalo Cura. Well, be careful, champ, that's the first and only rule, said Epifanio, letting go of his arm and smiling and giving him a hug and taking him out to eat at the only place that served posole in the center of Santa Teresa at that murky time of night. (526–527)

The more seasoned Epifanio has a keener sense of the dangers involved in attempting to uncover the truth, and he knows that the duration and effectiveness of their partnership will depend on taking care.

Relationships of mutual support also develop among the journalists reporting on the murders of women in Santa Teresa. As we have seen, Fate provides support for Guadalupe Roncal when she goes to interview Klaus Haas in prison. His "company and protection" are not imposed paternalistically but offered in response to her request and in exchange for access to the chief suspect (299). This bond is fragile: Fate is tempted to abandon his Mexican colleague when following her car to the prison, but Rosa Amalfitano is "strongly opposed" to the idea (345), perhaps because she and Guadalupe were drawn to each other immediately: "It didn't take Guadalupe Roncal and Rosa Amalfitano more than a minute to share their respective woes" (344). So one bond reinforces another.

A comparable solidarity emerges between the North American journalists Mary-Sue Bravo and Josué Hernández Mercado. Both attend the press conference at which Klaus Haas announces the identity of the man whom he believes to be the Santa Teresa serial killer. Hernández Mercado is the only journalist present who fails to observe the protocol of calling the police for their official response (611). After the press conference, Mary-Sue Bravo sees him by chance in a restaurant with a brawny man who looks like a policeman, but when she goes back to speak to her colleague, the brawny man is gone (611). A week later, she learns that Hernández Mercado has gone missing (615). She travels to Green Valley, where he worked, and there she meets the boy "of eighteen, maybe seventeen" who reported on his disappearance (620). Her inspection of Hernández Mercado's house reveals no clues, and she decides to drop the story, reckoning that he has probably gone to another state to avoid paying debts. The boy reporter, however, calls a week later to ask about the progress of her investigation and points out that if Hernández Mercado had chosen to leave, he would have taken with him the books that he had written and published. Mary-Sue realizes that he is right (630). Once again, a bond that was about to break is reinforced by a third party.

The world of *2666* is not socially atomized; it contains forms of cooperation and solidarity that emerge interstitially in "small affinity groups," which are not exactly or always groups of friends.[23] Commenting on an episode in *The Savage Detectives*, Jean Franco writes: "What has replaced 'patria o muerte' is 'amistad o muerte'—the fragile and transient bond of friendship between men, leaving women ambiguously on the margins."[24]

This is largely true: friendship matters greatly in Bolaño's fiction, and the worlds that his books construct are predominantly masculine and masculinist.[25] It would be unconvincing to argue otherwise on the basis of exceptional female characters such as Cesárea Tinajero or Auxilio Lacouture, however well they exemplify bravery and endurance. Nevertheless it would not be accurate to say that in Bolaño's fiction only fragile friendships between men stand between the totalitarian state and anarchy (understood as a war of all against all), or between the criminal and the outraged citizen.

For a start, the emergent forms of solidarity that I have been discussing sometimes involve women, as in the cases of the journalists, discussed above. And at the end of *2666* we see relations of mutual support developing among the women who visit the Santa Teresa prison. In 2001, after an absence of two years, Lotte Haas returns to see her son:

> That same day she visited the prison and felt happy when a little old woman recognized her.
> "Bless your eyes, you're back, ma'am," said the old woman.
> "Oh, Monchita, how are you?" said Lotte as she gave her a long hug.
> "As you can see, dear, still barely holding on," answered the old woman. (888)

Although, as Franco writes, in Bolaño's work, "chains of friendship and connection are broken by distance, time and death,"[26] links can be made or renewed at a late stage. Just before the end of *2666*, the aging Lotte Haas, for example, befriends her son's lawyer, Isabel Santolaya (885), and reconnects with her brother Hans, whom she has not seen since she was a child (890). Furthermore, the obstinacy of Bolaño's amateur detectives in searching for the disappeared shows that the sense of connection can persist in spite of distance, time, and death. Everything that we know about Azucena Esquivel Plata, whose life was discussed in the third section of chapter 4, leads us to suppose that only assassination could stop her trying to find out what happened to her friend Kelly Rivera Parker. As for Arturo Belano and Ulises Lima, the pair of friends at the center of *The Savage Detectives*, they go their separate ways in Port Vendres (SD 248), but in "Death of Ulises" an enduring attachment draws Belano to the apartment where Lima used to live, and this pilgrimage acquaints him with the dead poet's "last disciples," by whom he is duly fêted (SE 133–134).

Finally, although friendship may enter into the forms of solidarity that emerge in Bolaño's fiction, it need not do so. Fate and Guadalupe Roncal barely know each other, and the same is true of Mary-Sue Bravo and Josué Hernández Mercado. From an Aristotelian point of view, it might be said that they have friendships motivated by usefulness, which are therefore inferior to and less durable than genuine friendships, motivated by admiration of virtue.[27] But to use Aristotle's categories here is to suggest that these relationships are somehow less than they should be, a judgment that the fiction does not invite us to make. Guadalupe Roncal is potentially useful to Fate in that she gives him access to Haas. Josué Hernández Mercado may provide Mary-Sue Bravo with material for a story. But neither Guadalupe nor Josué is simply being used. Fate and Mary-Sue are both trying to help their colleagues, and all four journalists are motivated by a common goal: to discover more of the truth behind the crimes. They are connected not by an inferior kind of friendship but by a solidarity based on a shared sense of what matters and a shared exposure to risk.

The associations that I have been examining are non- or anti-institutional. Epifanio Galindo and Lalo Cura are aware of the corruption and negligence among their superior officers, especially in the judicial police: "Those fucking *judiciales* never solve a case, Epifanio said to Lalo Cura" (462). They know, for example, that Inspector Ortiz Rebolledo has covered up the involvement of a fellow *judicial* in the killing of Esther Perea Peña (625). Their loyalty is not to the institution that employs them but to an ideal that it is globally failing to serve. To do their jobs well, they have to take risky personal initiatives. Similarly, Fate and Mary-Sue Bravo must struggle with their editors to write what they feel are the truly important stories. Mary-Sue eventually obtains permission to investigate the disappearance of Josué Hernández Mercado (619), but when Fate proposes "a sketch of the industrial landscape in the third world, a piece of *reportage* about the current situation in Mexico, a panorama of the border, a serious crime story"

(294–295), he is told to concentrate on the boxing match that he has been sent to cover.

Insofar as it privileges voluntary associations over hierarchical institutions, Bolaño's fiction has an anarchist ethos, in line with the principles defended by Bakunin and Kropotkin.[28] It is significant that the Mexican anarchist Ricardo Flores Magón was a beacon for the original visceral realists—"the one who always inspired us was Flores Magón," says Amadeo Salvatierra (SD 276)—and that the young poets who are reviving or reinventing the movement drink a toast to him (276). For Bolaño, however, as opposed to the great anarchist agitators of the nineteenth and early twentieth centuries, the utopian horizon has receded into an uncertain future: first the Left must find a way "out of the pit of shame and futility" (LEE 218). This outlook is likely to seem ineffective to revolutionaries intent on seizing state power and irresponsible to reformers attached to due process. Bolaño's work, including his criticism and interviews, is also anarchist in a purely critical way: it stigmatizes attraction to institutionally vested power and prestige. If courage and generosity are the cardinal virtues in his fictional universe, there is a salient vice that is not the opposite of either and has no convenient one-word name. It is the particular kind of servility targeted by Flaubert when he writes of Homais in *Madame Bovary* that "he was incapable, by temperament, of staying away from a famous person," and of Dambreuse in *Sentimental Education* that he worshipped "authority so fervently that he would have paid for the privilege of selling himself."[29] Bolaño is systematically merciless in his treatment of characters who feel this kind of magical, magnetic attraction to the famous and the powerful.

Jesús Fernández Gómez in *Nazi Literature in the Americas* deems Hitler to be "Europe's providential savior, but says little more about him. Physical proximity to power, however, moves him to tears" (NLA 39). In *By Night in Chile*, Sebastián Urrutia Lacroix is enchanted by the presence of Pinochet, as we saw in chapter 6. In *2666*, attraction to power is presented less comically. Almendro, alias El Cerdo (The Pig), a writer and publisher turned cultural bureaucrat who met Archimboldi in Mexico City, considers the pros and cons of requesting an ambassadorship or a post as a cultural attaché in Europe: "One of the pros, absolutely, would be the chance to write again. . . . One of the cons, no question about it, was the physical separation from power. Distancing oneself from power is never good, he'd discovered that early on, before he'd been granted real power, when he was head of the house that tried to publish Archimboldi" (102). That is, when literature was still his primary concern. The case of El Cerdo prompts Amalfitano to tell a story about the fate of the Mexican intellectual:

> At some point your shadow has quietly slipped away . . . your shadow is lost and you, momentarily, forget it. And so you arrive on a kind of stage, without your shadow, and you start to translate reality or reinterpret it or sing it. The stage is really a proscenium and upstage there's an enormous tube, something like a mine shaft or the gigantic opening of a mine. . . . From the opening of the mine come unintelligible noises. . . . The point is, no one sees, really sees, the mouth of the mine. Stage machinery, the play of light and shadows, a trick of time, hides the real shape of the opening from the gaze of the audience. In fact, only the spectators who are closest to the stage, right up against the orchestra pit, can see the shape of something behind the dense veil of camouflage. . . . The other spectators can't see anything beyond the proscenium, and it's fair to say they'd rather not. Meanwhile, the shadowless intellectuals are always facing the audience, so unless they have eyes in the backs of their heads, they can't see anything. They only hear the sounds that come from deep in the mine. And they translate or reinterpret or re-create them. Their work, it goes without saying, is of a very low standard. They employ rhetoric where they sense a hurricane, they try to be eloquent where they sense fury unleashed, they strive to maintain the discipline of meter where there's only a deafening and hopeless silence. They say cheep cheep, bow wow, meow meow, because they're incapable of imagining an animal of colossal proportions, or the absence of such an animal. (121–122)

At the end of his tirade, Amalfitano declares that he has been "talking nonsense" (123), but the scene that he describes has a clear allegorical sense. Mexican writers and intellectuals, all of whom work for the state, however critical of the state they may be (121), are reduced to the condition of pets;

but to translate the reality on which they have turned their backs, rather than traducing it with rhetoric, eloquence, and conventions, they would need to be colossal wild animals. They would need to be "barbaric writers," not as Raoul Delorme is in *Distant Star* (131–132) but as Archimboldi is in *2666*: "a Germanic barbarian, an artist in a state of permanent incandescence" (839). The shadowless Mexican intellectuals recall Adalbert von Chamisso's Peter Schlemihl, who let the devil take his shadow in exchange for Fortunatus's bottomless purse. They have not consciously struck any bargains; their shadows have simply slipped away, but this is clearly a result of their docility with respect to state power. Surrender to the state has denatured them.

Amalfitano is certainly not an exemplar of mental balance, but he is no fool, and although this rant is hyperbolic, it chimes with what Bolaño said in his own name on the question of writers and power, as here in "The Myths of Cthulhu":

> And García Márquez never taught us more than when he welcomed the Pope in Havana, wearing patent leather boots—García, not the Pope, who I guess would have been wearing sandals—along with Castro, who was booted too. I can still remember the smile that García Márquez was not quite able to contain on that grand occasion. Half-closed eyes, taut skin as if he'd just had a face-lift, slightly puckered lips, Saracen lips as Amado Nervo would have said, green with envy. (IG 158)

In Bolaño's eyes, the author of *No One Writes to the Colonel*, a "simply perfect" novel (B 49), is doubly dishonored by the pleasure that he apparently takes in associating with Castro and the Pope. It is not just that Bolaño agreed with Lord Acton that "great men are almost always bad men";[30] he also seems to have felt that proximity to those who exercise power, whether or not they are personally bad, inevitably has a corrupting influence on writers.

This is an allergy rather than a worked-out position, and not entirely reasonable, but reasons for it can be found in the trajectory of a writer who came to maturity in societies governed by corrupt and repressive institutions. Not only was Bolaño closely acquainted with state criminality under

Pinochet in Chile (LEE 214–215), he also spent nine formative years in Mexico, beginning in 1968, when the Institutional Revolutionary Party sent the armed forces to occupy the campus of the UNAM and crush a student demonstration in Tlatelolco, killing at least 44 people.[31] In Spain, where he arrived in 1977, two years after General Franco's death, Bolaño never became a citizen or occupied a salaried position or joined a political party. In a recently published letter, written in 1986, he declared: "I consider myself a communist, although I've never had a membership card and never will. If I was presented with one, I imagine I'd give it back straight away, or at least before they could take it off me again."[32] Bolaño won a number of literary prizes but was never awarded a fellowship, grant, or residency.[33] Unlike many Latin American writers, he never held a diplomatic post or worked as a cultural attaché, as he points out in "I Can't Read" (SE 92). His first book with a major publisher appeared in 1996, almost twenty years after his arrival in Europe. He was not alone during those years: he had the support of his family, his wife, and his friends, but he owed less to political, educational, or literary institutions than most contemporary writers. Carlos Franz reports that when asked, during a visit to Chile, how he felt about his recent success, Bolaño replied, "It's come too late" (2008: 114). Certainly it came too late to alter his visceral anarchism.

POETRY

When Jean Franco remarks that Bolaño "often sounds like a romantic anarchist,"[34] I take it that she is using the terms pejoratively to suggest an attitude that is outdated and irresponsible. Franco does not go so far as to say that Bolaño *is* a romantic anarchist, but I will, because I believe that the terms can be used in a nonpejorative and descriptively accurate way. I have already argued that there is a sense in which Bolaño not only "often sounds like" an anarchist but is one. In this section and the next I will explain what is specifically romantic about his anarchism. To put it in a nutshell, Bolaño is a *romantic* anarchist in the way that he privileges poetry (broadly defined) and not only identifies it with the virtue of courage, as we saw in chapter 5, but also extends the concept synecdochically so that it comes to signify a stance that I will call "neotenic openness."

Bolaño began his literary career as a poet and continued to write poetry up until his death,[35] although from 1992 on he devoted most of his energy to novels and stories, hoping to provide for his family, quixotically it must have seemed, at least until the success of *The Savage Detectives*.[36] He once said that "writing in prose is a terrible lapse of taste [*es de un mal gusto bestial*]" (B 76), a quip echoed by Ernesto San Epifanio in *The Savage Detectives*: "Poetry is more than enough for me, although sooner or later I'm bound to commit the vulgarity of writing stories" (SD 46). The remark, like many that Bolaño made in passing, was intended to be provocative, but I think it would be a mistake to discount it as pure provocation. It is neither straight-forwardly ironic nor entirely sincere.[37]

If Bolaño believed that poetry was nobler than prose, it was not just because of its ancient lineage, to which he was fond of alluding (he was especially attached to the earliest poet in the Palatine Anthology: Archilocus [BP 57–59, 161]), but also because, in the long battle of the genres, it is the great loser, preserved from mercantile corruption (if not from other kinds) by its marginality. In *2666*, Marco Antonio Guerra makes this point in a conversation with Amalfitano: "Poetry is the one thing that isn't contaminated, the only thing that isn't part of the game. . . . Only poetry— and let me be clear, only some of it—is good for you, only poetry isn't shit" (226). We should not be too quick to assume, however, that young Guerra is speaking for Bolaño here or that he understands poetry in the same way. After all, he also says that "the human being, broadly speaking, is the closest thing there is to a rat" (219). Guerra's mention of Trakl, who worked as a pharmacist in Vienna, reminds Amalfitano of a young pharmacist he knew in Barcelona, who preferred the "perfect exercises" of the masters to their "great, imperfect, torrential works" (227). This, for Amalfitano, indicates not refined taste but a lack of nerve: "They want to watch the great masters spar, but they have no interest in real combat, when the great masters struggle against that something, that something that terrifies us all, that something that cows us and spurs us on, amid blood and mortal wounds and stench"

(227). Watching "real combat" may not be pleasant, but the pharmacist's purism is impoverishing, and so, by implication, is Guerra's "grandiloquent" rejection of all prose (227).

Bolaño said in an interview that the best poetry of the twentieth century had been written in prose—"James Joyce's *Ulysses* contains *The Waste Land*, and it's better than *The Waste Land*" (B 103)—and he described Pedro Lemebel as "the best poet of my generation, though he doesn't write poetry" (BP 81). Using the term "poetry" in this way poses obvious problems of vagueness, which have been underlined astringently by the French poet Jacques Roubaud: "Poetry only exists in poems; and in concatenations, assemblages, and constructions of poems. . . . Poetry is not something vague, undifferentiated, an ectoplasmic and sentimental master key [*passe-partout*]. To say that poetry is everywhere is to say that, in fact, it's nowhere."[38] Friedrich Schlegel approaches this extreme when, in "Dialogue on Poetry" (1800), he "dissolves the concept of poetry in the idea of a 'natural poetry,' which is nothing other than nature itself, or the earth," as Jean-Luc Nancy and Philippe Lacoue-Labarthe have written.[39] But Bolaño does not go quite so far. He uses the term "poetry" in an honorific fashion, not only to distinguish a superior class of composition in verse but also to include admired works in prose, much as Coleridge, in *Biographia Literaria* (1817), grants full poetic status to "the writings of Plato, and Jeremy Taylor, and Burnet's *Theory of the Earth*," adding that "poems of any length neither can be, nor ought to be, all poetry."[40] Sometimes, like John Stuart Mill in "What Is Poetry?" (1833), Bolaño extends the notion further to include nonverbal arts, as when, in *Distant Star*, the narrator concludes that Lorenzo, an all-around performer and artist of life, is at least the equal of Juan Stein and Diego Soto: "Sometimes I think he was the best poet of the three. But usually I see them all together" (DS 76).[41]

These romantic understandings of what poetry is are certainly vaguer than Roubaud's formalist delimitation, but their vagueness has been useful in expansive defenses of the art, from the Schlegel brothers to Les Murray,[42] because it facilitates extension of the concept to include a range of widely valued things. In Bolaño's fiction, poetry as product and practice stands for something larger. Just before *The Savage Detectives* was published in the

United States, Jonathan Galassi of Farrar, Straus and Giroux told the *Washington Post*: "it's a metaphor, you know, it's not literally a novel about poets. It's about poetic temperament in the world. It's romantic. It's about young idealists coming up against corruption and tragedy."[43] This was said before the book's surprising success, and Galassi sounds slightly nervous about the effect that the description "a novel about poets" might have on potential readers (an effect that he was well positioned to gauge, being a poet as well as a publisher). *The Savage Detectives* is, literally, a novel about poets, but Galassi was right to point out that poetry in the novel also stands for something more than a kind of verbal composition, even if that kind is capacious enough to include *Ulysses* and the *crónicas* of Pedro Lemebel.

At the end of part II of *The Savage Detectives*, Amadeo Salvatierra says:

> Like so many Mexicans, I too gave up poetry. Like so many thousands of Mexicans, I too turned my back on poetry. Like so many hundreds of thousands of Mexicans, I too, when the moment came, stopped writing and reading poetry. From then on, my life proceeded along the drabbest course you can imagine. (SD 520–521)

It is not that writing and reading poetry were sufficient in themselves to make his life colorful. Those activities were part of an open, adventurous way of living that he gave up "when the moment came," but which he recovers, if temporarily, thanks to the visit of Belano and Lima. It is significant that at the end of the night spent talking with the young poets, Salvatierra opens the windows of his apartment and turns out the light. Like part III of *The Savage Detectives*, which ends with the unanswered riddle, "What's outside the window?" and a drawing of a window frame that seems to be dissolving, part II eludes conclusion by means of an opening out.

Amadeo Salvatierra's attitude to his visitors differs strikingly from that of the leader of the stridentist movement, Manuel Maples Arce. Belano visits Maples Arce and leaves a set of interview questions. When he returns to pick up the answers, the senior poet instructs his maid to tell the novice that he is not at home, then listens to their conversation from behind a closed door: "If he comes back to see me, I thought, I'll be justified, if he shows up here one day, without calling first, to talk to me, to listen to me tell my old stories, to submit his poems for my consideration, I'll be justified" (SD 161). Maples Arce stands on his dignity and expects Belano to come to him as a disciple, earning access to the master by persisting and submitting. The contrast with Amadeo's welcome could not be clearer: "My dear boys, I said to them, I'm so glad to see you, come right in, make yourselves at home, and as they filed down the hall . . . , I skipped joyfully ahead into the kitchen, where I got out a bottle of Los Suicidas mezcal" (SD 127). Maples Arce may not have turned his back on the reading and writing of poetry, but the routine continuation of those activities has not been enough to prevent psychosclerosis. He is like the aging poets described by Alejandro Zambra in "Against Poets (I)":

> Occasionally a merciful reporter asks them what the point of poetry is in this dehumanized, consumerist world. They sigh and answer as they have always answered: that only poetry will save the world; that in the midst of confusion we have to search for true words and hold onto them. They say it without conviction, routinely, but they are absolutely right.[44]

OPENNESS

In Bolaño's fiction, poetry stands synecdochically for what Giorgio Agamben, in *Idea of Prose*, calls "neotenic openness [*illatenza neotenica*],"[45] or to translate more awkwardly, taking into account Agamben's use of *illatenza* as an equivalent of the German term *Unverborgenheit* (as used by Heidegger) and the Greek *aletheia*, "neotenic unconcealedness."[46] Discussing the "infantile vocation of human language," the fact that the human ability to speak is not written into the genetic code but must be acquired by contact with the outside world during an initial phase of indetermination, Agamben writes, "the attempt to imitate the natural germen in order to transmit immortal and codified values in which neotenic openness once more shuts itself off in a specific tradition is precisely the characteristic of a degraded culture."[47] Neotenic openness, to allow the expression its broadest sense, is a youthful openness preserved beyond the age at which it is typically lost, and therefore a quality that is distinctly manifest only in individuals who are at least relatively old, like Amadeo Salvatierra or Benno von Archmiboldi at the end of *2666*. The biological term "neoteny" was coined by Julius Kollman in 1885, and refers to the persistence of larval or juvenile traits in the adult form of an animal.[48] The traits concerned may be behavioral as well as physiological, for example playfulness in domestic dogs.[49] From a sociological point of view, behavioral neoteny in humans could be characterized as resistance to what Pierre Bourdieu calls social aging:

> Social aging is nothing other than the slow renunciation or disinvestment (socially assisted and encouraged) which leads agents to adjust their aspirations to their objective chances, to espouse their condition, become what they are and make do with what they have, even if this entails deceiving themselves as to what they are and what they have, with collective complicity, and accepting bereavement of all the "lateral possibles" they have abandoned along the way.[50]

This is precisely what key characters in Bolaño's fiction—Belano, Lima, Ansky, and Archimboldi among them—refuse to do. In this respect, Efraim Ivanov, the "Cervantes of Soviet science fiction," and his ghostwriter Boris Ansky, in *2666*, contrast in a stark and significant way. Ivanov believes that a real writer is "basically a responsible person with a certain level of maturity" who knows that he has a series of institutions behind him: "the Writers' Association, the Artists' Syndicate, the Confederation of Literary Workers, Poets' House" (*2666* 714). Ansky, on the contrary, lives "his whole life in rabid immaturity because the revolution, the one true revolution, is also immature" (741).

Speaking of his infrarealist youth in Mexico, Bolaño explicitly linked poetry with an active openness: "For me, to be a poet was at once to be a revolutionary and to be totally open to any cultural manifestation, any sexual expression, well, open to everything, to any experimentation with drugs" (B 38). In his fiction, however, openness is not simply readiness to party. Often it means being open to an ethical demand, and like detective work it has a contemplative as well as an active aspect. It involves attentiveness, a quality that certain of Bolaño's characters possess to an extraordinary degree, notably B in "Last Evenings on Earth" and Belano in "Photos," as we saw in the final section of chapter 2. Like the narrator of "Labyrinth," these characters are overinterpreters, prone to what experimental psychologists call apophenia. Recent work by De Young, Grazioplene, and Peterson situates apophenia within the Openness/Intellect domain of personality traits (one of the so-called "Big Five" domains), and suggests that the proclivity to overinterpret is associated with openness to experience.[51] The association is marked, at any rate, in the cases of those characters in Bolaño's fiction who practice savage or wild detection: B and Belano, as we have seen, but also Auxilio Lacouture in *Amulet,* who is convinced that a vase in Pedro Garfías's apartment is a secret door to hell (A 6), or, on an intellectual plane, Amalfitano in *2666,* who draws geometrical figures linking the names of famous and obscure thinkers to form patterns that, in retrospect, he regards as verging on the absurd (2666 191–194).

In Bolaño's work, openness is preserved largely by persistence. In "Muse," he presents his truant teenage self, also portrayed in "The Grub" (LEE 60–73), as the benchmark by which to measure decline: "And even if the years pass/and the Roberto Bolaño of the Alameda/and the Librería de Cristal/is transformed,/is paralyzed//becomes older and stupider/you'll stay just as beautiful" (UU 809). Body and mind may lose their agility, but that will hardly matter as long as the poet continues to follow the muse's "radiant trail" (809). Few of the poets in *The Savage Detectives,* however, maintain the fidelity declared in "Muse." The novel's second part is tragic not just because the visceral realist group is dispersed and some of its members die, but also because many of them, like Amadeo Salvatierra, turn their backs on poetry or explicitly repudiate it.

Laura Jáuregui enrolls in study for a biology degree (SD 134) and, in 1976, sums up the shortcomings of the visceral realists like this: "the real problem was that they were almost all at least twenty and they acted like they were barely fifteen" (154). The gifted Font twins dissociate themselves from the group (159, 297–298). Xóchitl García continues writing poetry after the movement's official demise (340) but later seems to give it up in favor of journalism (348). When Clara Cabeza accosts Ulises Lima in Parque Hundido on behalf of her employer, Octavio Paz, Lima identifies himself as "the second-to-last visceral realist poet left in Mexico" (479). By this stage, most of the group's former members have moved on. They feel that they have grown up. But on this point *The Savage Detectives* is not entirely impartial, in spite of its multiple perspectives: the novel intimates that their growing up has been a closing down, as we can see by examining the monologues of Laura Jáuregui and Daniel Grossman, in which repudiating poetry (as opposed to merely turning away from it, as Amadeo has done), is linked to self-deception and self-destruction.

Laura Jáuregui claims that no one ever took visceral realism seriously, "not deep down" (134), and in the course of a sleepless night, she comes to see it as a rhetorical instrument invented by Belano:

> It occurred to me that it was all a message for me. It was a way of saying don't leave me, see what I'm capable of, stay with me. And then I realized that deep down the guy was a creep. Because it's one thing to fool yourself and another thing entirely to fool everybody else. The whole visceral realism thing was a love letter, the demented strutting of a dumb bird in the moonlight, something essentially cheap and meaningless. (134–135)

This may not be entirely deluded, but it is at best a half-truth, for it disregards the group's other founder, Ulises Lima: *he* takes visceral realism seriously, for reasons that have nothing to do with her. Laura is deceiving herself, at least in part.

Years after the group has broken up, in the course of a road trip from Puerto Ángel back to Mexico City, Daniel Grossman and Norman Bolzman reminisce about the time when Ulises Lima came to visit them and Claudia in Tel Aviv. Daniel says that he and Claudia liked the fact that Ulises was strange because back then they thought they were "going to be writers and would have given anything to belong to that essentially pathetic group, the visceral realists. Youth is a scam" (427). This is very different from Amadeo Salvatierra's admission that he too turned his back on poetry. Daniel is repudiating poetry as a youthful illusion. Rather than admitting that his life has shrunk, he claims to have matured. Rather than facing the fear of being "no good" as a writer, the fear that, according to Boris Ansky, "afflicts most citizens who, one fine (or dark) day choose to make the practice of writing . . . an integral part of their lives" (2666 722), he dismisses writing itself as a kind of fraud to which the young are prone. He has not simply moved on but tried to cut himself off from an earlier part of his life.

The repudiation of poetry is thematized again in the story "Enrique Martín." The eponymous character is a Spanish poet who writes bad poems in both Castilian and Catalan: "Enrique *wanted* to be a poet, and he threw himself into this endeavor with all his energy and willpower. He was tenacious in a blind, uncritical way, like the bad guys in westerns, falling like flies, but persevering, determined to take the hero's bullets, and in the end there was something likeable about this tenacity; it gave him an aura, a kind of literary sanctity" (LEE 27). His tenacity, however, has limits. A few years after first meeting the narrator, Enrique tells him that he has stopped writing poetry: "when I looked up he was smiling as if to say, I've grown up, I've realized you can enjoy art without making a fool of yourself, without keeping up some pathetic pretense of being a writer" (30). Instead of simply concentrating on his career, however, he has started contributing articles on UFO sightings to a magazine called *Questions & Answers* (39–40). One night, Enrique visits the narrator in a rather nervous state and gives him a packet of papers for safekeeping: "It isn't poetry, he said with a smile. . . . What is it? I asked. Nothing, just some stuff" (36). Years later, Belano hears that Enrique has hanged himself in his apartment, after covering the walls with numbers. He tries to find out why, but his investigation is fruitless. Before moving house, he opens the packet:

> I thought I'd find numbers and maps, maybe some sign that might explain his death. There were fifty A4 sheets, neatly bound. There were no maps or coded messages on any of them, just poems, mainly in the style of Miguel Hernández, but there were also some imitations of León Felipe, Blas de Otero, and Gabriel Celaya. That night I couldn't get to sleep. My turn to flee had come. (51)

Enrique Martín was not able, in the end, fully to renounce poetry. He may have stopped writing poems, but sensing that he was in some kind of danger, he wanted the poems that he had written to be kept safe, so he entrusted them to another poet. The truly "pathetic pretense" in his case was not pretending to be a writer but pretending to have stopped wanting to be one. Perhaps that desire was symptomatic of a delusion from the start, but the unsuccessful attempt to excise it not only destroys Enrique's "aura," his "literary sanctity," it also seems to deprive him of the Hölderlinian "poet's courage" discussed in chapter 5, a capacity to endure dependent on trust and belief. As the narrator puts it at the beginning of the story, "A poet can endure anything. . . . We grew up with this conviction" (32).

The cases of Laura Jáuregui, Daniel Grossman, and Enrique Martín, in which the repudiation of poetry as a youthful illusion is associated with self-deception and self-destruction, suggest that the neotenic openness for which poetry stands in Bolaño's fiction is a quality maintained by persistence, by resisting social pressures to move on, "grow up," and espouse an assigned condition. But certain ways of trying to hold onto youth may also be self-deceptive and self-destructive. Daniel Grossman's friend Norman Bolzman does not seem to agree that "youth is a scam." Once "ultranormal Norman" (SD 427), he has become more than a little strange by the time he and Daniel recollect Ulises Lima's visit to Tel Aviv. He is conscious of having lost something over the years but believes that it can be recovered intact: "We can get back into the game whenever we want to" (427). What he has lost and what the "game" is are questions that remain unanswered, but we know that since splitting up with Claudia his relationships with women have been "relatively cool" (425), and that he regards his impotence as "a symptom . . . not a problem" (425). Children interest him in a new way:

> Then he talked about children, children in general and the children of Puerto Ángel in particular, asking me what I thought about the children of Puerto Ángel, and the truth is I didn't think *anything* about the children of the town we were leaving behind, I mean, I hadn't even noticed them! and then Norman looked at me and said: each time I think of them it centers me. Just like that: It centers me. And I thought: it would be

better if he watched the highway instead of me, and I also thought: something's up. (425)

Norman goes on to interpret a dream that Claudia recounted to him one morning on the telephone, in which there were colors and a battle in the background, drifting away:

> She dreamed about the children we hadn't had. Fuck off, I said. That was the meaning of the dream. So according to you, the battle drifting away is the children you didn't have? More or less, said Norman, that was the shadows fighting. And the colors? They're what's left, a shitty abstraction of what's left [*la pinche abstracción de lo que queda*]. (SD 426; LDS 453)

The last sentence is ambiguous: the colors may be a poor abstract representation or they may represent the poor abstraction of a childless life. It may be that Norman is yearning to be anchored or centered in life by children of his own, or, as the preceding discussion of his impotence hints, that his sexual desire is reorienting itself toward children. We will never know, because his speeding leads to an accident that kills him and seriously injures Daniel. Norman's unrealistic conviction that we can recover everything we have lost contrasts with Daniel's revisionary "realism," according to which none of it was worth having in the first place. While Daniel's attitude cuts off a part of his past, Norman's is coupled with a recklessness that ends up cutting his life short.

The story of Norman Bolzman implies that fixation on the irremediably lost comports serious dangers for the self and for others, and that fidelity to one's past can take limiting and perverse forms. Neotenic openness is a matter of becoming as well as remaining. When asked in 2001 about his "state of maturity," Bolaño replied: "I'm afraid that, as far the important things go, I'm still an immature person. And that's not easy; don't go thinking we're born immature; it's something you have to work on really hard" (B 30). Like his quip about writing in prose, this is meant to be provocative. But, again, I think it would a mistake to dismiss it out of hand. What could it mean to become, rather than to remain, immature?

The question is vast, but it can be answered with a degree of precision in the context of the "artist's novel" that is "The Part About Archimboldi" in *2666*. One thing that becoming immature could mean, for a writer, is to lose oneself more fully in the construction of an imaginary world, as children often do in play, while using the written word to stabilize that construction over time. This kind of absorption is what makes the activity of arranging words and mental images gratifying for Archimboldi, who thinks of his own books and his plans for future books as "a game insofar as he derived pleasure from writing, a pleasure similar to that of the detective on the heels of the killer" (2666 817). Becoming immature in this sense would be equivalent to attaining the paradoxical human maturity that, according to Nietzsche, consists in "rediscovering the seriousness that we had towards play when we were children,"[52] or approaching the condition of the genius as defined by Baudelaire in an article on the late-blooming Constantin Guys: "genius is nothing more nor less than childhood recovered at will."[53]

To the extent that it is gamelike, artistic composition requires a provisional withdrawal from practicalities. As Roger Caillois remarks, "play is essentially a separated occupation, carefully isolated from the rest of existence."[54] Engaging seriously in the game of writing means moving beyond the totalizing formulations of the infrarealist manifesto—"Our ethic is Revolution, our aesthetic is Life: one-single-thing"[55]—and acknowledging some degree of separation between life and art, accepting that the writer's responsibilities are divided. If this is to betray an avant-garde ideal, Bolaño was betraying it already in his infrarealist youth, when, as Guadalupe Ochoa remembers, his regular habits and work ethic distinguished him from the other members of the group: "From a certain time of night, he would shut himself in to read and write, on the principle that if I'm a writer, what I do is write. . . . While the rest of us partied on, Roberto would religiously go home."[56]

However committed and sincere their statements of intent, imaginative writers must risk irresponsibility insofar as they cannot know in advance whether or not their work will work, in three senses of the word. First, will it work for them? Will they be satisfied with the results of their work? Second, will it work for a publisher, as an item in a symbolic and commercial marketplace? And third, will it be taken up by readers, producing significant effects on cultural traditions and more broadly in the world? There is always a high probability that the answer to one or more of those questions will be no, and that the decisions taken in order to accomplish the work will not be retrospectively justifiable. In a famous paper, Bernard Williams proposed the notion of "moral luck" and applied it to this sort of situation. As an illustrative example he took the case of the painter Gauguin, who abandoned his wife and children and sailed off to Tahiti in search of conditions more propitious to his painting:

> If he fails . . . then he did the wrong thing, not just in the sense in which that platitudinously follows, but in the sense that having done the wrong thing in those circumstances he has no basis for the thought that he was justified in acting as he did. If he succeeds, he does have a basis for that thought. . . . even if Gauguin can be ultimately justified, that need not provide him with any way of justifying himself to others, or at least to all others. Thus he may have no way of bringing it about that those who suffer from his decision will have no justified ground of reproach. Even if he succeeds, he will not acquire a right that they accept what he has to say; if he fails, he will not even have anything to say.[57]

Williams chose this example because it is extreme and throws the nature of the problem into relief. But even if an artist or a writer has made a choice whose effects on others are less acute, such as temporarily relying on the income of a spouse or relative in order to concentrate on creative work, the fundamental problem is the same. He or she cannot "do something which is thought to be essential to rationality and to the notion of justification itself, which is that one should be in a position to apply the justifying considerations at the time of the choice and in advance of knowing whether one was right (in the sense of its coming out right)" (24). Following Pierre-Michel Menger, I argued in chapter 1 that literary writing is "modeled by uncertainty"; I would add now, in the wake of Williams, that it is a risky undertaking even in undramatic cases that pose no imminent threat to the writer's life, because significant portions of that life are, in the long run, at stake. Becoming immature may mean accepting this risk, and immersing oneself in the game, as Archimboldi does, acquiring a "confidence" that has more to do with trust and deep concentration on the work under way than with self-assurance or a sense of achievement: "Archimboldi's writing, the process of creation or the daily routine in which this process peacefully unfolded, gathered strength and something that for want of a better word might be called confidence [*confianza*]" (2666 817; 2666s 1022).

The trust that Archimboldi places in the game turns out to be justifiable: his work works in the first two senses indicated above, at least. His writing proceeds smoothly, and he is able to complete one book after another to his own satisfaction without apparent difficulty: "Writing was easy, because all he needed was a notebook and a pencil" (2666 768). On reading the manuscript of his second book, *The Endless Rose*, the publisher Bubis decides that Archimboldi belongs to the very exclusive category of authors not to be abandoned, however their books fare in the marketplace (815). Before too long, a substantial reading public begins to endorse this commitment (837). As to whether his work will work in the third sense, Archimboldi remains skeptical—"This 'confidence' didn't signify the end of doubt, of course, much less that the writer believed his work had some value" (817)—but that is partly because he wisely concentrates on doing his work rather than monitoring its reception and curating his reputation.

"The Part About the Critics" explores the effects that Archimboldi's work is having in the world, which although unspectacular are indubitably real. In spite of what W. H. Auden wrote in his elegy for W. B. Yeats, poetry (and the same could be said of imaginative literature in general) can make things happen, as Louis Macneice pointed out, disagreeing with his friend:

> The fallacy lies in thinking that it is the *function* of art to make things happen and that the effect of art upon actions is something either direct or calculable. It is an historical fact that art can make things happen and Auden in his reaction from a rigid Marxism seems . . . to have been straying towards the Ivory Tower.[58]

In "7, Middagh Street," Paul Muldoon's Louis goes further. Having said that Auden in America has "set himself up . . . as a Dutch master/intent only on painting an oyster," he takes issue with the famous line: "poetry can make things happen—/not only can, but *must*—/and the very painting of that oyster/is in itself a political gesture."[59] The word "must" should, I think, be understood here as expressing not an obligation but a fact: poetry *necessarily* makes things happen, although those things may and often do seem derisory in the face of a grave wrong. As Macneice implies, the effects of imaginative writing are indirect and incalculable. There is no way of knowing beforehand what they will turn out to be, and this kind of uncertainty, like those discussed in the final section of chapter 1, is illustrated by Bolaño's fiction.

Even when a piece of imaginative writing remains unpublished, its effects may be significant. At the end of "Enrique Martín," the shamefaced poet's manuscript makes it clear to the narrator that his turn to flee has come (LEE 41). In *2666*, Boris Ansky's notebook, improbably preserved from destruction, ignites Hans Reiter's enthusiasm for literature and shows him a way to defy the reign of semblance: "Only Ansky's wandering isn't semblance, he thought, only Ansky at fourteen isn't semblance" (741). Published but very obscure writing may also inflect the course of a life. In "Vagabond in France and Belgium," B makes a pilgrimage to Masnuy Saint-Jean, searching for traces of Henri Lefebvre, whose name he has discovered in an old issue of *Luna Park* (LEE 173). "Why are you so interested in him?" asks his friend M. "Because nobody else is, says B. And because he was good" (187). Similarly, Arturo Belano and Ulises Lima set out for Sonora in search of Cesárea Tinajero on the strength of a single published poem and the reminiscences of her old stridentist companions. This capacity to move readers geographically as well as emotionally is of course shared by better-known authors. Carlos Wieder too inspires quests: "Certain enthusiasts set off into the wide world intending, if not to bring him back to Chile, at least to have their photos taken with the great man" (DS 107). And Espinoza, Pelletier, and Norton journey to Santa Teresa in the hope of finding the writer who brought them together.

Archimboldi's work gives rise to communities and rivalries. It draws its readers into a fictional world that unfolds like an endless rose and, in so doing, opens onto the wider world from which it sprang. Indirectly, it brings the European academics Pelletier and Espinoza to the realization that they will never be fully satisfied by scholarship (2666 29); it removes them from the conference circuit and confronts them with the daily life of a border city in northern Mexico. While Espinoza pursues his romance with Rebeca the rug vendor and has "forgotten all about the books by Archimboldi hidden away in his suitcase" (150), Pelletier buys a French-Spanish dictionary and starts deciphering the local papers. "I want to find out what's going on in this city," he says (137).

What I have said about the effects of Archimboldi's work applies also to the novels and stories of Roberto Bolaño. They have inspired pilgrimages to Blanes, Mexico City, and Sonora, some of which, like those of Dunia Gras, Leonie Meyer-Kreuler, and Montserrat Madariaga Caro, have in turn led to the writing and publication of valuable books. Bolaño's fiction has given rise to communities and rivalries. And as I argued in chapter 1, it sends us back to what is happening among us here and now, provisionally confirming Robert Filiou's declaration: "art is what makes life more interesting than art," only to remind us that, far from rendering itself obsolete, art can only produce this effect by inhabiting the life that it transfigures.

All the indications are that Bolaño's work is working in the third sense indicated above, that it is being taken up and integrated into traditions of literary and popular culture, and that coming years will see it monumentalized and officialized. Understandably, some of Bolaño's early readers have mixed feelings about this process.[60] But even a body of work preceded by a stout reputation meets its readers one by one, and affects them in unforeseeable ways. Precisely because this critical study participates in the process of monumentalization, I would like to end it by remembering that the "incalculably diffusive" effects of Bolaño's fiction (to borrow an expression from George Eliot),[61] the effects that leave no public trace and do not accumulate in any obvious way, may be vital nonetheless, like the indirect effects of the laughter at the end of "The Part About the Crimes": "Even on the poorest streets people could be heard laughing. Some of those streets were completely dark, like black holes, and the laughter that came from who knows where was the only sign, the only beacon that kept residents and strangers from getting lost" (633).

APPENDIX

VICTIMS IN "THE PART ABOUT THE CRIMES" AND *HUESOS EN EL DESIERTO*

NAME OF VICTIM AND DATE ON WHICH BODY FOUND IN 2666. (PAGE REFERENCE IN SPANISH/ ENGLISH EDITIONS)	FEATURES IN COMMON WITH CORRESPONDING REAL CASE (AS DOCUMENTED IN *HUESOS EN EL DESIERTO*). THE NUMBERS REFER TO THE AGES OF THE VICTIMS.	SOLVED/UNSOLVED IN 2666	NAME OF REAL VICTIM AND DATE ON WHICH BODY FOUND, ACCORDING TO *HUESOS EN EL DESIERTO* (PAGE REFERENCE)	FEATURES IN COMMON WITH CORRESPONDING FICTIONAL CASE IN 2666. THE NUMBERS REFER TO THE AGES OF THE VICTIMS.
1. Esperanza Gómez Saldaña January 1993 (444/354)		unsolved	1. Alma Chavira Farel January 23, 1993 (273)	
2. Luisa Celina Vázquez Five days later (445/354)		solved: domestic violence	2. Angelina Luna Villalobos January 25, 1993 (273)	
3. Unidentified Mid-February 1993 (446/355)		unsolved	3. Unidentified February 17, 1993 (273)	
4. Isabel Urrea March 1993 (446/355)	radio reporter, shot in the forehead	unsolved	4. Jessica Lizalde León March 14, 1993 (273)	radio reporter, shot in the face

(continued)

NAME OF VICTIM AND DATE ON WHICH BODY FOUND IN 2666. (PAGE REFERENCE IN SPANISH/ENGLISH EDITIONS)	FEATURES IN COMMON WITH CORRESPONDING REAL CASE (AS DOCUMENTED IN *HUESOS EN EL DESIERTO*). THE NUMBERS REFER TO THE AGES OF THE VICTIMS.	SOLVED/UNSOLVED IN 2666	NAME OF REAL VICTIM AND DATE ON WHICH BODY FOUND, ACCORDING TO *HUESOS EN EL DESIERTO* (PAGE REFERENCE)	FEATURES IN COMMON WITH CORRESPONDING FICTIONAL CASE IN 2666. THE NUMBERS REFER TO THE AGES OF THE VICTIMS.
5. Isabel Cansino A month later (April 1993) (448/357)		unsolved	5. Luz de la O. García April 21, 1993 (273)	
6. Unidentified May 1993 (450/358)	wearing shorts, five months pregnant, strangled	unsolved	6. Unidentified May 3, 1993 (273)	wearing shorts, five months pregnant, strangled
7. Guadalupe Rojas Three days later (450/359)		solved: domestic violence		
8. Unidentified Last dead woman of May 1993 (451/360)	fair skin, light hair, found on the slopes of Cerro Estrella	unsolved	7. Unidentified May 13, 1993 (273)	fair skin, light hair, found on the slopes of Cerro Bola

9. Emilia Mena Mena June 1993 (466/372)	stabbed and burned (though the burning may not have been deliberate)	unsolved (the main suspect was her boyfriend, who disappeared)	8. Verónica Huitrón Quezada June 5, 1993 (273)	stabbed and burned
10. Unidentified Five days later (467/373)	stake driven through her, fractured skull possibly principal cause of death	unsolved	9. Unidentified June 10, 1993 (273)	branch driven through her, died of a fractured skull
11. Margarita López Santos June 1993 (469/375)	16, medical examiner unable to determine cause of death due to state of body	unsolved	10. Guadalupe Ivonne Estrada Salas June 14, 1993 (273)	16, decomposition of body prevented identification of cause of death
12. Unidentified September 1993 (486/389)	in a car in the Buenavista subdivision	unsolved	11. Unidentified August 28, 1993 (272)	in a Mustang in the Senecú subdivision
13. Gabriela Morón Two weeks later (September 1993) (488/390)	18, shot by her boyfriend	solved: domestic violence	12. Marcela Santos García September 17, 1993 (272)	18, shot, apparently by her boyfriend
14. Marta Navales Gómez October 1993 (489/391)	20, found in the dump of the Arsenio Farrell industrial park	unsolved	13. Mireya Hernández Méndez October 14, 1993 (272)	20, found in the dump of the Juárez industrial park

(continued)

NAME OF VICTIM AND DATE ON WHICH BODY FOUND IN 2666. (PAGE REFERENCE IN SPANISH/ ENGLISH EDITIONS)	FEATURES IN COMMON WITH CORRESPONDING REAL CASE (AS DOCUMENTED IN *HUESOS EN EL DESIERTO*). THE NUMBERS REFER TO THE AGES OF THE VICTIMS.	SOLVED/UNSOLVED IN 2666	NAME OF REAL VICTIM AND DATE ON WHICH BODY FOUND, ACCORDING TO *HUESOS EN EL DESIERTO* (PAGE REFERENCE)	FEATURES IN COMMON WITH CORRESPONDING FICTIONAL CASE IN 2666. THE NUMBERS REFER TO THE AGES OF THE VICTIMS.
15. "Elsa Luz Pintado" (carrying ID of Elsa Luz Pintado, but that was not her real identity) October 1993 (489/391)	body in advanced state of decomposition, employee at Hipermercado del Norte	unsolved	14. Tomasa Salas Calderón October 14, 1993 (272)	advanced state of decomposition, employee at Hipermart
16. Andrea Pacheco Martínez Mid–November 1993 (490/392)	13, kidnapped on her way out of Vocational School 16	unsolved	15. Esmeralda Leyva Rodríguez November 15, 1993 (272) 13,	kidnapped on her way out of Vocational School 27
17. Felicidad Jiménez Jiménez December 20, 1993 (491/392)	found at home, piece of wood jammed in her vagina, killed by her son	solved: domestic violence	16. Yolanda Tapia December 15, 1993 (272)	found at home, wood in her vagina, said to have been killed by her son

17. Unidentified January 11, 1994 (272)			white Lycra shorts, flowered blouse
18. Emilia García Hernández February 11, 1994 (272)			killed in the La Mallelón nightclub; apparently by girls who also worked there
19. María Rocío Cordero March 11, 1994 (272)			11, found in a drainage pipe
20. Lorenza Isela González April 25, 1994 (272)			index and little fingers mutilated, strangled and wounded in chest; owner of Safari bar said to have been involved

18. Unidentified Date of death: January 1–6, 1994 (500/399)		unsolved	hot pants, shirt with big black flower stamped on the chest and a red flower on the back
19. Leticia Contreras Zamudio (500/400)		unsolved	killed in the La Riviera nightclub; two other girls from the club charged with the murder but later declared innocent
20. Penélope Méndez Becerra (503/402)		unsolved	11, found in a drainage pipe
21. Lucy Anne Sander (508/406)		unsolved	26, found near the border fence, a few yards past some gas tanks (see case 21 in *Huesos en el desierto*: Donna Maurine Striplin Boggs)
22. América García Cifuentes Two days later (515/411)		unsolved	both hands missing index and little finger, strangled and wounded in chest; owner of Serafino's bar questioned

(*continued*)

NAME OF VICTIM AND DATE ON WHICH BODY FOUND IN 2666. (PAGE REFERENCE IN SPANISH/ENGLISH EDITIONS)	FEATURES IN COMMON WITH CORRESPONDING REAL CASE (AS DOCUMENTED IN *HUESOS EN EL DESIERTO*). THE NUMBERS REFER TO THE AGES OF THE VICTIMS.	SOLVED/UNSOLVED IN 2666	NAME OF REAL VICTIM AND DATE ON WHICH BODY FOUND, ACCORDING TO *HUESOS EN EL DESIERTO* (PAGE REFERENCE)	FEATURES IN COMMON WITH CORRESPONDING FICTIONAL CASE IN 2666. THE NUMBERS REFER TO THE AGES OF THE VICTIMS.
23. Mónica Durán Reyes Two weeks later, May 1994 (515/412)	12, found alongside Santa Teresa–Puebla Azul highway, raped and strangled	unsolved	21. Donna Maurine Striplin Boggs May 12, 1994 (272)	26, found on bank of Río Bravo, in front of the Esmeralda refinery (see case 21 in *2666*: Lucy Anne Sander)
24. Rebeca Fernández de Hoyos A month later (516/412)	33, found in her house, strangled	unsolved	22. Gladys Yaneth Fierro Vargas May 8, 1994 (271)	12, found 300 meters from Juárez-Porvenir highway, strangled and raped
25. Isabel, a.k.a. "La Vaca" August 1994 (522/417)	solidly built, 5'5" (1.65 meters), dark-skinned, dark curly hair; suspects: "El Chilango" and "El Mariachi"	solved: suspects confessed	23. María Agustina Hernández June 25, 1994 (271)	around 35, found in her house, strangled
			24. Patricia, a.k.a. "La Burra" August 8, 1994 (271)	1.63 meters, solidly built, dark-skinned, curly hair; suspects: "El Cuervo" and "El Mariachi"

26. Unidentified October 1994 (530/423)	wearing a gold ring with a black stone, inscribed with the name of an English academy in the center of the city	unsolved	25. Unidentified October 25, 1994 (271)	wearing a ring from the Academia Comercial Hidalgo
27. Unidentified November 1994 (531/424)	about 30, found on a building site	unsolved	26. Unidentified November 9, 1994 (271)	about 30, found on a building site
28. Silvana Pérez Arjona November 1994 (532/425)	15, thin, dark-skinned, hair half scorched off	solved: domestic violence	27. Guillermina Hernández November 20, 1994 (271)	15, thin, dark-skinned, body scorched
29. Unidentified January 5, 1995 (562/449)	skeleton, in a farming cooperative	unsolved	28. Unidentified January 10, 1995 (271)	bones, in a farming cooperative
30. Claudia Pérez Millán January 15, 1995 (563/449)	black sweater, wrapped in a white blanket, 31	unsolved	29. María Cristina Quezada Mauricio January 15, 1995 (271)	black sweater, yellow blanket, 31
31. María de la Luz Romero February 1995 (564/450)	14	unsolved	30. Miriam Adriana Vázquez February 24, 1995	14

(continued)

NAME OF VICTIM AND DATE ON WHICH BODY FOUND IN 2666. (PAGE REFERENCE IN SPANISH/ ENGLISH EDITIONS)	FEATURES IN COMMON WITH CORRESPONDING REAL CASE (AS DOCUMENTED IN HUESOS EN EL DESIERTO). THE NUMBERS REFER TO THE AGES OF THE VICTIMS.	SOLVED/UNSOLVED IN 2666	NAME OF REAL VICTIM AND DATE ON WHICH BODY FOUND, ACCORDING TO HUESOS EN EL DESIERTO (PAGE REFERENCE)	FEATURES IN COMMON WITH CORRESPONDING FICTIONAL CASE IN 2666. THE NUMBERS REFER TO THE AGES OF THE VICTIMS.
32. Sofía Serrano April 1995 (565/451)	found in a hotel	unsolved (cause of death: overdose of bad cocaine, which may have been given to her knowingly)	31. Fabiola Zamudio April 17, 1995 (271)	found in a hotel
33. Olga Paredes Pacheco April 1995 (566/452)	25	unsolved	32. Karina Daniela Gutiérrez April 21, 1995 (271)	25
34. Paula García Zapatero July 1995 (569/454)	19, jeans, low-cut white blouse, cowboy boots	unsolved	33. Araceli Rosaura Martínez Montáñez July 4, 1995 (270)	19, jeans, white blouse, coffee-colored boots
35. Rosaura López Santana July 1995 (569/454)	body dumped behind the PEMEX tanks, pantyhose	unsolved	34. Erika García Moreno July 16, 1995 (270)	body found behind PEMEX, pantyhose

36. Aurora Muños Álvarez, August 1995 (575/459)	28, had gotten into a black Peregrino with two men she seemed to know	unsolved	35. Gloria Olivas Morales, August 6, 1995 (270)	28, kidnapped along with two men
37. Emilia Escalante Sanjuán, August 1995 (576/460)	33, police report (as opposed to medical examiner's report) gives alcohol poisoning as cause of death	unsolved	36. Patricia Cortés Campos, August 8, 1995 (270)	33, police report gives "intoxication" as cause of death
38. Estrella Ruiz Sandoval, A week later (576/460)	17	unsolved	37. "Elizabeth Castro García", August 17, 1995 (270)	17
39. Mónica Posadas, One day later (576/460)	20, "three-way" rape	unsolved	38. Gloria Escobedo Piña, August 20, 1995 (270)	20, "three-way" rape
40. Unidentified, Two days later (578/462)	18–22	unsolved	39. Unidentified, August 22, 1995 (270)	18–20
41. Unidentified, Same day (578/462)	Found 100 feet from previous victim, state of body made it impossible to determine cause of death	unsolved	40. Unidentified, August 22, 1995 (270)	Found near previous victim, dead for 60–90 days, cause of death unknown

(continued)

NAME OF VICTIM AND DATE ON WHICH BODY FOUND IN 2666. (PAGE REFERENCE IN SPANISH/ENGLISH EDITIONS)	FEATURES IN COMMON WITH CORRESPONDING REAL CASE (AS DOCUMENTED IN *HUESOS EN EL DESIERTO*). THE NUMBERS REFER TO THE AGES OF THE VICTIMS.	SOLVED/UNSOLVED IN 2666	NAME OF REAL VICTIM AND DATE ON WHICH BODY FOUND, ACCORDING TO *HUESOS EN EL DESIERTO* (PAGE REFERENCE)	FEATURES IN COMMON WITH CORRESPONDING FICTIONAL CASE IN 2666. THE NUMBERS REFER TO THE AGES OF THE VICTIMS.
42. Jacqueline Ríos A week later (579/462)	25, black underwear, white tennis shoes	unsolved	41. Miriam de los Ángeles Deras August 27, 1995 (270)	25, black underwear, white tennis shoes
43. Marisa Hernández Silva First days of September 1995 (580/463)	17, disappeared at beginning of July (one breast severed, other nipple bitten off)	unsolved	42. Silvia Elena Rivera Morales September 1, 1995 (269)	17, dead for 45 to 60 days
44. Unidentified Three days later (584/466)	hands bound with the strap of a woman's purse (one breast severed, other nipple bitten off)	unsolved	43. Unidentified September 5, 1995 (269)	hands tied with the strap of a woman's purse
45. Unidentified Same day (584/466)	rotting body, Jokko brand jeans	unsolved	44. Unidentified September 10, 1995 (269)	rotting body, Braxton brand jeans

46. Unidentified End of September 1995 (584/466)	Lee jeans (right breast severed, left nipple bitten off)	unsolved	45. Olga Alicia Carrillo September 9, 1995 (269)	Lee jeans
47. Adela García Estrada November 1995 (617/493)	15, right breast severed, left nipple bitten off	unsolved	46. Adriana Torres Márquez November 11, 1995 (268)	15, right breast severed, left nipple bitten
48. Unidentified A week later (618/493)	about 19, gray pants underneath black pants	unsolved	47. Unidentified November 18, 1995 (268)	18, gray pants underneath black pants
49. Beatriz Concepción Roldán Four days later (618/494)	22, prime suspect: her partner, Evodio Cifuentes	unsolved	48. Ignacia Morales Soto November 23, 1995 (268)	22, prime suspect: Juan Escajeda
50. Michelle Requejo December 1995 (619/495)	black blouse, black tennis shoes, hands tied behind her back	unsolved	49. Rosa Isella Quintanilla December 15, 1995 (268)	black blouse, black tennis shoes, tied up
51. Rosa López Larios December 1995 (621/496)	body discovered behind a PEMEX tower	unsolved	50. Elizabeth Gómez December ?, 1995 (268)	body discovered on a PEMEX sports field, prime suspect a municipal policeman

(continued)

NAME OF VICTIM AND DATE ON WHICH BODY FOUND IN 2666. (PAGE REFERENCE IN SPANISH/ENGLISH EDITIONS)	FEATURES IN COMMON WITH CORRESPONDING REAL CASE (AS DOCUMENTED IN HUESOS EN EL DESIERTO). THE NUMBERS REFER TO THE AGES OF THE VICTIMS.	SOLVED/UNSOLVED IN 2666	NAME OF REAL VICTIM AND DATE ON WHICH BODY FOUND, ACCORDING TO HUESOS EN EL DESIERTO (PAGE REFERENCE)	FEATURES IN COMMON WITH CORRESPONDING FICTIONAL CASE IN 2666. THE NUMBERS REFER TO THE AGES OF THE VICTIMS.
52. Ema Contreras December 1995 (623/498)	shot by her partner, a policeman	solved: domestic violence	51. Laura Ana Inere December ?, 1995 (268)	shot
53. Unidentified Beginning of February 1996 (626/500)	Tarahumara woman	unsolved		
54. Unidentified March 1996 (627/501)	10 years old (more or less), found near Casas Negras highway	unsolved	52. Unidentified March 9, 1996 (268)	9–12, Casas Grandes highway
55. Unidentified A few days later (628/503)		unsolved	53. Unidentified March 13, 1996 (268)	
56. Unidentified A week later (629/503)		unsolved	54. Unidentified March 18, 1996 (268)	

57. Unidentified Almost at the same time (630/503)	unsolved	55. Unidentified March 23, 1996 (268)	
58. Beverly Beltrán Hoyos As March (1996) came to an end (630/504)	16	unsolved	56. Guadalupe Verónica Castro Pando March 28, 1996 (268)	15
59. Unidentified Same day (631/504)		unsolved	57. Unidentified March 29, 1996 (268)
			58. Unidentified March 29, 1996 (268)
60. Unidentified The first week of April 1996 (634/507)	unsolved	59. Ignacia Morales April ?, 1996 (268)
		60. Josefina Reyes Salazar April ?, 1996 (268)
		61. Isalda Chávez April ?, 1996 (268)

(*continued*)

NAME OF VICTIM AND DATE ON WHICH BODY FOUND IN 2666. (PAGE REFERENCE IN SPANISH/ENGLISH EDITIONS)	FEATURES IN COMMON WITH CORRESPONDING REAL CASE (AS DOCUMENTED IN *HUESOS EN EL DESIERTO*). THE NUMBERS REFER TO THE AGES OF THE VICTIMS.	SOLVED/UNSOLVED IN 2666	NAME OF REAL VICTIM AND DATE ON WHICH BODY FOUND, ACCORDING TO *HUESOS EN EL DESIERTO* (PAGE REFERENCE)	FEATURES IN COMMON WITH CORRESPONDING FICTIONAL CASE IN 2666. THE NUMBERS REFER TO THE AGES OF THE VICTIMS.
61. Unidentified The last week in April 1996 (635/507)		unsolved	62. Rosario García Leal April 7, 1996	
62. Paula Sánchez Garcés June 1996 (636/508)	dancer at El Pelicano, shot by her husband	solved: domestic violence (but culprit not arrested)	63. Rosario Fátima Rodríguez April 28, 1996 (267)	
63. Unidentified A few days later (637/509)		unsolved	64. Aracely June 7, 1996 (267)	dancer at La Bahia, shot by her husband
64. Erica Mendoza At the end of June 1996 (639/509)		solved: domestic violence	65. Unidentified June 10, 1996 (267)	
			66. Elizabeth Ontiveros López June 26, 1996 (267)	

65. Unidentified July 1996 (641/513)	unsolved	clenched in the victim's hand was a kind of grass called *zacate*, the only thing that grew in the area	67. Unidentified July 7, 1996 (267)	holding local plants in her fist
66. Guadalupe Elena Blanco Shortly afterward (642/513)	unsolved		68. Sandra Luz Juárez Vázquez July 10, 1996 (267)	
67. Linda Vázquez A little later (642/514)	solved: gang violence		69. Unidentified July ?, 1996 (267)	
68. Marisol Camarena End of July 1996 (645/516)	unsolved	body dropped into a drum of corrosive acid, only her hands and feet were still whole, identified by silicone implants, kidnapped by 17 men; the victim's servant and her daughter escaped	70. Rocío Miranda Agüero July 30, 1996 (267)	body dropped into a drum of corrosive acid, only her hands and feet were still whole, identified by silicone implants, kidnapped by 17 men; the victim's servant and her daughter escaped
69. Marina Rebolledo First half of August 1996 (645/516)	unsolved	13, yellow shorts, white blouse, white socks, didn't come back from walking her sister to work at a *maquiladora*	71. Sonia Ivette Sánchez Ramírez August 9, 1996 (267)	13, yellow shorts, white blouse, white socks, didn't come back from walking her sister to work at a *maquiladora*

(continued)

NAME OF VICTIM AND DATE ON WHICH BODY FOUND IN 2666. (PAGE REFERENCE IN SPANISH/ENGLISH EDITIONS)	FEATURES IN COMMON WITH CORRESPONDING REAL CASE (AS DOCUMENTED IN *HUESOS EN EL DESIERTO*). THE NUMBERS REFER TO THE AGES OF THE VICTIMS.	SOLVED/UNSOLVED IN 2666	NAME OF REAL VICTIM AND DATE ON WHICH BODY FOUND, ACCORDING TO *HUESOS EN EL DESIERTO* (PAGE REFERENCE)	FEATURES IN COMMON WITH CORRESPONDING FICTIONAL CASE IN 2666. THE NUMBERS REFER TO THE AGES OF THE VICTIMS.
70. Angélica Nevares First half of August 1996 (645/516)		unsolved	72. Soledad Beltrán August 15, 1996 (266)	
71. Perla Beatriz Ochoterena August 17, 1996 (646/516)	("In the letter it said: all those dead girls" [517])	solved: suicide	73. Alma Leticia (Patricia) Palafox Zavala August 16, 1996 (266)	
72. Unidentified August 20, 1996 (647/517)		unsolved	74. Unidentified August 20, 1996 (266)	
73. Adela García Ceballos (648/518)		solved: domestic violence		
74. Lola Reynolds The last day of September 1996 (650/520)		unsolved	75. Perla Hopkins September 30, 1996 (266)	

75. Janet Reynolds The last day of September 1996 (650/520)		unsolved		
76. Unidentified October 1996 (650/520)	red-painted nails	unsolved	76. Unidentified October 31, 1996 (266)	red-painted nails
77. María Sandra Rosales Zepeda Beginning of November 1996 (653/522)	prostitute, shot by men traveling in a black Suburban	unsolved	77. Norma Leticia de la Cruz Bañuelos November 2, 1996 (266)	prostitute, shot by men traveling in a dark vehicle
78. Luisa Cardona Pardo Middle of November 1996 (656/524)	found in Podestá ravine, put up a struggle	unsolved	78. Leticia García Rosales November 14, 1996 (266)	found in a ravine, put up a struggle
79. Unidentified Three days later (658/525)	found in Podestá ravine, tattoo on left thigh	unsolved	79. Unidentified November 18, 1996 (266)	tattoo on wrist
			80. Unidentified November 31 [sic], 1996 (266)	

(continued)

NAME OF VICTIM AND DATE ON WHICH BODY FOUND IN 2666. (PAGE REFERENCE IN SPANISH/ ENGLISH EDITIONS)	FEATURES IN COMMON WITH CORRESPONDING REAL CASE (AS DOCUMENTED IN *HUESOS EN EL DESIERTO*). THE NUMBERS REFER TO THE AGES OF THE VICTIMS.	SOLVED/UNSOLVED IN 2666	NAME OF REAL VICTIM AND DATE ON WHICH BODY FOUND, ACCORDING TO *HUESOS EN EL DESIERTO* (PAGE REFERENCE)	FEATURES IN COMMON WITH CORRESPONDING FICTIONAL CASE IN 2666. THE NUMBERS REFER TO THE AGES OF THE VICTIMS.
80. Estefanía Rivas December 1996 (659/527)	shot in the back of the head	unsolved	81. Susana Mejía Flores December 6, 1996 (266)	shot in the head
81. Herminia Noriega December 1996 (659/527)	(half-sister of Estefanía Rivas), shot in the back of the head	unsolved	82. Brenda Mejía Flores December 6, 1996 (266)	(sister of Susana), shot in the head
			83. Unidentified January ?, 1997 (266)	
			84. Unidentified January 16, 1997 (265)	
82. Guadalupe Guzmán Prieto The second week of March 1997 (682/545)	11, dead for about a month, strangled, "possible that that killer had hanged the girl with his hands"	unsolved	85. Cinthia Rocío Acosta Alvarado March 11, 1997 (265)	10, dead for a month, strangled, probably hanged with hands

83. Jazmín Torres Dorantes Four days later (682/546)	11, slopes of Cerro Estrella, more than 15 stab wounds	unsolved	86. Ana María Gardea Villalobos March 14, 1997 (265)
84. Carolina Fernández Fuentes Two days later (683/546)		unsolved	87. Maribel Palomino Arvizo March 21, 1997 (265)
85. Unidentified Three days later (684/547)	right breast mutilated, nipple of left breast torn off	unsolved	
86. Unidentified The last week of March 1997 (685/547)		unsolved	
87. Elena Montoya The next day (685/548)		unsolved	88. Silvia Guadalupe Díaz March 29, 1997 (265)
88. Irene González Reséndiz The last day of March 1997 (686/549)		unsolved	

slopes of Cerro Bela, 15 stab wounds

(continued)

NAME OF VICTIM AND DATE ON WHICH BODY FOUND IN 2666. (PAGE REFERENCE IN SPANISH/ENGLISH EDITIONS)	FEATURES IN COMMON WITH CORRESPONDING REAL CASE (AS DOCUMENTED IN *HUESOS EN EL DESIERTO*). THE NUMBERS REFER TO THE AGES OF THE VICTIMS.	SOLVED/UNSOLVED IN 2666	NAME OF REAL VICTIM AND DATE ON WHICH BODY FOUND, ACCORDING TO *HUESOS EN EL DESIERTO* (PAGE REFERENCE)	FEATURES IN COMMON WITH CORRESPONDING FICTIONAL CASE IN 2666. THE NUMBERS REFER TO THE AGES OF THE VICTIMS.
89. Michele Sánchez Castillo April 6, 1997 (699/559)	found next to a soft drink bottling plant, bits of scalp adhering to iron bar, white-beaded black pants pulled down to knees, pink blouse pulled up over breast, fought her attacker, not raped	unsolved	89. Miriam Águilar Rodríguez April 11, 1997 (265)	found behind a soft drink bottling plant, bits of scalp adhering to block of cement, white-flecked black pants pulled down to knees, pink blouse pulled up over breast, successfully resisted rape
90. Unidentified April 12, 1997 (705/564)	black pants, green blouse, tennis shoes, advanced state of decomposition	unsolved	90. Unidentified April 16, 1997 (265)	dark pants, green blouse, tennis shoes, advanced state of decomposition
			91. Unidentified May 15, 1997 (265)	
			92. Marcela Hernández Macías May 19, 1997 (264)	

91. Aurora Cruz Barrientos May 1997 (711/569)	18, killed in her home, multiple stab wounds	unsolved	93. Amelia Lucio Borjas May 29, 1997 (264)	18, killed in her home, 9 stab wounds in thorax
92. Sabrina Gómez Demetrio June 1, 1997 (715/573)	.	unsolved	94. Verónica Beltrán May 31, 1997 (264)	
93. Aurora Ibañez Medel June 1997 (716/573)		unsolved		
94. Unidentified July 1997 (718/575)	between 20 and 25, in a sewage ditch, sock on her right foot, two rings on her left hand	unsolved	95. Unidentified July 9, 1997 (264)	between 20 and 30, in a sewage ditch, sock on her left foot, two fantasy rings on her left hand
95. Ana Muñoz Sanjuán September 1997 (719/576)		unsolved	96. Martha Gutiérrez García September 9, 1997 (264)	
96. María Estela Ramos September 1997 (721/577)		unsolved	97. María Irma Plancarte Luna September 28, 1997 (264)	

(continued)

NAME OF VICTIM AND DATE ON WHICH BODY FOUND IN 2666. (PAGE REFERENCE IN SPANISH/ENGLISH EDITIONS) THE NUMBERS REFER TO THE AGES OF THE VICTIMS.	FEATURES IN COMMON WITH CORRESPONDING REAL CASE (AS DOCUMENTED IN HUESOS EN EL DESIERTO). THE NUMBERS REFER TO THE AGES OF THE VICTIMS.	SOLVED/UNSOLVED IN 2666	NAME OF REAL VICTIM AND DATE ON WHICH BODY FOUND, ACCORDING TO HUESOS EN EL DESIERTO (PAGE REFERENCE)	FEATURES IN COMMON WITH CORRESPONDING FICTIONAL CASE IN 2666. THE NUMBERS REFER TO THE AGES OF THE VICTIMS.
97. Unidentified October 7, 1997 (724/579)	near baseball fields, bite marks on left nipple (half torn off), one leg shorter than the other, more than 35 stab wounds	unsolved	98. Unidentified October 3, 1997 (264)	PEMEX sports field, one leg shorter than the other, about 50 stab wounds
			99. Brenda Esther Alfaro Luna October 13, 1997 (264)	
98. Leticia Borrego García October 10, 1997 (728/583)	half buried, near PEMEX soccer field	unsolved	100. Virginia Rodríguez Beltrán October 13, 1997 (264)	half-buried, sports field behind PEMEX
99. Lucía Domínguez Roa October 10, 1997 (732/586)		unsolved		

100. Rosa Gutiérrez Centeno, October 14, 1997 (739/591)	38	unsolved	101. Juana Íñiguz Mares, October 21, 1997 (264)	38
101. Unidentified, Beginning of November 1997 (743/595)	Cerro La Asunción, bones	unsolved	102. Unidentified, November 7, 1997 (264)	Cerro Bola, bones
102. Angélica Ochoa, November 12, 1997 (748/599)	shot in the street	unsolved	103. Norma Julissa Ramos Muñoz, November 8, 1997 (264)	shot in the street
103. Rosario Marquina, November 16, 1997 (754/603)	clothes hidden in bushes, black leggings and red panties, disappeared while out dancing	unsolved	104. Eréndira Buendía Muñoz, November 7, 1997 (264)	clothes beside the body, black leggings and red panties, disappeared while out dancing
104. María Elena Torres, November 25, 1997 (758/607)	32, stabbed in the neck	unsolved	105. María Teresa Rentería Salazar, November 30, 1997 (263)	32, stabbed in the neck
105. Úrsula González Rojo, December 1, 1997 (764/611)	found in a stream bed, dark-skinned, hair dyed black, pants caught around ankles, stab wounds	unsolved	106. Aracely Núñez Santos, December 1, 1997 (263)	found in a stream bed, dark-skinned, hair dyed black, pants around ankles, stab wounds

(continued)

NAME OF VICTIM AND DATE ON WHICH BODY FOUND IN 2666. (PAGE REFERENCE IN SPANISH/ ENGLISH EDITIONS)	FEATURES IN COMMON WITH CORRESPONDING REAL CASE (AS DOCUMENTED IN *HUESOS EN EL DESIERTO*). THE NUMBERS REFER TO THE AGES OF THE VICTIMS.	SOLVED/UNSOLVED IN 2666	NAME OF REAL VICTIM AND DATE ON WHICH BODY FOUND, ACCORDING TO *HUESOS EN EL DESIERTO* (PAGE REFERENCE)	FEATURES IN COMMON WITH CORRESPONDING FICTIONAL CASE IN 2666. THE NUMBERS REFER TO THE AGES OF THE VICTIMS.
106. Juana Marín Lozada December 3, 1997 (769/616)	dressed, fracture of cervical vertebrae	unsolved	107. Amalia María de los Dolores Saucedo Díaz de León December 3, 1997 (263)	dressed, fracture of cervical vertebrae
107. Unidentified December 10, 1997 (775/620)	bones, by Casas Negras highway, leggings and tennis shoes near body	unsolved	108. Unidentified December 8, 1997 (263)	bones, by Casas Grandes highway, pants and tennis shoes near body
108. Esther Perea Peña December 15, 1997 (781/625)	24, shot in a dance hall	officially solved but probably a cover-up	109. Rosa Margarita Arellanes García December 9, 1997 (263)	24, shot in a dance hall

109. Unidentified December 19, 1997 (788/630)	navy blue pants, black belt, dead for approximately a year	unsolved
110. Unidentified December 1997 (790/632)		unsolved
110. Unidentified December 21, 1997	navy blue pants, black belt, dead for months	

NB: The real cases are listed here in the order in which they follow one another in *Huesos en el desierto* (respecting González Rodríguez's minor departures from chronological order).

Total murders in *2666*: 109. Unsolved: 98 (90 percent). Solved: 11 (10 percent, counting case 62 [in *2666*] as solved and case 108 as unsolved). Seventy-three correspondences between fictional cases and real cases have been indicated in bold. This number is disputable, since some of the correspondences are based on a single common feature, which may be simply coincidental. Four more correspondences could be conjectured on the basis of a single common feature such as age (cases 58 and 100 in *2666*), "red-painted nails" (case 76), or the presence of a tattoo (case 79). Features common to many of the cases, such as the victim's long, dark hair or evidence of vaginal and anal rape, have not been regarded as sufficient basis for a correspondence. It is interesting that most of the correspondences are grouped in two blocks: cases 8–52 and 101–109 in *2666*. There are many more correspondences in the first half of "The Part About the Crimes" than in the second half. The most significant detail revealed by the comparison of the real and fictional cases is that if we include Perla Beatriz Ochoterena among the fictional victims (since her suicide is connected to the murders: she leaves a note referring to "all those dead girls" [*2666* 517]), their number *exactly* matches that of the real victims in Juárez in the years 1995–1998 as recorded in *Huesos en el desierto*.

NOTES

INTRODUCTION

1. Mónica Maristain, *El hijo de Míster Playa: Una semblanza de Roberto Bolaño* (Oaxaca de Juárez: Almadía, 2012), 21; Andrés Neuman, "La fuente y el desierto," in *Roberto Bolaño. Estrella cercana. Ensayos sobre su obra*, ed. Augusta López Bernasocchi and José Manuel López de Abiada (Madrid: Verbum, 2012), 318–319; Oswaldo Zavala, *Siembra de nubes* (Praxis: Mexico, 2011), 161.
2. Ricardo Piglia, "Theses on the Short Story," *New Left Review* 70 (2011): 63.
3. Cora Diamond, *The Realistic Spirit: Wittgenstein, Philosophy and the Mind* (Cambridge, Mass.: MIT Press, 1995), 309.
4. Friedrich Nietzsche, *Untimely Meditations*, ed. Daniel Breazeale, trans. R. J. Hollingdale (Cambridge: Cambridge University Press, 1997), 112.
5. Claudia Card, *Confronting Evils: Terrorism, Torture, Genocide* (Cambridge: Cambridge University Press, 2010), 18.
6. Jean Franco, "Questions for Bolaño," *Journal of Latin American Cultural Studies* 18, nos. 2–3 (2009): 216.

1. THE ANOMALOUS CASE OF ROBERTO BOLAÑO

1. Robert Amutio, "Paroles de traducteur," in *Les astres noirs de Roberto Bolaño*, ed. Karim Benmiloud and Raphaël Estève (Bordeaux: Presses Universitaires de Bordeaux, 1997), 220.
2. Francine Prose, "The Folklore of Exile," *The New York Times*, July 9, 2006.
3. Scott Esposito, "The Dream of Our Youth," *Hermano Cerdo*, April 2008, http://hermanocerdo.anarchyweb.org/index.php/2008/04/the-dream-of-our-youth/.

4. Leon Neyfakh, "The Status Galley: How to Pick Up Girls with the New Roth," *The New York Observer*, June 17, 2008.

5. "Bolaño-mania," *The Economist*, November 20, 2008.

6. Ilan Stavans, "Willing Outcast: How a Chilean-born Iconoclast Became a Great Mexican Novelist," *The Washington Post*, May 6, 2007.

7. Jean Franco, "Questions for Bolaño," *Journal of Latin American Cultural Studies* 18, nos. 2–3 (2009): 207.

8. Tom Tivnan and Philip Stone, "Review of 2009: Author-ised," *The Bookseller*, January 29, 2010, http://www.thebookseller.com/feature/review-2009-author-ised.html.

9. Pierre Bourdieu, *The Rules of Art: Genesis and Structure of the Literary Field*, trans. Susan Emanuel (Stanford: Stanford University Press, 1996), 79.

10. Pierre Bourdieu, *Pascalian Meditations*, trans. Richard Nice (Oxford: Polity Press, 2000), 92.

11. Bourdieu, *The Rules of Art*, 77–81.

12. Horacio Castellanos Moya, *La metamorfosis del sabueso* (Santiago, Chile: Universidad Diego Portales, 2011), 117.

13. On Skármeta, Allende, and the post-Boom, see Donald Shaw, *The Post-Boom in Spanish American Fiction* (Albany: State University of New York Press, 1998), 78, 88, 220.

14. Edmundo Paz Soldán, "Roberto Bolaño: Literatura y apocalípsis," in *Roberto Bolaño: La experiencia del abismo*, ed. Fernando Moreno (Santiago, Chile: Lastarria, 2011), 34.

15. "Roberto Bolaño," interview by Fernando Villagrán, *Off the Record*, Universidad Católica de Valparaíso Televisión, 1998, http://www.youtube.com/watch?v=qNhTTqu5Vsw.

16. This response is not included in the interview as it is published in BP 354–369 and B 62–72.

17. Alberto Medina, "Arts of Homelessness: Roberto Bolaño or the Commodification of Exile," *Novel: A Forum on Fiction* 42, no. 3 (2009): 553.

18. Montserrat Madariaga Caro, *Bolaño infra* (Santiago, Chile: RIL Editores, 2010), 143–151.

19. André Breton, *The Lost Steps*, trans. Mark Polizzotti (Lincoln and London: University of Nebraska Press, 1996), 78–79.

20. Mónica Maristain, *El hijo de Míster Playa: Una semblanza de Roberto Bolaño* (Oaxaca de Juárez: Almadía, 2012), 107, 184.

21. On Bolaño's conception of the literary field as a battlefield, see Carlos Franz, "Roberto Bolaño: una pasión helada," *Letras libres* 26 (2003), http://www.letraslibres.com/index.php?art=9196, and Rafael Eduardo Gutiérrez Giraldo, *De la literatura como un oficio peligroso: Crítica y ficción en la obra de Roberto Bolaño* (Ph.D. diss., Pontificia Universidade Católica do Rio de Janeiro, 2010), 67, http://www2.dbd.puc-rio.br/pergamum/tesesabertas/0610675_10_pretextual.pdf.

22. Roman Jakobson, "Linguistics and Poetics," in *Selected Writings*, vol. 3 (The Hague and Paris: Mouton, 1981), 27.

23. Leo Spitzer, *La enumeración caótica en la poesía moderna*, trans. Raimundo Lida (Buenos Aires: Coni, 1945), 25–27.

24. Jonathan Beckman, "Death and the Maidens," *The Literary Review* 363 (March 2009): 51.

25. Castellanos Moya, *La metamorfosis del sabueso*, 116.

26. Sigmund Freud, "Some Character Types Met with in Psychoanalytic Work," in *The Standard Edition of the Complete Psychological Works of Sigmund Freud*, ed. James Strachey, vol. 14 (London: The Hogarth Press, 1957), 316–318.

27. See Benedictus de Spinoza, *Complete Works*, ed. Michael L. Morgan, trans. Samuel Shirley and others (Indianapolis: Hackett, 2002), 283; and Gilles Deleuze, *Spinoza: Practical Philosophy*, trans. Robert Hurley (San Francisco: City Lights, 1988), 71, 62–63, 100.

28. Ignacio Echevarría, "Bolaño Extraterritorial," in *Bolaño salvaje*, ed. Edmundo Paz Soldán and Gustavo Faverón Patriau (Barcelona: Candaya, 2008), 444.

29. See Spinoza, *Complete Works*, 319; and Deleuze, *Spinoza*, 28.

30. Roberto Bolaño, "Entrevista a Roberto Bolaño," interview by Mihály Dés, *Lateral: Revista de cultura* 5, no. 40 (1998): 8; Carmen Boullosa, "El agitador y las fiestas," in *Bolaño salvaje*, ed. Edmundo Paz Soldán and Gustavo Faverón Patriau (Barcelona: Candaya, 2008), 424.

31. Jules Huret, *Enquête sur l'évolution littéraire* (Paris: Charpentier, 1891), 65; Arthur Rimbaud, *Collected Poems*, trans. Oliver Bernard (Harmondsworth: Penguin, 1986), 319.

32. Alejandro Zambra, *Formas de volver a casa* (Barcelona: Anagrama, 2011), 164.

33. "On Bolaño," *N + 1*, November 12, 2008, http://www.nplusonemag.com/bola-o.

34. On Bolaño's attitude to young writers, see B 124, and Andrés Neuman, "La fuente y el desierto," in *Roberto Bolaño. Estrella cercana. Ensayos sobre su obra*, ed. Augusta López Bernasocchi and José Manuel López de Abiada (Madrid: Verbum, 2012), 319.

35. Javier Cercas, "Bolaño en Gerona: Una amistad," in *Archivo Bolaño 1977–2003*, ed. Juan Insua (Barcelona: Centro de Cultura Contemporánea de Barcelona, 2013), 61.

36. For a detailed study of the reception of Bolaño's fiction in English translation, see Wilfrido H. Corral, *Bolaño traducido: Nueva literatura mundial* (Madrid: Escalera, 2011).

37. Josefina Ludmer, interview by Magalí Ventura and Karina Micheletto, *Matando más enanos . . .* (blog), April 8, 2007, http://matandomasenanos.blogspot.com/2007/04/josefina-ludmer.html.

38. Sarah Pollack, "Latin America Translated (Again): Roberto Bolaño's *The Savage Detectives* in the United States," *Comparative Literature* 61, no. 3 (2009): 362.

39. Darío Jaramillo Agudelo, "Mago de un solo truco," *El País*, April 4, 2007.

40. Natasha Wimmer, "Natasha Wimmer on Translating 2666," interview by Alan Page, *Vulture*, November 14, 2008, http://www.vulture.com/2008/11/natasha_wimmer_on_translating.html.

41. Cited in Javier Cercas, "Print the Legend," *El País*, April 14, 2007.

42. Jorge Luis Borges, *Selected Non-Fictions*, ed. Eliot Weinberger, trans. Esther Allen, Suzanne Jill Levine, and Eliot Weinberger (New York: Penguin, 1999), 54.

43. "What is characteristic of great geniuses is their faculty of generalizing and their power of creation. They create types, each of which epitomizes a class, and by doing so they enrich the consciousness of mankind. . . . Shakespeare is formidable in this regard. He was not a man, he was a continent: he contained whole crowds of great men, entire landscapes. Writers like him do not worry about *style*: they are powerful in spite of all their faults and because of them. When it comes to us, the little men, our value depends on finished execution. Hugo, in this century, will rout all his contemporaries, even though he is full of

bad things: but what lung-power! What inspiration! I will risk a proposition here that I wouldn't dare utter to anyone else: that very great men often write very badly—and bravo for them" (Gustave Flaubert, *The Letters of Gustave Flaubert 1830–1857*, ed. and trans. Francis Steegmuller [London: Faber, 1979], 171).

44. Nicole Krauss has said that she was influenced by Bolaño when writing *Great House*: "He's one of those writers who absolutely changed everything for me" (interview with Juliet Linderman, *Jewcy Magazine*, October 27, 2010, http://www.jewcy.com/arts-and-culture/jewcy-interviews-nicole-krauss). Similarly, the Japanese novelist Akiko Otake has written: "I read the fourteen short stories [of *Llamadas telefónicas* in the Japanese translation] and felt that something inside me changed. The stories left me with a tactile impression. I felt that the author, more than the stories themselves, had influenced my life, which was a rare experience" (comments on Kinokuniya booklog, 2009, http://booklog.kinokuniya.co.jp/ohtake/archives/2009/10/post_52.html, trans. Masako Ogawa). Commenting on the Chinese translation of *2666*, the novelist Yu Hua has predicted that Bolaño will have an influence on Chinese writing comparable to that of García Márquez: "These two great works are just like two different trees in the vast world of Latin American literature. . . . Chinese writers will surely find inspiration in *2666*, just as they have in *Solitude* over the decades" (Wu Ziru, "The Chinese Edition of Bolaño's *2666* Newly Released," *Global Times*, December 25, 2011).

45. César Aira, "Particularidades absolutas," *Nueve Perros* 1 (2001): 11.

46. Andrew Wylie, "Bolaño Studies," *The New York Times*, December 5, 2008.

47. Esposito, "The Dream of Our Youth"; Pollack, "Latin America Translated (Again)," 357–359; Castellanos Moya, *La metamorfosis del sabueso*, 118–123; Christopher Domínguez Michael, *La sabiduría sin promesa* (Santiago, Chile: Ediciones Universidad Diego Portales, 2009), 99; Juan Antonio Masoliver Ródenas, "Palabras contra el tiempo," in *Bolaño salvaje*, ed. Edmundo Paz Soldán and Gustavo Faverón Patriau (Barcelona: Candaya, 2008), 310–311.

48. Marcel Proust, *By Way of Sainte-Beuve*, trans. Sylvia Townsend Warner (London: Chatto and Windus, 1958), 92.

49. C. S. Lewis and E. M. W. Tillyard, *The Personal Heresy: A Controversy* (Oxford: Oxford University Press, 1939), 2.

50. Ibid., 24, 32.

51. Roland Barthes, *Image, Text, Music*, trans. Stephen Heath (London: Fontana, 1977), 145–47.

52. Alexander Nehamas, "Writer, Text, Work, Author," in *Literature and the Question of Philosophy*, ed. Anthony Cascardi (Baltimore: Johns Hopkins University Press, 1987), 278.

53. Roland Barthes, *The Pleasure of the Text*, trans. Richard Miller (New York: Hill and Wang, 1975), 27.

54. Madariaga, *Bolaño infra*, 68.

55. Itamar Even-Zohar, "Translated Literature in the Polysystem," in *The Translation Studies Reader*, ed. Lawrence Venuti (New York and London: Routledge, 2004), 201.

56. Jonathan Lethem, "The Departed," *The New York Times*, November 12, 2008.

57. Barbara Epler, "Roberto Bolaño in the USA," in *Archivo Bolaño 1977–2003*, ed. Juan Insua (Barcelona: Centro de Cultura Contemporánea de Barcelona, 2013), 168.

58. Two of his stories, "Cell Mates" and "Joanna Silvestri," have appeared in *Playboy*.

59. Cited in David Smith, "Women Are Still a Closed Book to Men," *The Observer*, May 29, 2005.

60. Over the last thirty years, the percentages of female winners of the Nobel Prize for Literature, the Pulitzer Prize for Fiction, the Man-Booker Prize, and the Rómulo Gallegos Prize are all below 50. Nevertheless, the percentages over the last 10 years are higher in each case. Nobel: 40 percent as against 23 percent; Man-Booker: 50 percent as against 40 percent; Pulitzer: 40 percent as against 37 percent; Rómulo Gallegos: 20 percent as against 14 percent.

61. In the "Note to the First Edition" of *2666*, Ignacio Echevarría speaks of the novel's "rash totalizing zeal" (2666 896). In a review, Sam Anderson called it Bolaño's "everything novel" ("Prose Poem: Roberto Bolaño's Brilliant, Messy, Everything Novel," *New York Magazine*, November 7, 2008, http://nymag.com/arts/books/reviews/52011/).

62. Don Anderson, "Visceral Realism in Bolaño's Sea of Seeming," *The Australian*, January 10, 2009.

63. In *The Encyclopedia of Twentieth-Century Fiction*, the teams line up as follows. Minimalists: Raymond Carver, Anne Beattie, Marilynne Robinson, Amy Hempel, Frederick Barthelme, Bobbie Ann Mason, Tobias Wolff, Jayne Anne Phillips, Richard Ford. Maximalists: David Foster Wallace, Jonathan Franzen, Richard Powers, Rick Moody, William T. Vollmann, Thomas Pynchon, Don DeLillo, Paul West (*The Encyclopedia of Twentieth-Century Fiction*, ed. Brian W. Shaffer and Patrick O'Donnell, 3 vols. [Chichester: Wiley-Blackwell, 2011], 3:706).

64. In a recently published letter, written in 1986, Bolaño claimed: "there is almost certainly no Chilean poet who knows the history of the Soviet Union during the Second World War better than I do" ("Autobiografía," *Granta 13: Mex* (2012): 277).

65. Henry James, "The Art of Fiction," in *The Portable Henry James*, ed. Morton Dauwen Zabel (Penguin: Harmondsworth, 1977), 402–403.

66. Virginia Woolf, *Women and Writing* (London: The Women's Press, 1979), 71.

67. Bourdieu, *Pascalian Meditations*, 144.

68. Pierre Bourdieu, *Distinction: A Social Critique of the Judgement of Taste*, trans. Richard Nice (London: Routledge and Kegan Paul, 1984), 323.

69. Alberto Manguel, review of *Nazi Literature in the Americas*, *The Guardian*, February 6, 2010.

70. Philip Larkin, *Required Writing: Miscellaneous Pieces 1955–1982* (London: Faber, 1983), 69.

71. César Aira, "Lo incomprensible," *ABC Cultural*, February 26, 2000: 23.

72. Lorin Stein, "Q&A with Lorin Stein," *Las obras de Roberto Bolaño* (blog), January 28, 2010, http://www.bolanobolano.com/tag/lorinstein/Stein; Natasha Wimmer, "The Translator's Task—To Disappear," interview by Matthew Shaer, *Christian Science Monitor*, January 16, 2009.

73. Scott Esposito, "*2666*—The Big Book of BEA?" *Conversational Reading* (blog), June 3, 2008, http://www.conversationalreading.com/2008/06/a-little-more-a.html.

74. Matthew J. Sagalnik, Peter Sheridan Dodds, and Duncan J. Watts, "Experimental Study of Inequality and Unpredictability in an Artificial Cultural Market," *Science* 311, no. 5762 (2006): 855–56.

75. Richard Caves, *Creative Industries: Contracts Between Art and Commerce* (Cambridge, Mass.: Harvard University Press, 2000), 371.

76. Pierre-Michel Menger, *Le travail créateur: S'accomplir dans l'incertain* (Paris: Hautes Études, Gallimard/Seuil, 2009), 317.

77. Ibid., 8.

2. BOLAÑO'S FICTION-MAKING SYSTEM

1. Javier Cercas, "Print the Legend," *El País,* April 14, 2007.

2. Nora Catelli, "El laboratorio Bolaño," *El País,* September 14, 2002.

3. Jorge Luis Borges, *Collected Fictions*, trans. Andrew Hurley (New York: Viking, 1998), 94.

4. Roland Barthes, *Image, Text, Music,* trans. Stephen Heath (London: Fontana, 1977), 92–95.

5. Guillermo Martínez, "Narrativa argentina hoy," *Guillermo Martínez* (blog), 2010, http://guillermo-martinezweb.blogspot.com/2011/06/Narrativa-argentina-hoy.html.

6. Daniel Aranda, "Originalité historique du retour de personnages balzaciens," *Revue d'histoire littéraire de la France* 101, no. 6 (2001): 1588.

7. Aranda, "Originalité historique," 1583; Fernand Lotte, "Le 'retour des personnages' dans 'La Comédie humaine,'" *Année balzacienne 1961*: 236–256.

8. Marcel Proust, *The Prisoner* and *The Fugitive*, trans. Carol Clark and Peter Collier (London: Penguin, 2003), 144.

9. Marcel Proust, *Correspondance*, ed. Philip Kolb, vol. 21 (Paris: Plon, 1993), 41.

10. P. F. Strawson, *Individuals: An Essay in Descriptive Metaphysics* (London: Routledge, 1959), 31.

11. Lotte, "Le 'retour des personnages,'" 258.

12. César Aira, *Las noches de Flores* (Barcelona: Mondadori, 2004), 29, 32.

13. Sergio Marras similarly regards *Distant Star* as the "main point of inflection" in Bolaño's fiction (*El héroe improbable* [Santiago de Chile: RIL editores, 2011], 31). A recently published letter to Waldo Rojas shows that *Distant Star* was finished by November 1995 (Roberto Bolaño, *De Blanes a Paris: Sobre una correspondencia de Roberto Bolaño a Waldo Rojas*, ed. Giordano Muzio and Nicolás Slachevsky [Santiago de Chile: Multitud, 2012]: n.p.).

14. The posthumously published volumes *The Unknown University* and *Woes of the True Policeman* functioned in comparable but significantly different ways. *Woes of the True Policeman* seems to have served as a structural model for *2666*. Its central character is Oscar Amalfitano, who reappears in "The Part About Amalfitano." In *Woes*, Amalfitano's daughter disappears with an unnamed black man (100), who prefigures Oscar Fate in *2666*. Like *2666*, *Woes* is composed of five parts: one is a "part about Archimboldi" (entitled "J. M. G. Arcimboldi") and another a "part about the crimes" ("Killers of Sonora"). But the posthumously published novel did not serve only as a source of characters and narrative ideas; textual material from it is also reproduced elsewhere. Padilla's letter about Raoul Delorme and the sect of "barbaric writers" (WTP 69–71) is recycled and expanded in chapter 10 of *Distant Star* (130–135). Padilla's classification of poets into "faggots, queers, sissies," etc. (WTP 3–5) is attributed to Ernesto San Epifanio in *The Savage Detectives* (72–74). The story about

the corporal who supposedly raped Arthur Rimbaud, affirmed as fact by the narrator of *Woes* (96–97), reappears in *The Savage Detectives* as "an amazing story" told by Ulises Lima (144–145). An anecdote recounted to Amalfitano in *Woes* (60–62) becomes "Another Russian Tale" (R 19–23). Pancho Monje's account of how he defended his employer's wife when the other two bodyguards ran away (WTP 184–189) figures as an episode in the life of Lalo Cura in *2666* (394–396), and Lalo Cura's genealogy (*2666* 554–558) reproduces that of Pancho Monje (WTP 178–183), with one significant difference: instead of being seduced by three students from Monterrey in 1968, Lalo's mother sleeps with two students from Mexico City in 1976.

The posthumous poetry collection *The Unknown University* was quarried in a similar way: Bolaño carefully prepared the typescript in 1993 (UU 817) and later took from it two sections of *Tres* (2000) and the entirety of *Antwerp* (2002), as well as material for *The Romantic Dogs* (1995) and *El último salvaje* (*The Last Savage*, 1995) (Ignacio Echevarría and Bruno Montané, "Editando a Bolaño," *Quimera* 314 [2010]: 41). In these cases of extraction (rather than expansion), the changes are minor.

15. Jorge Guzmán Tapia, *En el borde del mundo: Memorias del juez que procesó a Pinochet*, trans. Oscar Luis Molina S. (Barcelona: Anagrama, 2005), 125, 143–144.

16. The fight at the end of *The Savage Detectives* takes place outside Villaviciosa, and Belano and Lima are last seen driving west (SD 573). In *2666*, the students, who have been in Villaviciosa, are looking for the highway to Ures or Hermosillo, both of which lie to the west, when they meet María Expósito (*2666* 558; Dunia Gras and Leonie Meyer-Kreuler, *El viaje imposible: En México con Roberto Bolaño* [Zaragoza: Tropo, 2010], 87–90).

17. There is another prefiguration of Lalo Cura in *Woes of the True Policeman*, where the genealogy and life of Pancho Monje, as pointed out in note 14 above, correspond closely to those of Lalo in *2666*. The characters' family names, moreover, are semantically linked: Monje (monk), Cura (priest). And to complicate matters further still, the story "William Burns" has been passed on to the narrator by "Pancho Monge" (with a g), "a policeman in Santa Teresa" (R 25).

As the Colombian Lalo prefigures the Mexican Lalo and is transfigured by him, so the Amalfitano of *Woes of the True Policeman* prefigures the Amalfitano of *2666*. In *Woes*, Amalfitano teaches literature; he has translated J. M. G. Arcimboldi's *The Endless Rose* (21); and he discovers his homosexuality after the death of his wife. Because of an affair with a student, he has been obliged to quit his job as a professor in Barcelona. The only university that will employ him is the University of Santa Teresa (28). In *2666*, Amalfitano teaches philosophy; he has translated Benno von Archimboldi's *The Endless Rose* (116); and the European critics suppose that he is homosexual when they see him with the rector's son, Marco Antonio Guerra (128), but their supposition is not confirmed. When Amalfitano is asked by his father's spirit if he is a queer, he replies with a calm *no* (208). He is living in Santa Teresa because he was convinced by Silvia Pérez, a professor whom he met in Buenos Aires, to go and teach there when his contract in Barcelona expired (199).

The writer Arc(h)imboldi presents an especially complex case of transfiguration. In *The Savage Detectives*, J. M. G. Arcimboldi is a French writer, "one of the greatest French

2. BOLAÑO'S FICTION-MAKING SYSTEM

novelists," according to Luis Sebastián Rosado (155), author of a novel entitled *The Endless Rose* (271). His properties are compatible with those of the more fully developed J. M. G. Arcimboldi of *Woes of the True Policeman*, in which *The Endless Rose*, although mentioned (21), is not among the seven novels summarized. By virtue of his initials and his French-ness, Arcimboldi brings to mind J. M. G. Le Clézio, winner of the Nobel Prize in 2008. In *2666*, Benno von Archimboldi, with an h, is the improbable pseudonym adopted by the German writer Hans Reiter, whose biography is quite distinct from that of J. M. G. Arcimboldi, yet whose bibliography includes *The Endless Rose* (2666 815). The French writer and the German have incompatible properties, and their names, though similar, are differ-ent, but to treat them simply as independent characters would be to miss the significant "dialogue" between them. Both names allude to that of the Milanese mannerist painter Giuseppe Arcimboldo (1527–1593), in whose work Boris Ansky in *2666* puzzlingly finds, as well as joy and terror, simplicity and "the end of semblance" (729, 734–735). With the mention of Arcimboldo and the allusions to his name, Bolaño may be indirectly figuring a feature of his fiction-making system, for the painter's way of representing whole objects that are also fragments of a larger and more loosely structured whole is analogous to the way *The Savage Detectives* and *2666* are made up of juxtaposed and interlocking stories (see Marras, *El héroe improbable*, 21–26).

18. Celina Manzoni, "Reescritura como desplazamiento y anagnórisis en *Amuleto*," in *Roberto Bolaño: La escritura como tauromaquia*, ed. Celina Manzoni (Buenos Aires: Corregidor, 2002), 176.

19. Paisley Livingston, "Nested Art," *The Journal of Aesthetics and Art Criticism* 61, no. 3 (2003): 238.

20. Gérard Genette, *Palimpsests*, trans. Channa Newman and Claude Doubinsky (Lincoln and London: University of Nebraska Press, 1997), 251.

21. Borges, *Collected Fictions*, 67.

22. Livingston, "Nested Art," 242.

23. As several critics have pointed out, Ramírez Hoffman's skywriting and Willy Schürholz's land art allude to formally similar projects undertaken by Raúl Zurita in 1982 and 1993. See Ina Jennerjahn, "Escritos en los cielos y fotografías del infierno. Las 'Acciones de arte' de Carlos Ramírez Hoffman, según Roberto Bolaño," *Revista de Crítica Literaria Latinoamericana* 28, no. 56 (2002): 74–80; María Luisa Fischer, "La memoria de las historias en *Estrella distante* de Roberto Bolaño," in *Bolaño salvaje*, ed. Edmundo Paz Soldán and Gustavo Faverón Patriau (Barcelona: Candaya, 2008), 153–154; Ignacio López-Vicuña, "The Violence of Writing: Liter-ature and Discontent in Roberto Bolaño's Chilean Novels," *Journal of Latin American Cultural Studies* 18, nos. 2–3 (2009): 159–160; Gareth Williams, "Sovereignty and Melancholic Paralysis in Roberto Bolaño," *Journal of Latin American Cultural Studies* 18, nos. 2–3 (2009): 133–136; Silvana Mandolessi, "El arte según Wieder: Estética y política de lo abyecto en *Estrella distan-te*," *Chasqui* 40, no. 2 (2011): 72–74; Helena Usandizaga, "Poesía y prosa en la obra de Roberto Bolaño," in *Roberto Bolaño. Estrella cercana. Ensayos sobre su obra*, ed. Augusta López Bernasoc-chi and José Manuel López de Abiada (Madrid: Verbum, 2012): 396–398; Jean Franco, *Cruel Modernity* (Durham and London: Duke University Press, 2013), 117–118.

24. Oulipo, *Oulipo Compendium*, ed. Harry Matthews and Alastair Brotchie (London: Atlas, 1998), 124.

25. In an early instance of the pseudosummary in Bolaño's work, Enric Rosquelles in *The Skating Rink* describes a novel by Remo Morán entitled *Saint Bernard*, which is also fundamentally ambiguous in that it "recounts the deeds of a dog of that breed, or a man named Bernard, later canonized, or a delinquent who goes by that alias" (SR 168).

26. Mark Ford, "Bolaño: On the Edge of the Precipice," *The New York Review of Books* 58, no. 15 (2011): 33.

27. Alan Pauls, "La solución Bolaño," in *Bolaño salvaje*, ed. Edmundo Paz Soldán and Gustavo Faverón Patriau (Barcelona: Candaya, 2008), 327. Philip Derbyshire writes: "The poets of the novel are poetically silent," which is true, but this silence results from a strategic choice on the part of the novelist and does not imply, as Derbyshire claims, "the loss or impossibility of poetry" or "the impossibility of poetic language as such" (*"Los detectives salvajes*: Line, Loss and the Political," *Journal of Latin American Cultural Studies* 18, nos. 2–3 [2009]: 168, 172, 174).

28. The speaker in "Ravings I," from *A Season in Hell*, says of his "infernal bridegroom": "Perhaps he possesses secrets for *transforming life*?" (Arthur Rimbaud, *Collected Poems*, trans. Oliver Bernard [Harmondsworth: Penguin, 1986], 322).

29. William Butler Yeats, *Collected Poems* (London: Macmillan, 1982), 278.

30. Andrés Ramírez is talking to Belano (SD 360–372).

31. Wolfgang Iser, "Indeterminacy and the Reader's Response in Prose Fiction," in *Aspects of Narrative*, ed. J. Hillis Miller (New York: Columbia University Press, 1971), 12.

32. Livingston, "Nested Art," 237.

33. The following novels are briefly described: *The Berlin Underworld* (5), *Bitzius* (6), *The Endless Rose* (815), *Rivers of Europe* (823), *Bifurcaria Bifurcata* (824), *Saint Thomas* (846), *The Blind Woman, The Black Sea, The Lottery Man, The Father* (847), and *The King of the Forest* (887). Of *The Garden, The Leather Mask,* and *D'Arsonval,* we know only that they concern England, Poland, and France, respectively (3), and that in *The Leather Mask* there is a mask made of human skin (106), which perhaps explains why Pelletier thinks that his lover Vanessa might read it as a horror novel (82). *Mitzi's Treasure* (4), *Railroad Perfection* (5–6), *The Head* (60), *Lüdicke* (783), *Inheritance* (837), and *The Return* (849) are simply mentioned, not described at all.

34. *Railroad Perfection* (a title reused in *2666*) consists of ninety-nine apparently unrelated two-page dialogues, which begin *in medias res* and break off inconclusively. On a second or third reading, an exegete may realize that many of the novel's diverse characters are avatars of a fundamental pair, reducible in turn to a single person, engaged in schizophrenic self-pursuit: "both are fleeing, or chasing each other, or one is chasing and the other is hiding" (WTP 158). As if that were not complicated enough, it is also possible to reconstruct a series of stories by connecting nonconsecutive dialogues. Like many of the pseudosummaries in *Nazi Literature in the Americas*, this one serves a ludic function.

35. Umberto Eco, *Interpretation and Overinterpretation*, ed. Stefan Collini (Cambridge: Cambridge University Press, 1992), 48–49.

36. Richard Rorty, "The Pragmatist's Progress," in *Interpretation and Overinterpretation*, ed. Stefan Collini (Cambridge: Cambridge University Press, 1992), 97.

37. Peter Brugger, "From Haunted Brain to Haunted Science: A Cognitive Neuroscience View of Paranormal and Pseudoscientific Thought," in *Hauntings and Poltergeists*, ed. James Houran and Rense Lange (Jefferson, N.C.: McFarland, 2001), 204.

38. Mónica Maristain, *El hijo de Míster Playa: Una semblanza de Roberto Bolaño* (Oaxaca de Juárez: Almadía, 2012), 187.

39. Sigmund Freud, "Psychoanalytic Notes on an Autobiographical Account of a Case of Paranoia (Dementia Paranoides)," in *The Standard Edition of the Complete Psychological Works of Sigmund Freud*, ed. James Strachey, vol. 12 (London: The Hogarth Press, 1957), 10.

40. Philippe Lançon, "69 raisons de danser avec Bolaño," *Libération*, June 26, 2003.

41. *Antología de la poesía surrealista*, ed. and trans. Aldo Pellegrini (Buenos Aires: Compañia General Fabril Editora, 1961), 228.

42. Robert Amutio, "Paroles de traducteur," in *Les astres noirs de Roberto Bolaño*, ed. Karim Benmiloud and Raphaël Estève (Bordeaux: Presses Universitaires de Bordeaux, 1997), 226.

43. Lançon, "69 raisons de danser avec Bolaño."

44. Eco, *Interpretation and Overinterpretation*, 48–49.

45. Raymond Roussel, *How I Wrote Certain of My Books*, trans. Trevor Winkfield (Ann Arbor, Mich.: Sun, 1977), 11.

3. SOMETHING IS GOING TO HAPPEN: NARRATIVE TENSION

1. Gustave Flaubert, *The Letters of Gustave Flaubert 1830–1857*, ed. and trans. Francis Steegmuller (London: Faber, 1979), 154.

2. E. M. Forster, *Aspects of the Novel* (Harmondsworth: Penguin, 1962), 33.

3. Alain Robbe-Grillet, *For a New Novel*, trans. Richard Howard (Evanston, Ill.: Northwestern University Press, 1989), 33. He did, however, go on to recognize, indirectly, that the target of his polemic was not storytelling as such, but a certain historically conditioned notion of what *counts* as a story, since he imagined critics of the future reflecting nostalgically on the era of the "new novel" and saying, "Look how, back in the fifties, people knew how to invent stories" (34).

4. B. S. Johnson, *Aren't You Rather Young to Be Writing Your Memoirs?* (London: Hutchinson, 1973), 14–15.

5. Mark Ford, "Bolaño: On the Edge of the Precipice," *The New York Review of Books* 58, no. 15 (2011): 36.

6. Robert McKee, *Story: Substance, Structure, Style, and the Principles of Screenwriting* (New York: Regan Books, 1997), 217, 338.

7. Jean-Marie Schaeffer, "Avant-propos," in Raphaël Baroni, *La tension narrative: Suspense, curiosité, surprise* (Paris: Seuil, 2007), 13.

8. Emma Kafalenos, "Emotions Induced by Narratives," *Poetics Today* 20, no. 3 (2008): 383.

9. Raphaël Baroni, *La tension narrative: Suspense, curiosité, surprise* (Paris: Seuil, 2007), 108.

10. Kafalenos, "Emotions Induced by Narratives," 384.

11. Meir Sternberg, "Telling in Time II: Chronology, Teleology, Narrativity," *Poetics Today* 13, no. 3 (1992): 524; Baroni, *La tension narrative*, 110.

12. Donald Beecher, "Suspense," *Philosophy and Literature* 31, no. 2 (2007): 256.

13. Ricardo Piglia, *Formas breves* (Barcelona: Anagrama, 2000), 105; "Theses on the Short Story," *New Left Review* 70 (2011): 63.

14. Piglia, "Theses on the Short Story," 63.

15. Guillermo Martínez, *La fórmula de la inmortalidad* (Seix Barral: Buenos Aires, 2005), 81.

16. Noël Carroll, *The Philosophy of Horror or Paradoxes of the Heart* (New York and London: Routledge, 1990), 130–136.

17. "There is no document of civilization which is not at the same time a document of barbarism" (Walter Benjamin, "Theses on the Philosophy of History," in *Illuminations*, ed. Hannah Arendt, trans. Harry Zohn [London: Fontana, 1973], 258).

18. "2666," *The New Yorker*, November 17, 2008, http://www.newyorker.com/arts/reviews/brief lynoted/2008/11/17/081117crbn_brieflynotedl.

19. Patricia Espinosa, "Tres libros de poesía del primer Bolaño: *Reinventar el amor, Fragmentos de la universidad desconocida* y *El último salvaje*," in *Roberto Bolaño: La experiencia del abismo*, ed. Fernando Moreno (Santiago de Chile: Lastarria, 2011), 64.

20. See SR 179; MP 119; NLA 193; DS 18, 66, 92; SD 567; LEE 25, 73, 103; IG 5; 2666 104, 261.

21. Noël Carroll, "The Paradox of Suspense," in *Suspense: Conceptualizations, Theoretical Analyses, and Empirical Explanation,* ed. Peter Vorderer, Hans J. Wulff, and Mike Friedrichsen (Mahwah, NJ: Lawrence Erlbaum Associates, 1996), 75; Tzvetan Todorov, *The Poetics of Prose*, trans. Richard Howard (Ithaca: Cornell University Press, 1977), 47.

22. Antoni Casas Ros, *Enigma* (Paris: Gallimard, 2010), 55.

23. Meir Sternberg, *Expositional Modes and Temporal Ordering in Fiction* (Baltimore and London: Johns Hopkins University Press, 1978), 244–245; "Telling in Time II," 519.

24. Baroni, *La tension narrative*, 108–109.

25. Gustavo Faverón Patriau, "El Rehacedor: 'El gaucho insufrible' y el ingreso de Bolaño en la tradición argentina," in *Bolaño salvaje*, ed. Edmundo Paz Soldán and Gustavo Faverón Patriau (Barcelona: Candaya, 2008), 378–399.

26. Baroni, *La tension narrative*, 305.

27. Ibid., 300.

28. Sternberg, "Telling in Time II," 524.

29. Mihály Dés, "Putas asesinas," in *Roberto Bolaño: La escritura como tauromaquia*, ed. Celina Manzoni (Buenos Aires: Corregidor, 2002), 198.

30. Piglia, *Formas breves*, 124.

4. AIMLESSNESS

1. Paul Ricoeur, *Time and Narrative*, trans. Kathleen McLaughlin and David Pellauer, vol. 3 (Chicago: University of Chicago Press, 1988), 246.

2. Hannah Arendt, *The Human Condition* (Chicago: University of Chicago Press, 1958), 186.

3. Pierre Bourdieu, *Raisons pratiques: Sur la théorie de l'action* (Paris: Seuil, 1994), 81–82.

4. Arendt, *The Human Condition*, 184.

5. Alasdair MacIntyre, *After Virtue* (Notre Dame: University of Notre Dame Press, 2007), 212.

6. MacIntyre, *After Virtue*, 212; Bernard Williams, "Life as Narrative," *European Journal of Philosophy* 17, no. 2 (2007): 305–314; Peter Lamarque, "On Not Expecting Too Much from Narrative," *Mind & Language* 19 (2004): 394.

7. Anthony Rudd, "In Defense of Narrative," *European Journal of Philosophy* 17, no. 1 (2007): 62.

8. For a recent survey of the debate, and a challenge to "narrative identity realism," which regards "narratively constituted selves as being real in some more ontologically significant sense than fictional constructs are," see Patrick Stokes, "Is Narrative Identity Four-Dimensionalist?" *European Journal of Philosophy* 20 (2012), Issue Supplement S1: E86–E106.

9. Rudd, "In Defense of Narrative," 60.

10. Marya Schectman, "Stories, Lives and Basic Survival: A Refinement and Defense of the Narrative View," in *Narrative and Understanding Persons*, ed. Daniel D. Hutto (Cambridge: Cambridge University Press, 2007), 159–161.

11. Jane Forsey, "Art and Identity: Expanding Narrative Theory," *Philosophy Today* 47, no. 2 (2003): 183.

12. Jeanette Bicknell, "Self Knowledge and the Limitations of Narrative," *Philosophy and Literature* 28 (2004): 402.

13. John Christman, "Narrative Unity as a Condition of Personhood," *Metaphilosophy* 35, no. 5 (2004): 710.

14. Galen Strawson, *Real Materialism and Other Essays* (Oxford: Oxford University Press, 2008), 189. Vendela Vida acknowledges a substantive debt to Strawson in the afterword of her novel *Let the Northern Lights Erase Your Name* (New York: Ecco, 2007).

15. Marya Schechtman, *The Constitution of Selves* (Ithaca, N.Y.: Cornell University Press, 1996), 105.

16. Strawson, *Real Materialism*, 201.

17. Schectman, "Stories, Lives and Basic Survival," 163.

18. Galen Strawson, "The Self," in *Models of the Self*, ed. Shaun Gallagher and Jonathan Shear (Thorverton, UK: Imprint Academic, 1997), 15.

19. Strawson, *Real Materialism*, 193.

20. Ibid., 207.

21. Joshua Landy, *Philosophy as Fiction: Self, Deception and Knowledge in Proust* (Oxford: Oxford University Press, 2004), 11.

22. Friedrich Nietzsche, *Untimely Meditations*, ed. Daniel Breazeale, trans. R. J. Hollingdale (Cambridge: Cambridge University Press, 1997), 112.

23. Strawson, *Real Materialism*, 205.

24. John Lippitt, "Getting the Story Straight: Kierkegaard, MacIntyre and Some Problems with Narrative," *Inquiry* 50 (2007): 49–50; Strawson, *Real Materialism*, 202; Samantha Vice, "Literature and the Narrative Self," *Philosophy* 78 (2003): 103.

25. Cora Diamond, *The Realistic Spirit: Wittgenstein, Philosophy and the Mind* (Cambridge, Mass.: MIT Press, 1995), 309–318.

26. Lippitt, "Getting the Story Straight," 52.

27. Pablo Berchenko, "El referente histórico chileno en *Nocturno de Chile* de Roberto Bolaño," in *La memoria de la dictadura: Nocturno de Chile, Roberto Bolaño; Interrupciones 2, Juan Gelman*, ed. Fernando Moreno (Paris: Ellipses, 2006), 17. Paula Aguilar points out a further resonance: Los Halcones (the Falcons) was the name of a repressive paramilitary group that operated in Mexico from 1966 to 1971 and participated in the Tlatelolco massacre on October 2, 1968. The group was established by Colonel Manuel Díaz Escobar, who was transferred to Chile shortly after the coup in 1973 and worked there as military attaché to the Mexican embassy ("Pobre memoria la mía: Literatura y melancolía en el contexto de la postdictadura chilena [*Nocturno de Chile* de Roberto Bolaño]," in *Bolaño salvaje*, ed. Edmundo Paz Soldán and Gustavo Faverón Patriau [Barcelona: Candaya, 2008], 136).

28. MacIntyre, *After Virtue*, 217. Susan Wolf's ampler conception of meaningfulness might, however, accommodate the life of Auxilio Lacouture, since it requires only that one be "actively and . . . somewhat successfully engaged in projects of independent worth," allows the projects to be brief, and does not stipulate that they should be connected to form a unified life story (*Meaning in Life and Why It Matters* [Princeton and Oxford: Princeton University Press, 2010], 28).

29. Strawson, *Real Materialism*, 198.

30. Landy, *Philosophy as Fiction*, 127.

31. Marcel Proust, *Finding Time Again*, trans. Ian Patterson (London: Penguin, 2003), 295.

32. According to Joshua Landy, Samuel Beckett was an artist who declined the project of creating a total Self: "Beckett, I think, accepts what Proust believes about what it would take to be a self; he accepts the nature of the difficulties standing in the way; he accepts that human beings experience an urge to overcome these difficulties, and to discover or create a coherent identity for themselves; *but he doesn't agree that this is a good thing*" (*How to Do Things with Fictions* [Oxford: Oxford University Press, 2012], 219–220, n. 93).

33. Kathleen V. Wilkes, "Know Thyself," in *Models of the Self*, ed. Shaun Gallagher and Jonathan Shear (Thorverton, UK: Imprint Academic, 1997), 27.

34. Strawson, *Real Materialism*, 225.

35. Schectman, "Stories, Lives and Basic Survival," 163.

36. Strawson, *Real Materialism*, 220.

5. DUELS AND BRAWLS: BORGES AND BOLAÑO

1. See Edwin Williamson, *Borges: A Life* (London: Penguin, 2004), 323, 353, 426.

2. Jorge Luis Borges, "Three Milongas," trans. David Young and Ana Cara-Walker, *World Literature Today* 62, no. 1 (1988): 10.

3. Jorge Luis Borges, *The Aleph and Other Stories (1933–1969)*, ed. and trans. Norman Thomas di Giovanni (Dutton: New York, 1970), 211.

4. Georg Wilhelm Friedrich Hegel, *Aesthetics: Lectures on the Fine Arts*, trans. T. M. Knox (Oxford: Oxford University Press, 1975), 89; Geoffrey Hartman, "Romanticism and

Anti-Self-Consciousness," in *Beyond Formalism: Literary Essays 1958–1970* (New Haven and London: Yale University Press, 1970), 309–310.

5. Percy Bysshe Shelley, *The Selected Poetry and Prose of Shelley*, ed. Harold Bloom (New York: New American Library, 1966), 448.

6. Rodrigo Fresán, "El samurái romántico," in *Bolaño salvaje*, ed. Edmundo Paz Soldán and Gustavo Faverón Patriau (Barcelona: Candaya, 2008), 294.

7. Friedrich Hölderlin, *Poems and Fragments*, trans. Michael Hamburger (London: Routledge and Kegan Paul, 1966), 201.

8. Walter Benjamin, "Two Poems by Friedrich Hölderlin: 'The Poet's Courage' and 'Timidity,'" in *Early Writings 1910–1917*, trans. Howard Eiland and others (Cambridge, Mass.: Harvard University Press, 2011), 192; "Zwei Gedichte von Friedrich Hölderlin, 'Dichtermut'—'Blödigkeit,'" in *Gesammelte Schriften*, ed. Rolf Tiedemann and Hermann Schweppenhäuser, vol. 2.1 (Frankfurt am Main: Suhrkamp Verlag, 1977), 125.

9. For a thorough overview of recent scholarship on "Timidity" and Benjamin's commentary, see May Mergenthaler, "The 'Paradox' of Poetic Courage: Hölderlin's Ode 'Timidity' and Benjamin's Commentary Reconsidered," *The Germanic Review* 85 (2010): 224–249.

10. Pío Baroja, *The Restlessness of Shanti Andia and Selected Stories*, trans. Anthony and Elaine Kerrigan (New York: Signet, 1962), 313.

11. Ernest J. Weinrib, "Duty to Rescue," in *Morality, Harm and the Law*, ed. Gerald Dworkin (Boulder: Westview, 1994), 141–143.

12. Ariel Dorfman, *Some Write to the Future*, trans. George Shivers with the author (Durham and London: Duke University Press, 1991), 37; see also Blas Matamoro, "La guerra borgiana," *Cuadernos hispanoamericanos* 585 (1999): 71.

13. Martín Kohan, "Mano a Mano," *Variaciones Borges* 27 (2009): 231.

14. Jorge Luis Borges, *Collected Fictions*, trans. Andrew Hurley (New York: Viking, 1998), 179.

15. See Steven Boldy, *A Companion to Jorge Luis Borges* (London: Tamesis, 2009), 125–128. The expression "a forking in time" is used by the sinologist Stephen Albert in "The Garden of Forking Paths" (Borges, *Collected Fictions*, 125).

16. Alan Pauls, *El factor Borges: Nueve ensayos ilustrados* (Buenos Aires: Fondo de Cultura Económica de Argentina, 2000), 41.

17. Borges, *Collected Fictions*, 231, translation modified; *Obras completas*, vol. 1 (Buenos Aires: Emecé, 1996), 578.

18. Jorge Luis Borges, *The Sonnets*, ed. and trans. Stephen Kessler (Penguin: Harmondsworth, 2011), 259.

19. Simon Critchley, *Infinitely Demanding: Ethics of Commitment, Politics of Resistance* (London: Verso, 2007), 48.

20. See Ignacio López-Vicuña, "The Violence of Writing: Literature and Discontent in Roberto Bolaño's Chilean Novels," *Journal of Latin American Cultural Studies* 18, nos. 2–3: 158; and on the symbolic conflict between the Tel Quel group and the Oulipo, see Clemens Arts, *Oulipo et Tel Quel: Jeux formels et contraintes génératrices* (Leiden: University of Leiden Press, 1999), 42–45.

21. Jorge Luis Borges, *Evaristo Carriego*, trans. Norman Thomas di Giovanni (New York: E. P. Dutton, 1984), 33.

22. For Alan Pauls, the major work was produced between the late 1930s and the early 1950s (*El factor Borges*, 32). Juan José Saer sets more generous temporal limits (1930–1960), but is also more severe in his comments on the texts written before and after this period (*La narracion-objeto* [Barcelona: Seix Barral, 1999], 127).

23. Jorge Luis Borges, *Doctor Brodie's Report*, trans. Norman Thomas di Giovanni in collaboration with the author (Penguin: Harmondsworth, 1976), 36–37.

24. Borges, *Collected Fictions*, 207.

25. Borges, *Doctor Brodie's Report*, 39.

26. Jorge Luis Borges, *The Book of Sand*, trans. Norman Thomas di Giovanni (Harmondsworth: Penguin, 1979), 22.

27. Williamson, *Borges: A Life*, 355–368.

28. Amélie Oksenberg Rorty, *Mind in Action: Essays in the Philosophy of Mind* (Boston: Beacon Press, 1988), 300–302. For a portrait of a courage addict, who "found his way into all kinds of fights when you'd never have guessed there was any fighting to be done," see "Cutty, One Rock," August Kleinzahler's memoir about the brief life of his brother (*Cutty, One Rock: Low Characters and Strange Places, Gently Explained* [New York: Farrar, Straus and Giroux, 2004], 120–155).

29. There is no justifiable homicide statute in the Mexican Federal Penal Code or in that of the state of Sonora. For a survey of U.S. legislation on the defense of others, see Marco F. Bendinelli and James T. Edsall, "Defense of Others: Origins, Requirements, Limitations, and Ramifications," *Regent University Law Review* 5, no. 153 (1995): 153–214; and for arguments in favor of the imminence requirement for the right to act in self-defense, see Kimberly Kessler Ferzan, "Defending Imminence: From Battered Women to Irak," *Arizona Law Review* 46, no. 213 (2004): 213–262.

30. Alain Badiou, *The Meaning of Sarkozy*, trans. David Fernbach (London: Verso, 2008), 73.

31. Enrique Lihn, *The Dark Room and Other Poems*, ed. Patricio Lerzundi, trans. Jonathan Cohen, John Felstiner, and David Unger (New York: New Directions, 1978), 96–101.

32. Benjamin, "Two Poems by Friedrich Hölderlin," 192.

6. EVIL AGENCIES

1. Claudia Card, *Confronting Evils: Terrorism, Torture, Genocide* (Cambridge: Cambridge University Press, 2010), 18.

2. Pablo Berchenko, "El referente histórico chileno en *Nocturno de Chile* de Roberto Bolaño," in *La memoria de la dictadura: Nocturo de Chile, Roberto Bolaño; Interrupciones 2, Juan Gelman*, ed. Fernando Moreno (Paris: Ellipses, 2006), 18.

3. Pedro Lemebel, *De perlas y cicatrices* (Santiago, Chile: Lom, 1996), 15.

4. On the legal concept of complicity, see Christopher Kutz, *Complicity: Ethics and Law for a Collective Age* (Cambridge: Cambridge University Press, 2007), 209.

5. Primo Levi, *The Drowned and the Saved*, trans. Raymond Rosenthal (New York: Summit, 1988), 40.

6. "Human Rights Trials in Chile and the Region," Human Rights Observatory, Universidad Diego Portales, Santiago, Chile, Bulletin no. 7, 2010, http://www.icso.cl/images/Paperss/observatorio7.pdf; "Caso Prats: Condenan a ex agentes de Pinochet," *La Nación*, July 1, 2008. According to the testimony of Michael Townley, Mariana Callejas was holding the detonator of the car bomb: "I'm sitting at the steering wheel, she's sitting on the other side. It's sitting in her lap. She picks it up and says what do I do. . . . She's fumbling with it, she's pushing it, whatever. It wasn't even turned on" (John Dinges, *The Condor Years: How Pinochet and His Allies Brought Terrorism to Three Continents* [New York and London: The New Press, 2004], 77).

7. Andrés Gómez Bravo, "Ha habido un aprovechamiento de la historia del taller de Lo Curro," *La Tercera*, November 6, 2010.

8. Louis-Ferdinand Céline, *Le style contre les idées* (Paris: Complexe, 1987), 66.

9. As an exemplar of heroic purity, Jünger is a telling choice: decorated in the First World War and associated with the von Stauffenberg bomb plot to assassinate Hitler in 1944, he was also the author of an article on "Nationalism and the Jewish Question" (1930), in which he argued that the Jews posed a threat to German unity: "The realization of the authentic German gestalt separates itself from the Jewish gestalt as clearly as transparent, unmoving water from oil, and takes the shape of a recognizable layer. . . . In the same measure in which the German will gains form and clarity, it would be crazy for a Jew to think that he can be German in Germany. He faces the final alternative: either to be a Jew or not to be" (cited in Elliot Y. Neaman, *A Dubious Past: Ernst Jünger and the Politics of Literature After Nazism* [Berkeley: University of California Press, 1999], 36).

10. See Ignacio López-Vicuña, "The Violence of Writing: Literature and Discontent in Roberto Bolaño's Chilean Novels," *Journal of Latin American Cultural Studies* 18, nos. 2–3 (2009): 164.

11. Mary Midgely, *Wickedness: A Philosophical Essay* (London: Routledge, 1984), 128.

12. Armando Uribe Arce, *El fantasma de la sinrazón y El secreto de la poesía* (Santiago, Chile: Be-uve-dráis editores, 2001), 13.

13. Adam Morton, *On Evil* (New York: Routledge, 2004), 48.

14. Gary Watson, "The Trouble with Psychopaths," in *Reasons and Recognition: Essays on the Philosophy of T. M. Scanlon*, ed. R. Jay Wallace, Rahul Kumar, and Samuel Freeman (New York: Oxford University Press, 2011), 324.

15. Immanuel Kant, *Religion Within the Boundaries of Mere Reason and Other Writings*, ed. and trans. Allen Wood and George di Giovanni (Cambridge: Cambridge University Press, 1998), 60.

16. At one moment only does the narrative adopt Wieder's point of view, during the air show over the Captain Lindstrom airstrip: "Then he flew over some railway sheds and what appeared to be disused factories, although down in the streets he could make out people dragging cardboard boxes, children climbing on fences, dogs. To the left, at nine o'clock, he recognized two enormous shantytowns, separated by the railway tracks" (DS 80). Given

what we know about Wieder's crimes by this stage in the novel, momentarily seeing through his eyes and looking down from a great height on what he would presumably consider to be human vermin is a perturbing experience, which provokes some of the unease felt by the narrator when he recognizes the aviator in a bar near the end of the novel. "For a nauseating moment I could see myself almost joined to him, like a vile Siamese twin, looking over his shoulder at the book he had opened" (DS 144).

17. Kant, *Religion Within the Boundaries of Mere Reason*, 60.

18. Card, *Confronting Evils*, 57.

19. Levi, *The Drowned and the Saved*, 47–60.

20. Card, *Confronting Evils*, 57.

21. As Ina Jennerjahn notes, Ramírez Hoffman/Wieder's exhibition "perverts" certain art actions of the Chilean neo-avant garde, which made use of photographic images of the disappeared ("Escritos en los cielos y fotografías del infierno. Las 'Acciones de arte' de Carlos Ramírez Hoffman, según Roberto Bolaño," *Revista de Crítica Literaria Latinoamericana* 28, no. 56 [2002]: 81).

22. Morton, *On Evil*, 95.

23. Greenwood is rather more optimistic than Romero. For him, "absolute evil" *is* random, but can be fought by learning how to "read" (DS 102).

24. Jean Franco, *Cruel Modernity* (Durham and London: Duke University Press, 2013), 119.

25. Hannah Arendt, *Eichmann in Jerusalem* (New York: Penguin, 2006), 287.

26. Isabelle Delpla, *Le mal en procès: Eichmann et les théodicées modernes* (Paris: Hermann, 2011), 154.

27. See Delpla, *Le mal en procès*, 106–108, 140–143.

28. Arendt, *Eichmann in Jerusalem*, 94–95.

29. Delpla, *Le mal en procès*, 62.

30. Arendt, *Eichmann in Jerusalem*, 106.

31. Christopher R. Browning, *Ordinary Men: Reserve Police Battalion 101 and the Final Solution in Poland* (London: Penguin, 2001), 76.

32. David Cesarani, *Eichmann: His Life and Crimes* (London: William Heinemann, 2004), 11–12; Delpla, *Le mal en procès*, 108, 140–143.

33. Delpla, *Le mal en procès*, 162.

34. See Morton, *On Evil*, 78–80.

35. J. M. Coetzee, *Elizabeth Costello: Eight Lessons* (Sydney: Random House, 2003), 167.

36. Arendt, *Eichmann in Jerusalem*, 252.

37. José Ramón Ruisánchez, "Fate o la inminencia," in *Roberto Bolaño: Ruptura y violencia en la literatura finisecular*, ed. Felipe A. Ríos Baeza (Mexico: Ediciones Eón, 2010), 395–396.

38. See *Archivo Bolaño 1977–2003*, ed. Juan Insua (Barcelona: Centro de Cultura Contemporánea de Barcelona, 2013), 104.

39. Paul Ricoeur, *Le mal: Un défi à la philosophie et à la théologie* (Geneva: Labor et Fides, 2004), 26.

40. Susan Neiman, "What's the Problem of Evil?" in *Rethinking Evil: Contemporary Perspectives*, ed. María Pía Lara (Berkeley and Los Angeles: University of California Press, 2001), 42; see also her *Evil in Modern Thought: An Alternative History of Philosophy* (Melbourne: Scribe, 2003), 68–70.

41. Stephen Greenblatt, *Will in the World: How Shakespeare Became Shakespeare* (London: Jonathan Cape, 2004), 323–324. See also Susan James, "Fruitful Imagining: On Catherine Wilson's 'Grief and the Poet,'" *British Journal of Aesthetics* 53, no. 1 (2013): 99; and Frank Kermode, *The Genesis of Secrecy: On the Interpretation of Narrative* (Cambridge, MA: Harvard University Press, 1979), 25.

42. Oswaldo Zavala, *Siembra de nubes* (Praxis: Mexico, 2011), 160.

7. A SENSE OF WHAT MATTERS

1. See Paul Ricoeur, *Time and Narrative*, trans. Kathleen McLaughlin and David Pellauer, vol. 3 (Chicago: University of Chicago Press, 1984), 59; Martha Nussbaum, *Love's Knowledge: Essays on Philosophy and Literature* (Oxford: Oxford University Press, 1990), 26; Gisèle Sapiro, *La responsabilité de l'écrivain: Littérature, droit et morale en France (XIXe–XXIe siècle)* (Paris: Seuil, 2011), 719.

2. E. M. Forster, *Aspects of the Novel* (Harmondsworth: Penguin, 1962), 82.

3. Jean Franco, "Questions for Bolaño," *Journal of Latin American Cultural Studies* 18, no. 2–3 (2009): 215.

4. Peter Goldie, *On Personality* (London: Routledge, 2004), 64.

5. John Doris, *Lack of Character: Personality and Moral Behavior* (Cambridge: Cambridge University Press, 2002), 2; Gilbert Harman, "The Nonexistence of Character Traits," *Proceedings of the Aristotelian Society* 100 (2000): 223.

6. John Stuart Mill, *On Liberty* (Harmondsworth: Penguin Classics, 1985), 68–69.

7. Immanuel Kant, *Groundwork of the Metaphysic of Morals*, trans. H. J. Paton (New York: Harper and Row, 1964), 96–98; Jens Timmermann, "Kantian Duties to the Self, Explained and Defended," *Philosophy* 18, no. 37 (2006): 505–530.

8. Nigel Warburton, *Freedom: An Introduction with Readings* (London and New York: Routledge, 2001), 54–56.

9. David Dyzenhaus, "John Stuart Mill and the Harm of Pornography," *Ethics* 102, no. 3 (1992): 550.

10. Catherine Wilson, *Moral Animals: Ideals and Constraints in Moral Theory* (Oxford: Oxford University Press, 2004), 298–299. For a consideration of the moral problems posed by prostitution that is both rigorous and realistic, see Martha Nussbaum, "'Whether from Reason or Prejudice': Taking Money for Bodily Services," *The Journal of Legal Studies* 27, S2 (1998): 693–723.

11. Ruwen Ogien, *L'éthique aujourd'hui: Maximalistes et minimalistes* (Paris: Gallimard, 2007), 196.

12. Ruwen Ogien, "Self-Other Asymmetry," *Les ateliers de l'éthique* 3, no. 1 (2008): 87.

13. Ruwen Ogien, *L'état nous rend-il meilleurs? Essai sur la liberté politique* (Paris: Gallimard, 2013), 102, 193–205.

14. Incidentally, this is not the case for Oscar Amalfitano in *Woes of the True Policeman*, who rediscovers *eros* with Padilla and his friends.

15. Jean Franco, *Cruel Modernity* (Durham and London: Duke University Press, 2013), 237.

16. Bernard Williams, *Moral Luck: Philosophical Papers 1973–1980* (Cambridge: Cambridge University Press, 1981), 49.

17. Georg Henrik Von Wright, *The Varieties of Goodness* (New York: Routledge and Kegan Paul, 1963), 53.

18. See Douglas N. Walton, *Courage: A Philosophical Investigation* (Berkeley: University of California Press, 1986), 52–55.

19. Franco, "Questions for Bolaño," 215.

20. Susan Wolf, *Meaning in Life and Why It Matters* (Princeton and Oxford: Princeton University Press, 2010), 28.

21. Robert Adams, "Comment," in Wolf, *Meaning in Life and Why It Matters*, 76.

22. In her response to Adams, Wolf concedes that *something* of value may be achieved by the very commitment to a project that, if successful, would be nonegocentrically valuable (Wolf, *Meaning in Life and Why It Matters*, 107).

23. On interstitial emergence, see Michael Mann, *The Sources of Social Power. Volume 1: A history of power from the beginning to A.D. 1760* (Cambridge: Cambridge University Press, 1986), 15–16; and Samuel Clark, *Living Without Domination: The Possibility of an Anarchist Utopia* (Aldershot: Ashgate, 2007), 59. The expression "small affinity groups" is borrowed from Simon Critchley, *Infinitely Demanding: Ethics of Commitment, Politics of Resistance* (London: Verso, 2007), 113–114.

24. Franco, "Questions for Bolaño," 211.

25. See the reservations expressed by the Spanish poet Olvido García Valdes in her appreciative personal essay "El poeta Roberto Bolaño," in *Archivo Bolaño 1977–2003*, ed. Juan Insua (Barcelona: Centro de Cultura Contemporánea de Barcelona, 2013), 116.

26. Franco, "Questions for Bolaño," 210.

27. Aristotle, *Nichomachean Ethics*, trans. Martin Ostwald (Indianapolis: Bobbs-Merrill, 1962), 218–220 [1156b].

28. "The life-giving order of freedom must be made solely from the bottom upwards. . . . Only individuals, united through mutual aid and voluntary association, are entitled to decide who they are, what they shall be, how they shall live" (Mikhail Bakunin, *Selected Writings*, ed. A. Lehning (New York: Grove Press, 1974), 206–207). "In a society developed on these [anarchist] lines, the voluntary associations which already now begin to cover all the fields of human activity would take a still greater extension so as to substitute themselves for the state in all its functions" (Peter Kropotkin, *The Conquest of Bread and Other Writings*, ed. Marshall Shatz [Cambridge: Cambridge University Press, 1995], 233).

29. Gustave Flaubert, *Madame Bovary*, trans. Lydia Davis (New York: Penguin, 2010), 286; *Sentimental Education*, trans. Robert Baldick (Harmondsworth: Penguin, 1964), 373.

30. Roland Hill, *Lord Acton* (New Haven: Yale University Press, 2000), 300.

31. Kate Doyle, "The Dead of Tlatelolco: Using the Archives to Exhume the Past," National Security Archive Electronic Briefing Book No. 201 (2006), http://www.gwu.edu/~nsarchiv/NSAEBB/NSAEBB201/index.htm; Fernando Herrera Calderón, "Contesting the State

from the Ivory Tower: Student Power, Dirty War and the Urban Guerrilla Experience in Mexico, 1965–1982" (Ph.D. diss., University of Minnesota, 2012), 5–15, http://conservancy. umn.edu/bitstream/122744/1/Calderon_umn_0130E_12574.pdf.

32. Roberto Bolaño, "Autobiografía," *Granta 13: Mex* (2012): 277.

33. In 1996 Bolaño applied, unsuccessfully, for a Guggenheim fellowship to complete *The Savage Detectives* (Jorge Herralde, *Para Roberto Bolaño* [Barcelona: Acantilado, 2005], 77).

34. Franco, "Questions for Bolaño," 216.

35. See Ignacio Echevarría, "Bolaño Extraterritorial," in *Bolaño salvaje*, ed. Edmundo Paz Soldán and Gustavo Faverón Patriau (Barcelona: Candaya, 2008), 436. A poem entitled "La muerte," dated 2003, was published on the Chilean website *Lanzallamas* (http://www. lanzallamas.org/) in March 2006. According to Carmen Pérez de Vega, Bolaño composed and revised this poem in the last weeks of his life ("Roberto Bolaño, el escritor cercano," paper presented at the Estrella distante conference, Universidad Andrés Bello, Viña del Mar, Chile, July 17, 2013).

36. Herralde, *Para Roberto Bolaño*, 34.

37. In a letter written in 1986, Bolaño reversed the provocation: "Writing poetry is a luxury that only academics with healthy bank accounts or those who live and suffer in the third world or those who don't know how to write can afford to indulge in. I don't fall into any of those categories" ("Autobiografía," 277–278).

38. Jacques Roubaud, *Poésie, etcetera: ménage* (Paris: Stock, 1995), 82.

39. Philippe Lacoue-Labarthe and Jean-Luc Nancy, *The Literary Absolute: The Theory of Literature in German Romanticism*, trans. Philip Barnard and Cheryl Lester (Albany: State University of New York Press, 1988), 92.

40. Samuel Taylor Coleridge, *Biographia Literaria* (London: Dent, 1975), 173.

41. See John Stuart Mill, *Mill's Essays on Literature and Society*, ed. J. B. Schneewind (New York: Collier, 1965), 103.

42. See Les Murray, *Blocks and Tackles: Articles and Essays, 1982 to 1990* (Sydney: Angus and Robertson, 1990), 171–175.

43. Cited in Bob Thomson, "A Writer Crosses Over," *The Washington Post*, April 8, 2007.

44. Alejandro Zambra, *No leer*, ed. Andrés Braithwaite (Santiago, Chile: Ediciones Universidad Diego Portales, 2010), 85.

45. Giorgio Agamben, *Idea of Prose*, trans. Michael Sullivan and Sam Whitsitt (Albany: State University Press of New York, 1995), 97; *Idea della prosa* (Milan: Feltrinelli, 1985), 70.

46. See the translator's note in Giorgio Agamben, *La potencia del pensamiento*, trans. Flavia Costa (Buenos Aires: Adriana Hidalgo editora, 2007), 190–191.

47. Agamben, *Idea of Prose*, 97.

48. Stephen Jay Gould, *Ontogeny and Phylogeny* (Cambridge and London: Harvard University Press, 1977), 179.

49. Sergio Pellis and Andrew Iwaniuk, "Evolving a Playful Brain: A Levels of Control Approach," *International Journal of Comparative Psychology* 17, no. 1 (2004): 95.

50. Pierre Bourdieu, *Distinction: A Social Critique of the Judgement of Taste*, trans. Richard Nice (London: Routledge and Kegan Paul, 1984), 105.

51. Colin G. De Young, Rachael G. Grazioplene, and Jordan B. Peterson, "From Madness to Genius: The Openness/Intellect Trait Domain as a Paradoxical Simplex," *Journal of Research in Personality* 46 (2012): 74.

52. Friedrich Nietzsche, *Beyond Good and Evil*, trans. Judith Nortman (Cambridge: Cambridge University Press, 2002), 62.

53. Charles Baudelaire, *The Painter of Modern Life and Other Essays*, trans. Jonathan Mayne (London: Phaidon, 1995), 8.

54. Roger Caillois, *Les jeux et les hommes* (Paris: Gallimard, 1967), 37.

55. Montserrat Madariaga Caro, *Bolaño infra* (Santiago, Chile: RIL editores, 2010), 146.

56. Ibid., 109.

57. Williams, *Moral Luck*, 23–24.

58. Louis Macneice, *The Poetry of W. B. Yeats* (New York: Oxford University Press, 1969), 192. Catherine Wilson makes a similar point in "Grief and the Poet": "Though Platonic scepticism over whether emotional engagement with fictions is improving may be justified, there is less reason to doubt that, like their counterparts originating in 'external' historical events and in 'internal' fantasies, literature-generated emotions influence our behaviour and decision-making in a variety of real-life contexts" (*British Journal of Aesthetics* 53, no. 1 [2013]: 91).

59. Paul Muldoon, *Meeting the British* (London: Faber, 1987), 56, 59.

60. The writer and critic Aura Estrada was one such early reader, according to Francisco Goldman ("2007/2666," *Dossier* 14 [2011]: 98).

61. George Eliot, *Middlemarch* (Harmondsworth: Penguin, 1965), 896.

BIBLIOGRAPHY

Adams, Robert. "Comment." In Susan Wolf, *Meaning in Life and Why It Matters*, 75–84. Princeton: Princeton University Press, 2010.

Agamben, Giorgio. *Idea della prosa*. Milan: Feltrinelli, 1985.

——. *Idea of Prose*. Trans. Michael Sullivan and Sam Whitsitt. Albany: State University of New York Press, 1995.

——. *La potencia del pensamiento*. Trans. Flavia Costa. Buenos Aires: Adriana Hidalgo editora, 2007.

Aguilar, Paula. "Pobre memoria la mía: literatura y melancolía en el contexto de la postdictadura chilena (*Nocturno de Chile* de Roberto Bolaño)." In *Bolaño salvaje*, ed. Edmundo Paz Soldán and Gustavo Faverón Patriau, 127–143. Barcelona: Candaya, 2008.

Aira, César. *Las noches de Flores*. Barcelona: Mondadori, 2004.

——. "Lo incomprensible." *ABC Cultural*, February 26, 2000, 22–23.

——. "Particularidades absolutas." *Nueve Perros* 1 (2001): 11–13.

Amutio, Robert. "Paroles de traducteur." In *Les astres noirs de Roberto Bolaño*, ed. Karim Benmiloud and Raphaël Estève, 219–228. Bordeaux: Presses Universitaires de Bordeaux, 1997.

Anderson, Don. "Visceral Realism in Bolaño's Sea of Seeming." *The Australian*, January 10, 2009.

Anderson, Sam. "Prose Poem: Roberto Bolaño's Brilliant, Messy, Everything Novel." *New York Magazine*, November 7, 2008. http://nymag.com/arts/books/reviews/52011/.

Antología de la poesía surrealista. Ed. and trans. Aldo Pellegrini. Buenos Aires: Compañia General Fabril Editora, 1961.

Aranda, Daniel. "Originalité historique du retour de personnages balzaciens." *Revue d'histoire littéraire de la France* 101, no. 6 (2001): 1573–1589.

Arendt, Hannah. *Eichmann in Jerusalem*. New York: Penguin, 2006.

——. *The Human Condition*. Chicago: University of Chicago Press, 1958.

Aristotle. *Nichomachean Ethics*. Trans. Martin Ostwald. Indianapolis: Bobbs-Merrill, 1962.

BIBLIOGRAPHY

Arts, Clemens. *Oulipo et Tel Quel. Jeux formels et contraintes génératrices.* Leiden: University of Leiden Press, 1999.

Badiou, Alain. *The Meaning of Sarkozy.* Trans. David Fernbach. London: Verso, 2008.

Bakunin, Mikhail. *Selected Writings.* Ed. A. Lehning. New York: Grove Press, 1974.

Baroja, Pío. *The Restlessness of Shanti Andia and Selected Stories.* Trans. Anthony and Elaine Kerrigan. New York: Signet, 1962.

Baroni, Raphaël. *La tension narrative: Suspense, curiosité, surprise.* Paris: Seuil, 2007.

Barthes, Roland. *Image, Text, Music.* Trans. Stephen Heath. London: Fontana, 1977.

——. *The Pleasure of the Text.* Trans. Richard Miller. New York: Hill and Wang, 1975.

Baudelaire, Charles. *The Painter of Modern Life and Other Essays.* Trans. Jonathan Mayne. London: Phaidon, 1995.

Beckman, Jonathan. "Death and the Maidens." *The Literary Review* 363 (March 2009): 50–51.

Beecher, Donald. "Suspense." *Philosophy and Literature* 31, no. 2 (2007): 255–279.

Bendinelli, Marco F. and James T. Edsall. "Defense of Others: Origins, Requirements, Limitations and Ramifications." *Regent University Law Review* 5, no. 153 (1995): 153–214.

Benjamin, Walter. "Theses on the Philosophy of History." In *Illuminations*, ed. Hannah Arendt, trans. Harry Zohn, 255–266. London: Fontana, 1973.

——. "Two Poems by Friedrich Hölderlin: 'The Poet's Courage' and 'Timidity.'" In *Early Writings 1910–1917*, trans. Howard Eiland and others, 171–196. Cambridge, Mass.: Harvard University Press, 2011.

——. "Zwei Gedichte von Friedrich Hölderlin, 'Dichtermut'—'Blödigkeit.'" In *Gesammelte Schriften*, ed. Rolf Tiedemann and Hermann Schweppenhäuser, vol. 2.1, 105–126. Frankfurt am Main: Suhrkamp Verlag, 1977.

Berchenko, Pablo. "El referente histórico chileno en *Nocturno de Chile* de Roberto Bolaño." In *La memoria de la dictadura: Nocturno de Chile, Roberto Bolaño; Interrupciones 2, Juan Gelman*, ed. Fernando Moreno, 11–20. Paris: Ellipses, 2006.

Bicknell, Jeanette. "Self-Knowledge and the Limitations of Narrative." *Philosophy and Literature* 28 (2004): 406–416.

Bioy Casares, Adolfo. *Borges.* Ed. Daniel Martino. Buenos Aires: Destino, 2006.

Bolaño, Roberto. *Amulet.* Trans. Chris Andrews. New York: New Directions, 2006. [A]

——. *Amuleto.* Barcelona: Anagrama, 1999.

——. *Archivo Bolaño 1977–2003.* Ed. Juan Insua. Barcelona: Centro de Cultura Contemporánea de Barcelona, 2013.

——. "Autobiografía" and "Manifiesto infrarrealista: Las fracturas de la realidad." *Granta 13: Mex* (2012): 274–284.

——. *Between Parentheses.* Trans. Natasha Wimmer. New York: New Directions, 2011. [BP]

——. *Bolaño por sí mismo.* Ed. Andrés Braithwaite. Santiago, Chile: Ediciones Universidad Diego Portales, 2006. [B]

——. *By Night in Chile.* Trans. Chris Andrews. New York: New Directions, 2003. [BNC]

——. *De Blanes a Paris: Sobre una correspondencia de Roberto Bolaño a Waldo Rojas.* Ed. Giordano Muzio and Nicolás Slachevsky. Santiago, Chile: Multitud, 2012.

——. *Los detectives salvajes.* Barcelona: Anagrama, 1998. [LDS]

——. *Distant Star.* Trans. Chris Andrews. New York: New Directions, 2004. [DS]

——. "Entrevista a Roberto Bolaño." Interview by Mihály Dés. *Lateral: Revista de cultura* 5, no. 40 (1998): 8–9.

——. *Estrella distante.* Barcelona: Anagrama, 1996. [ED]

——. *The Insufferable Gaucho.* Trans. Chris Andrews. New York: New Directions, 2010. [IG]

——. *Last Evenings on Earth.* Trans. Chris Andrews. New York: New Directions, 2006. [LEE]

——. *The Last Interview and Other Conversations.* Trans. Sybil Pérez. New York: Melville House, 2009. [LI]

——. *La literatura nazi en América.* Barcelona: Seix Barral, 1996. [LNA]

——. *Monsieur Pain.* Trans. Chris Andrews. New York: New Directions, 2010. [MP]

——. *Nazi Literature in the Americas.* Trans. Chris Andrews. New York: New Directions, 2008. [NLA]

——. *Putas asesinas.* Barcelona: Anagrama, 2001. [PA]

——. *The Return.* Trans. Chris Andrews. New York: New Directions, 2010. [R]

——. "Roberto Bolaño." Interview by Fernando Villagrán. *Off the Record.* Universidad Católica de Valparaíso Televisión, 1998. http://www.youtube.com/watch?v=qNhTTqu5Vsw.

——. *The Savage Detectives.* Trans. Natasha Wimmer. New York: Farrar, Straus and Giroux, 2006. [SD]

——. *The Secret of Evil.* Trans. Chris Andrews and Natasha Wimmer. New York: New Directions, 2012. [SE]

——. *The Skating Rink.* Trans. Chris Andrews. New York: New Directions, 2009. [SR]

——. *2666.* Barcelona: Anagrama, 2004. [2666s]

——. *2666.* Trans. Natasha Wimmer. New York: Picador/Farrar, Straus and Giroux, 2008. [2666]

——. *The Unknown University.* Trans. Laura Healey. New York: New Directions, 2013. [UU]

——. *Woes of the True Policeman.* Trans. Natasha Wimmer. New York: Farrar, Straus and Giroux, 2012. [WTP]

"Bolaño-mania." *The Economist,* November 20, 2008.

Boldy, Steven. *A Companion to Jorge Luis Borges.* London: Tamesis, 2009.

Borges, Jorge Luis. *The Aleph and Other Stories (1933–1969).* Ed. and trans. Norman Thomas di Giovanni. New York: Dutton, 1970.

——. *The Book of Sand.* Trans. Norman Thomas di Giovanni. Harmondsworth: Penguin, 1979.

——. *Collected Fictions.* Trans. Andrew Hurley. New York: Viking, 1998.

——. *Doctor Brodie's Report.* Trans. Norman Thomas di Giovanni in collaboration with the author. Harmondsworth: Penguin, 1976.

——. *Evaristo Carriego.* Trans. Norman Thomas di Giovanni. New York: Dutton, 1984.

——. *Obras completas.* Vol. 1. Buenos Aires: Emecé, 1996.

——. *Selected Non-Fictions.* Ed. Eliot Weinberger. Trans. Esther Allen, Suzanne Jill Levine, and Eliot Weinberger. New York: Penguin, 1999.

——. *The Sonnets.* Ed. and trans. Stephen Kessler. Harmondsworth: Penguin, 2011.

——. "Three Milongas." Trans. David Young and Ana Cara-Walker. *World Literature Today* 62, no. 1 (1988): 9–10.

Boullosa, Carmen. "El agitador y las fiestas." In *Bolaño salvaje,* ed. Edmundo Paz Soldán and Gustavo Faverón Patriau, 417–429. Barcelona: Candaya, 2008.

Bourdieu, Pierre. *Distinction: A Social Critique of the Judgement of Taste*. Trans. Richard Nice. London: Routledge and Kegan Paul, 1984.

——. *Pascalian Meditations*. Trans. Richard Nice. Oxford: Polity Press, 2000.

——. *Raisons pratiques: Sur la théorie de l'action*. Paris: Seuil, 1994.

——. *The Rules of Art: Genesis and Structure of the Literary Field*. Trans. Susan Emanuel. Stanford: Stanford University Press, 1996.

Breton, André. *The Lost Steps*. Trans. Mark Polizzotti. Lincoln and London: University of Nebraska Press, 1996.

Browning, Christopher R. *Ordinary Men: Reserve Police Battalion 101 and the Final Solution in Poland*. London: Penguin, 2001.

Brugger, Peter. "From Haunted Brain to Haunted Science: A Cognitive Neuroscience View of Paranormal and Pseudoscientific Thought." In *Hauntings and Poltergeists*, ed. James Houran and Rense Lange, 195–213. Jefferson, N.C.: McFarland and Company, 2001.

Brugnolo, Stefano and Laura Luche. "Recordar sin recordar: Figuras de desplazamiento en *Nocturno de Chile* de Roberto Bolaño." *Amerika* 3 (2010): http://amerika.revues.org/1479.

Caillois, Roger. *Les jeux et les hommes*. Paris: Gallimard, 1967.

Card, Claudia. *Confronting Evils: Terrorism, Torture, Genocide*. Cambridge: Cambridge University Press, 2010.

Carroll, Noël. "The Paradox of Suspense." In *Suspense: Conceptualizations, Theoretical Analyses, and Empirical Explanation*, ed. Peter Vorderer, Hans J. Wulff, and Mike Friedrichsen, 71–91. Mahwah, N.J.: Lawrence Erlbaum Associates, 1996.

——. *The Philosophy of Horror or Paradoxes of the Heart*. New York and London: Routledge, 1990.

Casas Ros, Antoni. *Enigma*. Paris: Gallimard, 2010.

"Caso Prats: condenan a ex agentes de Pinochet." *La Nación*, July 1, 2008.

Castellanos Moya, Horacio. *La metamorfosis del sabueso*. Santiago, Chile: Universidad Diego Portales, 2011.

Catelli, Nora. "El laboratorio Bolaño." *El País,* September 14, 2002.

Caves, Richard. *Creative Industries: Contracts between Art and Commerce*. Cambridge, Mass.: Harvard University Press, 2000.

Céline, Louis-Ferdinand. *Le style contre les idées*. Paris: Complexe, 1987.

Cercas, Javier. "Bolaño en Gerona: Una amistad." In *Archivo Bolaño 1977–2003*, ed. Juan Insua, 59–65. Barcelona: Centro de Cultura Contemporánea de Barcelona, 2013.

——. "Print the Legend." *El País,* April 14, 2007.

Cesarani, David. *Eichmann: His Life and Crimes*. London: William Heinemann, 2004.

Chamisso, Adalbert von. *Peter Schlemihl*. Trans. Leopold von Loewenstein-Wertheim. London: John Calder, 1957.

Christman, John. "Narrative Unity as a Condition of Personhood." *Metaphilosophy* 35, no. 5 (2004): 695–713.

Clark, Samuel. *Living Without Domination: The Possibility of an Anarchist Utopia*. Aldershot: Ashgate, 2007.

Coetzee, J. M. *Elizabeth Costello: Eight Lessons*. Sydney: Random House, 2003.

Coleridge, Samuel Taylor. *Biographia Literaria*. London: Dent, 1975.

Corral, Wilfrido H. *Bolaño traducido: Nueva literatura mundial.* Madrid: Escalera, 2011.

Critchley, Simon. *Infinitely Demanding: Ethics of Commitment, Politics of Resistance.* London: Verso, 2007.

Deleuze, Gilles. *Spinoza: Practical Philosophy.* Trans. Robert Hurley. San Francisco: City Lights, 1988.

Delpla, Isabelle. *Le mal en procès: Eichmann et les théodicées modernes.* Paris: Hermann, 2011.

Derbyshire, Philip. "*Los detectives salvajes*: Line, Loss and the Political." *Journal of Latin American Cultural Studies* 18, nos. 2–3 (2009): 167–176.

Dés, Mihály. "Putas asesinas." In *Roberto Bolaño: La escritura como tauromaquia*, ed. Celina Manzoni, 197–198. Buenos Aires: Corregidor, 2002.

De Young, Colin G., Rachael G. Grazioplene, and Jordan B. Peterson. "From Madness to Genius: The Openness/Intellect Trait Domain as a Paradoxical Simplex." *Journal of Research in Personality* 46 (2012): 63–78.

Diamond, Cora. *The Realistic Spirit: Wittgenstein, Philosophy and the Mind.* Cambridge, Mass.: MIT Press, 1995.

Dinges, John. *The Condor Years: How Pinochet and His Allies Brought Terrorism to Three Continents.* New York and London: The New Press, 2004.

Domínguez Michael, Christopher. *La sabiduría sin promesa.* Santiago, Chile: Ediciones Universidad Diego Portales, 2009.

Dorfman, Ariel. *Some Write to the Future.* Trans. George Shivers with the author. Durham and London: Duke University Press, 1991.

Doris, John. *Lack of Character: Personality and Moral Behavior.* Cambridge: Cambridge University Press, 2002.

Doyle, Kate. "The Dead of Tlatelolco: Using the Archives to Exhume the Past." National Security Archive Electronic Briefing Book No. 201 (2006). http://www.gwu.edu/~nsarchiv/NSAEBB/NSAEBB201/index.htm.

Dyzenhaus, David. "John Stuart Mill and the Harm of Pornography." *Ethics* 102, no. 3 (1992): 534–551.

Echevarría, Ignacio. "Bolaño Extraterritorial." In *Bolaño salvaje*, ed. Edmundo Paz Soldán and Gustavo Faverón Patriau, 431–445. Barcelona: Candaya, 2008.

Echevarría, Ignacio and Bruno Montané. "Editando a Bolaño." *Quimera* 314 (2010): 39–43.

Eco, Umberto. *Interpretation and Overinterpretation.* Ed. Stefan Collini. Cambridge: Cambridge University Press, 1992.

Eliot, George. *Middlemarch.* Harmondsworth: Penguin, 1965.

The Encyclopedia of Twentieth-Century Fiction. Ed. Brian W. Shaffer and Patrick O'Donnell, 3 vols. Chichester: Wiley-Blackwell, 2011.

Epler, Barbara. "Roberto Bolaño in the USA." In *Archivo Bolaño 1977–2003*, ed. Juan Insua, 167–169. Barcelona: Centro de Cultura Contemporánea de Barcelona, 2013.

Espinosa, Patricia. "Tres libros de poesía del primer Bolaño: *Reinventar el amor, Fragmentos de la universidad desconocida* y *El último salvaje*." In *Roberto Bolaño: La experiencia del abismo*, ed. Fernando Moreno, 63–78. Santiago, Chile: Lastarria, 2011.

Esposito, Scott. "The Dream of Our Youth." *Hermano Cerdo*, April 2008. http://hermanocerdo.anarchyweb.org/index.php/2008/04/the-dream-of-our-youth/.

———. "2666—The Big Book of BEA?" *Conversational Reading* (blog), June 2008. http://www.conversationalreading.com/2008/06/a-little-more-a.html.

Even-Zohar, Itamar. "Translated Literature in the Polysystem." In *The Translation Studies Reader*, ed. Lawrence Venuti, 199–204. New York and London: Routledge, 2004.

Faverón Patriau, Gustavo. "El Rehacedor: 'El gaucho insufrible' y el ingreso de Bolaño en la tradición argentina." In *Bolaño salvaje*, ed. Edmundo Paz Soldán and Gustavo Faverón Patriau, 371–415. Barcelona: Candaya, 2008.

Filiou, Robert. *L'art est ce qui rend la vie plus intéressante que l'art/El arte es lo que hace la vida más interesante que el arte.* Paris: Les presses du reel, 2003.

Fischer, María Luisa. "La memoria de las historias en *Estrella distante* de Roberto Bolaño." In *Bolaño salvaje*, ed. Edmundo Paz Soldán and Gustavo Faverón Patriau, 145–162. Barcelona: Candaya, 2008.

Flaubert, Gustave. *The Letters of Gustave Flaubert 1830–1857.* Ed. and trans. Francis Steegmuller. London: Faber, 1979.

———. *Madame Bovary.* Trans. Lydia Davis. New York: Penguin, 2010.

———. *Sentimental Education.* Trans. Robert Baldick. Harmondsworth: Penguin, 1964.

Ford, Mark. "Bolaño: On the Edge of the Precipice." *The New York Review of Books* 58, no. 15 (October 13, 2011): 33–36.

Forsey, Jane. "Art and Identity: Expanding Narrative Theory." *Philosophy Today* 47, no. 2 (2003): 176–190.

Forster, E. M. *Aspects of the Novel.* Harmondsworth: Penguin, 1962.

Franco, Jean. *Cruel Modernity.* Durham and London: Duke University Press, 2013.

———. "Questions for Bolaño." *Journal of Latin American Cultural Studies* 18, no. 2–3 (2009): 207–217.

Franz, Carlos. "Roberto Bolaño: una pasión helada." *Letras libres* 26 (November 2003), http://www.letraslibres.com/index.php?art=9196.

———. "Una tristeza insoportable: Ocho hipótesis sobre la mela-cholé de B." In *Bolaño salvaje*, ed. Edmundo Paz Soldán and Gustavo Faverón Patriau, 103–115. Barcelona: Candaya, 2008.

Fresán, Rodrigo. "El samurái romántico." In *Bolaño salvaje*, ed. Edmundo Paz Soldán and Gustavo Faverón Patriau, 293–303. Barcelona: Candaya, 2008.

Freud, Sigmund. "Psychoanalytic Notes on an Autobiographical Account of a Case of Paranoia (Dementia Paranoides)." In *The Standard Edition of the Complete Psychological Works of Sigmund Freud*, ed. James Strachey, vol. 12, 1–88. London: The Hogarth Press, 1958.

———. "Some Character Types Met with in Psychoanalytic Work." In *The Standard Edition of the Complete Psychological Works of Sigmund Freud*, ed. James Strachey, vol. 14, 309–333. London: The Hogarth Press, 1957.

García Valdés, Olvido. "El poeta Roberto Bolaño." In *Archivo Bolaño 1977–2003*, ed. Juan Insua, 109–117. Barcelona: Centro de Cultura Contemporánea de Barcelona, 2013.

Genette, Gérard. *Palimpsests.* Trans. Channa Newman and Claude Doubinsky. Lincoln and London: University of Nebraska Press, 1997.

Goldie, Peter. *On Personality.* London: Routledge, 2004.

Goldman, Francisco. "2007/2666." *Dossier* 14 (2011): 97–99.

Gómez Bravo, Andrés. "Ha habido un aprovechamiento de la historia del taller de Lo Curro." *La Tercera*, November 6, 2010.

González, Mónica. "Fallo del caso Prats: Una travesía de 36 años que estalla en el corazón del Ejército." CIPER: Centro de Investigación Periodística, Actualidad y entrevistas, July 8, 2010. http://ciperchile.cl/2010/07/08/fallo-del-caso-prats-una-travesia-de-36-anos-que-estalla-en-el-corazon-del-ejercito/.

González Rodríguez, Sergio. *Huesos en el desierto*. Barcelona: Anagrama, 2002.

Gould, Stephen Jay. *Ontogeny and Phylogeny*. Cambridge, Mass.: Harvard University Press, 1977.

Gras, Dunia and Leonie Meyer-Kreuler. *El viaje imposible: En México con Roberto Bolaño*. Zaragoza: Tropo, 2010.

Greenblatt, Stephen. *Will in the World: How Shakespeare Became Shakespeare*. London: Jonathan Cape, 2004.

Gutiérrez Giraldo, Rafael Eduardo. "De la literatura como un oficio peligroso: Crítica y ficción en la obra de Roberto Bolaño." Ph.D. diss., Pontifícia Universidade Católica do Rio de Janeiro, 2010. http://www2.dbd.puc-rio.br/pergamum/tesesabertas/0610675_10_pretextual.pdf.

Guzmán Tapia, Jorge. *En el borde del mundo: Memorias del juez que procesó a Pinochet*. Trans. Oscar Luis Molina S. Barcelona: Anagrama, 2005.

Harman, Gilbert. "The Nonexistence of Character Traits." *Proceedings of the Aristotelian Society* 100 (2000): 223–226.

Hartman, Geoffrey. "Romanticism and Anti-Self-Consciousness." In *Beyond Formalism: Literary Essays 1958–1970*, 298–310. New Haven: Yale University Press, 1970.

Hegel, Georg Wilhelm Friedrich. *Aesthetics: Lectures on the Fine Arts*. Trans. T. M. Knox. Oxford: Oxford University Press, 1975.

Herralde, Jorge. *Para Roberto Bolaño*. Barcelona: Acantilado, 2005.

Herrera Calderón, Fernando. "Contesting the State from the Ivory Tower: Student Power, Dirty War and the Urban Guerrilla Experience in Mexico, 1965–1982." Ph.D. diss., University of Minnesota, 2012. http://conservancy.umn.edu/bitstream/122744/1/Calderon_umn_0130E_12574.pdf

Hill, Roland. *Lord Acton*. New Haven: Yale University Press, 2000.

Hölderlin, Friedrich. *Poems and Fragments*. Trans. Michael Hamburger. London: Routledge and Kegan Paul, 1966.

——. *Selected Verse*. Trans. Michael Hamburger. London: Anvil, 1986.

"Human Rights Trials in Chile and the Region." Human Rights Observatory, Universidad Diego Portales, Santiago, Chile, Bulletin no. 7, 2010. http://www.icso.cl/images/Paperss/observatorio7.pdf.

Huret, Jules. *Enquête sur l'évolution littéraire*. Paris: Charpentier, 1891.

Iser, Wolfgang. "Indeterminacy and the Reader's Response in Prose Fiction." In *Aspects of Narrative*, ed. J. Hillis Miller, 1–45. New York: Columbia University Press, 1971.

James, Henry. "The Art of Fiction." In *The Portable Henry James*, ed. Morton Dauwen Zabel, 387–414. Harmondsworth: Penguin, 1977.

James, Susan. "Fruitful Imagining: On Catherine Wilson's 'Grief and the Poet.'" *British Journal of Aesthetics* 53, no. 1 (2013): 97–101.

Jakobson, Roman. "Linguistics and Poetics." In *Selected Writings*, vol. 3, 18–51. The Hague and Paris: Mouton, 1981.

Jaramillo Agudelo, Darío. "Mago de un solo truco." *El País*, April 4, 2007.

Jennerjahn, Ina. "Escritos en los cielos y fotografías del infierno. Las 'Acciones de arte' de Carlos Ramírez Hoffman, según Roberto Bolaño." *Revista de crítica literaria latinoamericana* 28, no. 56 (2002): 69–86.

Johnson, B. S. *Aren't You Rather Young to Be Writing Your Memoirs?* London: Hutchinson, 1973.

Kafalenos, Emma. "Emotions Induced by Narratives." *Poetics Today* 20, no. 3 (2008): 377–384.

Kant, Immanuel. *Groundwork of the Metaphysic of Morals*. Trans. H. J. Paton. New York: Harper and Row, 1964.

——. *Religion Within the Boundaries of Mere Reason and Other Writings*. Ed. and trans. Allen Wood and George di Giovanni. Cambridge: Cambridge University Press, 1998.

Kermode, Frank. *The Genesis of Secrecy: On the Interpretation of Narrative*. Cambridge, Mass.: Harvard University Press, 1979.

Kessler Ferzan, Kimberly. "Defending Imminence: From Battered Women to Irak." *Arizona Law Review* 46, no. 213 (2004): 213–262.

Kleinzahler, August. *Cutty, One Rock: Low Characters and Strange Places, Gently Explained*. New York: Farrar, Straus and Giroux, 2004.

Kohan, Martín. "Mano a Mano." *Variaciones Borges* 27 (2009): 225–232.

Krauss, Nicole. Interview with Juliet Linderman. *Jewcy Magazine*, October 27, 2010. http://www.jewcy.com/arts-and-culture/jewcy-interviews-nicole-krauss.

Kropotkin, Peter. *The Conquest of Bread and Other Writings*. Ed. Marshall Shatz. Cambridge: Cambridge University Press, 1995.

Kutz, Christopher. *Complicity: Ethics and Law for a Collective Age*. Cambridge: Cambridge University Press, 2007.

Lacoue-Labarthe, Philippe and Jean-Luc Nancy. *The Literary Absolute: The Theory of Literature in German Romanticism*. Trans. Philip Barnard and Cheryl Lester. Albany: State University of New York Press, 1988.

Lamarque, Peter. "On Not Expecting Too Much from Narrative." *Mind and Language* 19 (2004): 393–408.

Lançon, Philippe. "69 raisons de danser avec Bolaño." *Libération*, June 26, 2003.

Landy, Joshua. *How to Do Things with Fictions*. Oxford: Oxford University Press, 2012.

——. *Philosophy as Fiction: Self, Deception and Knowledge in Proust*. Oxford: Oxford University Press, 2004.

Larkin, Philip. *Required Writing: Miscellaneous Pieces 1955–1982*. London: Faber, 1983.

Lemebel, Pedro. *De perlas y cicatrices*. Santiago, Chile: Lom, 1996.

Lethem, Jonathan. "The Departed." *The New York Times*, November 12, 2008.

Levi, Primo. *The Drowned and the Saved*. Trans. Raymond Rosenthal. New York: Summit, 1988.

Lewis, C. S. and E. M. W. Tillyard. *The Personal Heresy: A Controversy*. Oxford: Oxford University Press, 1939.

Lihn, Enrique. *The Dark Room and Other Poems*. Ed. Patricio Lerzundi. Trans. Jonathan Cohen, John Felstiner, and David Unger. New York: New Directions, 1978.

Lippitt, John. "Getting the Story Straight: Kierkegaard, MacIntyre and Some Problems with Narrative." *Inquiry* 50 (2007): 34–69.

Livingston, Paisley. "Nested Art." *The Journal of Aesthetics and Art Criticism* 61, no. 3 (2003): 233–246.

López-Vicuña, Ignacio. "The Violence of Writing: Literature and Discontent in Roberto Bolaño's Chilean Novels." *Journal of Latin American Cultural Studies* 18, nos. 2–3 (2009): 155–166.

Lotte, Fernand. "Le 'retour des personnages' dans 'La Comédie humaine.'" *Année balzacienne* 1961: 227–281.

Ludmer, Josefina. Interview by Magalí Ventura and Karina Micheletto. *Matando más enanos . . .* (blog), April 8, 2007. http://matandomasenanos.blogspot.com/2007/04/josefina-ludmer.html.

MacIntyre, Alasdair. *After Virtue*. Notre Dame: University of Notre Dame Press, 2007.

Mandolessi, Silvana. "El arte según Wieder: estética y política de lo abyecto en *Estrella distante*." *Chasqui* 40, no. 2 (2011): 65–79.

Mann, Michael. *The Sources of Social Power. Volume 1: A History of Power from the Beginning to A.D. 1760*. Cambridge: Cambridge University Press, 1986.

Manzoni, Celina. "Recorridos urbanos, fantasmagoria y espejismo en *Amuleto*." In *Roberto Bolaño: Una literatura infinita*, ed. Fernando Moreno, 173–186. Poitiers: Centre de Recherches Latino-amércaines, 2005.

——. "Reescritura como desplazamiento y anagnórisis en Amuleto." In *Roberto Bolaño: La escritura como tauromaquia*, ed. Celina Manzoni, 175–184. Buenos Aires: Corregidor, 2002.

McKee, Robert. *Story: Substance, Structure, Style, and the Principles of Screenwriting*. New York: Regan Books, 1997.

Macneice, Louis. *The Poetry of W. B. Yeats*. New York: Oxford University Press, 1969.

Madariaga Caro, Montserrat. *Bolaño infra*. Santiago, Chile: RIL editores, 2010.

Manguel, Alberto. Review of *Nazi Literature in the Americas*. *The Guardian*, February 6, 2010.

Maristain, Mónica. *El hijo de Míster Playa: Una semblanza de Roberto Bolaño*. Oaxaca de Juárez: Almadía, 2012.

Marras, Sergio. *El héroe improbable*. Santiago, Chile: RIL editores, 2011.

Martínez, Guillermo. *La fórmula de la inmortalidad*. Buenos Aires: Seix Barral, 2005.

——. "Narrativa argentina hoy." *Guillermo Martínez* (blog), 2011. http://guillermo-martinezweb. blogspot.com/2011/06/Narrativa-argentina-hoy.html.

Masoliver Ródenas, Juan Antonio. "Palabras contra el tiempo." In *Bolaño salvaje*, ed. Edmundo Paz Soldán and Gustavo Faverón Patriau, 305–318. Barcelona: Candaya, 2008.

Matamoro, Blas. "La guerra borgiana." *Cuadernos hispanoamericanos* 585 (1999): 71–78.

Medina, Alberto. "Arts of Homelessness: Roberto Bolaño or the Commodification of Exile." *Novel: A Forum on Fiction* 42, no. 3 (2009): 546–554.

Menger, Pierre-Michel. *Le Travail créateur: S'accomplir dans l'incertain*. Paris: Hautes Études, Gallimard/Seuil, 2009.

Mergenthaler, May. "The 'Paradox' of Poetic Courage: Hölderlin's Ode 'Timidity' and Benjamin's Commentary Reconsidered." *The Germanic Review* 85 (2010): 224–249.

Midgely, Mary. *Wickedness: A Philosophical Essay*. London: Routledge, 1984.

Mill, John Stuart. *Mill's Essays on Literature and Society*. Ed. J. B. Schneewind. New York: Collier, 1965.

——. *On Liberty*. Harmondsworth: Penguin Classics, 1985.

Morton, Adam. *On Evil*. New York: Routledge, 2004.

Muldoon, Paul. *Meeting the British*. London: Faber, 1987.

Murray, Les. *Blocks and Tackles: Articles and Essays, 1982 to 1990*. Sydney: Angus and Robertson, 1990.

Neaman, Elliot Y. *A Dubious Past: Ernst Jünger and the Politics of Literature After Nazism*. Berkeley: University of California Press, 1999.

Nehamas, Alexander. "Writer, Text, Work, Author." In *Literature and the Question of Philosophy*, ed. Anthony Cascardi, 265–291. Baltimore: Johns Hopkins University Press, 1987.

Neiman, Susan. *Evil in Modern Thought: An Alternative History of Philosophy*. Melbourne: Scribe, 2003.

——. "What's the Problem of Evil?" In *Rethinking Evil: Contemporary Perspectives*, ed. María Pía Lara, 27–45. Berkeley and Los Angeles: University of California Press, 2001.

Neuman, Andrés. "La fuente y el desierto." In *Roberto Bolaño. Estrella cercana. Ensayos sobre su obra*, ed. Augusta López Bernasocchi and José Manuel López de Abiada, 317–322. Madrid: Verbum, 2012.

Neyfakh, Leon. "The Status Galley: How to Pick up Girls with the New Roth." *The New York Observer*, June 17, 2008.

Nietzsche, Friedrich. *Beyond Good and Evil*. Trans. Judith Nortman. Cambridge: Cambridge University Press, 2002.

——. *Untimely Meditations*. Ed. Daniel Breazeale. Trans. R. J. Hollingdale. Cambridge: Cambridge University Press, 1997.

Nino, Carlos Santiago. *Radical Evil on Trial*. New Haven: Yale University Press, 1996.

Nussbaum, Martha. *Love's Knowledge: Essays on Philosophy and Literature*. Oxford: Oxford University Press, 1990.

——. "'Whether from Reason or Prejudice': Taking Money for Bodily Services." *The Journal of Legal Studies* 27 (1998) S2: 693–723.

Ogien, Ruwen. *L'État nous rend-il meilleurs? Essai sur la liberté politique*. Paris: Gallimard, 2013.

——. *L'éthique aujourd'hui: Maximalistes et minimalistes*. Paris: Gallimard, 2007.

——. "Self-Other Asymmetry." *Les Ateliers de l'éthique* 3, no. 1 (2008): 79–89.

Oksenberg Rorty, Amélie. *Mind in Action: Essays in the Philosophy of Mind*. Boston: Beacon Press, 1988.

"On Bolaño." *N + 1*, November 12, 2008. http://www.nplusonemag.com/bola-0.

Otake, Akiko. Comments on Kinokuniya booklog, 2009. http://booklog.kinokuniya.co.jp/ohtake/archives/2009/10/post_52.html.

Oulipo. *Oulipo Compendium*. Ed. Harry Matthews and Alastair Brotchie. London: Atlas, 1998.

Pauls, Alan. *El factor Borges: Nueve ensayos ilustrados*. Buenos Aires: Fondo de Cultura Económica de Argentina, 2000.

——. "La solución Bolaño." In *Bolaño salvaje*, ed. Edmundo Paz Soldán and Gustavo Faverón Patriau, 319–332. Barcelona: Candaya, 2008.

Paz Soldán, Edmundo. "Roberto Bolaño: Literatura y apocalípsis." In *Roberto Bolaño: La experiencia del abismo*, ed. Fernando Moreno, 25–35. Santiago, Chile: Lastarria, 2011.

Pellis, Sergio and Andrew Iwaniuk. "Evolving a Playful Brain: A Levels of Control Approach." *International Journal of Comparative Psychology* 17, no. 1 (2004): 92–118.

Piglia, Ricardo. *Formas breves*. Barcelona: Anagrama, 2000.

——. "Theses on the Short Story." *New Left Review* 70 (2011): 63–66.

Pollack, Sarah. "Latin America Translated (Again): Roberto Bolaño's *The Savage Detectives* in the United States." *Comparative Literature* 61, no. 3 (2009): 346–365.

Prose, Francine. "The Folklore of Exile." *The New York Times*, July 9, 2006.

Proust, Marcel. *By Way of Sainte-Beuve*. Trans. Sylvia Townsend Warner. London: Chatto and Windus, 1958.

——. *Correspondance*. Ed. Philip Kolb. Vol. 21. Paris: Plon, 1993.

——. *Finding Time Again*. Trans. Ian Patterson. London: Penguin, 2003.

——. *The Prisoner and the Fugitive*. Trans. Carol Clark and Peter Collier. London: Penguin, 2003.

Ricoeur, Paul. *Le mal: Un défi à la philosophie et à la théologie*. Geneva: Labor et Fides, 2004.

——. *Time and Narrative*. Trans. Kathleen McLaughlin and David Pellauer. Vol. 1. Chicago: University of Chicago Press, 1984.

——. *Time and Narrative*. Trans. Kathleen McLaughlin and David Pellauer. Vol. 3. Chicago: University of Chicago Press, 1988.

Rimbaud, Arthur. *Collected Poems*. Trans. Oliver Bernard. Harmondsworth: Penguin, 1986.

Robbe-Grillet, Alain. *For a New Novel*. Trans. Richard Howard. Evanston, Ill.: Northwestern University Press, 1989.

Rorty, Richard. "The Pragmatist's Progress." In *Interpretation and Overinterpretation*, ed. Stefan Collini, 89–108. Cambridge: Cambridge University Press, 1992.

Roubaud, Jacques. *Poésie, etcetera: ménage*. Paris: Stock, 1995.

Roussel, Raymond. *How I Wrote Certain of My Books*. Trans. Trevor Winkfield. Ann Arbor: Sun, 1977.

Rudd, Anthony. "In Defense of Narrative." *European Journal of Philosophy* 17, no. 1 (2007): 60–75.

Ruisánchez, José Ramón. "Fate o la inminencia." In *Roberto Bolaño: Ruptura y violencia en la literatura finisecular*, ed. Felipe A. Ríos Baeza, 385–397. Mexico City: Ediciones Eón, 2010.

Saer, Juan José. *La narracion-objeto*. Barcelona: Seix Barral, 1999.

Sagalnik, Matthew J., Peter Sheridan Dodds, and Duncan J. Watts. "Experimental Study of Inequality and Unpredictability in an Artificial Cultural Market." *Science* 311, no. 5762 (2006): 854–856.

Sapiro, Gisèle. *La responsabilité de l'écrivain: Littérature, droit et morale en France (XIXe–XXIe siècle)*. Paris: Seuil, 2011.

Schaeffer, Jean-Marie. "Avant-propos." In Raphaël Baroni, *La tension narrative: Suspense, curiosité, surprise*, 11–15. Paris: Seuil, 2007.

Schechtman, Marya. *The Constitution of Selves*. Ithaca, N.Y.: Cornell University Press, 1996.

——. "Stories, Lives and Basic Survival: A Refinement and Defense of the Narrative View." In *Narrative and Understanding Persons*, ed. Daniel D. Hutto, 155–178. Cambridge: Cambridge University Press, 2007.

Shaw, Donald. *The Post-Boom in Spanish American Fiction*. Albany: State University of New York Press, 1998.

Shelley, Percy Bysshe. *The Selected Poetry and Prose of Shelley*. Ed. Harold Bloom. New York: New American Library, 1966.

Smith, David. "Women Are Still a Closed Book to Men." *The Observer*, May 29, 2005.

Spinoza, Benedictus de. *Complete Works*. Ed. Michael L. Morgan. Trans. Samuel Shirley and others. Indianapolis: Hackett, 2002.

Spitzer, Leo. *La enumeración caótica en la poesía moderna*. Trans. Raimundo Lida. Buenos Aires: Coni, 1945.

Stavans, Ilan. "Willing Outcast: How a Chilean-born Iconoclast Became a Great Mexican Novelist." *The Washington Post*, May 6, 2007.

Stein, Lorin. "Q&A with Lorin Stein." *Las obras de Roberto Bolaño* (blog), January 28, 2010. http://www.bolanobolano.com/tag/lorinstein/.

Sternberg, Meir. *Expositional Modes and Temporal Ordering in Fiction*. Baltimore and London: Johns Hopkins University Press, 1978.

——. "Telling in Time II: Chronology, Teleology, Narrativity." *Poetics Today* 13, no. 3 (1992): 463–541.

Stokes, Patrick. "Is Narrative Identity Four-Dimensionalist?" *European Journal of Philosophy* 20, Issue Supplement S1 (2010): E86–E106.

Strawson, Galen. *Real Materialism and Other Essays*. Oxford: Oxford University Press, 2008.

——. "The Self." In *Models of the Self*, ed. Shaun Gallagher and Jonathan Shear, 1–24. Thorverton, UK: Imprint Academic, 1997.

Strawson, P. F. *Individuals: An Essay in Descriptive Metaphysics*. London: Routledge, 1959.

Thomson, Bob. "A Writer Crosses Over." *The Washington Post*, April 8, 2007.

Timmermann, Jens. "Kantian Duties to the Self, Explained and Defended." *Philosophy* 18, no. 37 (2006): 505–530.

Tivnan, Tom and Philip Stone. "Review of 2009: Author-ised." *The Bookseller*, January 29, 2010. http://www.thebookseller.com/feature/review-2009-author-ised.html.

Todorov, Tzvetan. *The Poetics of Prose*. Trans. Richard Howard. Ithaca, N.Y.: Cornell University Press, 1977.

"2666." *The New Yorker*, November 17, 2008. http://www.newyorker.com/arts/reviews/brieflynoted/2008/11/17/081117crbn_brieflynotedl.

Uribe Arce, Armando. *El fantasma de la sinrazón y El secreto de la poesía*. Santiago, Chile: Be-uve-dráis editores, 2001.

Usandizaga, Helena. "Poesía y prosa en la obra de Roberto Bolaño." In *Roberto Bolaño. Estrella cercana. Ensayos sobre su obra*, ed. Augusta López Bernasocchi and José Manuel López de Abiada, 377–404. Madrid: Verbum, 2012.

Verlaine, Paul. *Les poètes maudits*. Paris: Léon Vannier, 1888.

Vice, Samantha. "Literature and the Narrative Self." *Philosophy* 78 (2003): 93–108.

Vida, Vendela. *Let the Northern Lights Erase Your Name*. New York: Ecco, 2007.

Von Wright, Georg Henrik. *The Varieties of Goodness*. New York: Routledge and Kegan Paul, 1963.

Walton, Douglas N. *Courage: A Philosophical Investigation*. Berkeley: University of California Press, 1986.

Warburton, Nigel. *Freedom: An Introduction with Readings*. London and New York: Routledge, 2001.

Washington Valdez, Diana. *The Killing Fields: Harvest of Women*. Burbank, Calif.: Peace at the Border, 2006.

Watson, Gary. "The Trouble with Psychopaths." In *Reasons and Recognition: Essays on the Philosophy of T. M. Scanlon*, ed. R. Jay Wallace, Rahul Kumar, and Samuel Freeman, 307–324. New York: Oxford University Press, 2011.

Weinrib, Ernest J. "Duty to Rescue." In *Morality, Harm and the Law*, ed. Gerald Dworkin, 134–144. Boulder, Colo.: Westview, 1994.

Wilkes, Kathleen V. "Know Thyself." In *Models of the Self*, ed. Shaun Gallagher and Jonathan Shear, 25–38. Thorverton, UK: Imprint Academic, 1999.

Williams, Bernard. "Life as Narrative." *European Journal of Philosophy* 17, no. 2 (2007): 305–314.

——. *Moral Luck: Philosophical Papers 1973–1980*. Cambridge: Cambridge University Press, 1981.

Williams, Gareth. "Sovereignty and Melancholic Paralysis in Roberto Bolaño." *Journal of Latin American Cultural Studies* 18, nos. 2–3 (2009): 125–140.

Williamson, Edwin. *Borges: A Life*. London: Penguin, 2004.

Wilson, Catherine. "Grief and the Poet." *British Journal of Aesthetics* 53, no. 1 (2013): 77–91.

——. *Moral Animals: Ideals and Constraints in Moral Theory*. Oxford: Oxford University Press, 2004.

Wimmer, Natasha. "Natasha Wimmer on Translating 2666." Interview by Alan Page. *Vulture*, November 14, 2008. http://www.vulture.com/2008/11/natasha_wimmer_on_translating.html.

——. "The Translator's Task—To Disappear." Interview by Matthew Shaer. *Christian Science Monitor*, January 16, 2009.

Wolf, Susan. *Meaning in Life and Why it Matters*. Princeton and Oxford: Princeton University Press, 2010.

Woolf, Virginia. *Women and Writing*. London: The Women's Press, 1979.

Wylie, Andrew. "Bolaño Studies." *The New York Times*, December 5, 2008.

Wu Ziru. 2011. "The Chinese Edition of Bolaño's *2666* Newly Released." *Global Times*, December 25, 2011.

Yeats, William Butler. *Collected Poems*. London: Macmillan, 1982.

Zambra, Alejandro. *Formas de volver a casa*. Barcelona: Anagrama, 2012.

——. *No leer*. Ed. Andrés Braithwaite. Santiago, Chile: Ediciones Universidad Diego Portales, 2010.

Zavala, Oswaldo. *Siembra de nubes*. Mexico City: Praxis, 2011.

INDEX

Roberto Bolaño is referred to as R B.